JACK TAR

and the

BABOON WATCH

INTERNATIONAL MARINE / McGRAW-HILL EDUCATION
CAMDEN, MAINE • NEW YORK • CHICAGO • SAN FRANCISCO
LISBON • LONDON • MADRID • MEXICO CITY • MILAN • NEW DELHI
SAN JUAN • SEOUL • SINGAPORE • SYDNEY • TORONTO

A Guide to
CURIOUS NAUTICAL KNOWLEDGE
for Landlubbers and Sea Lawyers Alike

JACK TAR

and the

BABOON WATCH

CAPTAIN FRANK LANIER

To my wife Marilou,
daughter Alyssa, and number one son Tristan
—thanks for keeping the wind in my sails.

1 2 3 4 5 6 7 8 9 10 11 12 13 14 15 QFR/QFR 1 9 8 7 6 5 4
ISBN 978-0-07-182526-9
MHID 0-07-182526-6
E ISBN 0-07-1824014

Library of Congress Cataloging-in-Publication Data is available from the Library of Congress.

McGraw-Hill Education books are available at special quantity discounts to use as premiums and sales promotions or for use in corporate training programs. To contact a representative, please e-mail us at bulksales@mheducation.com.

Questions regarding the content of this book should be addressed to www.internationalmarine.com

Questions regarding the ordering of this book should be addressed to
McGraw-Hill Education
Customer Service Department
P.O. Box 547
Blacklick, OH 43004
Retail customers: 1-800-262-4729
Bookstores: 1-800-722-4726

All illustrations (excepting those on pages i, iii, v, and xiii–top left) from *Century* magazine.

Contents

− Contents −

– Contents –

– Contents –

— Contents —

– Contents –

— Contents —

– Contents –

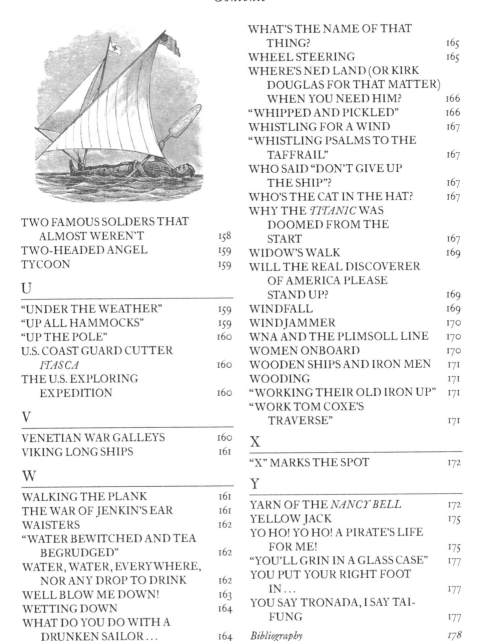

Preface

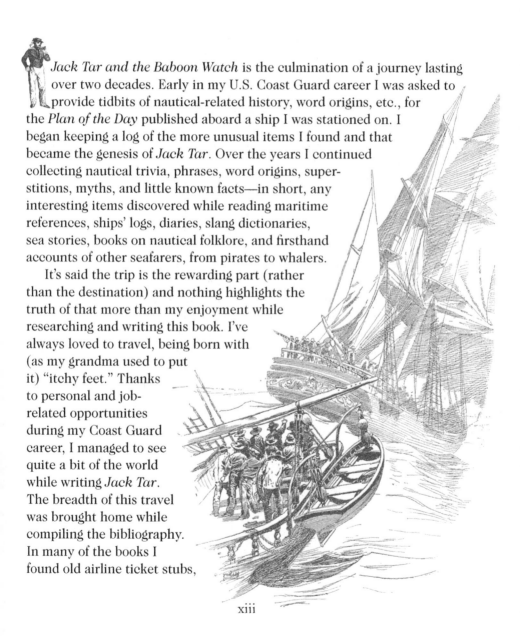

Jack Tar and the Baboon Watch is the culmination of a journey lasting over two decades. Early in my U.S. Coast Guard career I was asked to provide tidbits of nautical-related history, word origins, etc., for the *Plan of the Day* published aboard a ship I was stationed on. I began keeping a log of the more unusual items I found and that became the genesis of *Jack Tar*. Over the years I continued collecting nautical trivia, phrases, word origins, super-stitions, myths, and little known facts—in short, any interesting items discovered while reading maritime references, ships' logs, diaries, slang dictionaries, sea stories, books on nautical folklore, and firsthand accounts of other seafarers, from pirates to whalers.

It's said the trip is the rewarding part (rather than the destination) and nothing highlights the truth of that more than my enjoyment while researching and writing this book. I've always loved to travel, being born with (as my grandma used to put it) "itchy feet." Thanks to personal and job-related opportunities during my Coast Guard career, I managed to see quite a bit of the world while writing *Jack Tar*. The breadth of this travel was brought home while compiling the bibliography. In many of the books I found old airline ticket stubs, impromptu place markers tucked in while reading on those long flights to the Caribbean, Hawaii, Australia, and beyond.

How fortunate I was to research and write about Magellan's circumnavigation and the riches of Spain's Manila galleons after a day driving around the island of Guam or walking the streets of Manila. I wrote about Hispaniola and the first buccaneers when visiting the Dominican Republic and Haiti, drafted bits of trivia about James Cook while living in Hawaii and traveling the islands of the South Pacific. Nothing puts you "in character" like beachcombing along North Carolina's Ocracoke Island after recounting Blackbeard's death, or looking at artifacts recovered from his flagship, *Queen Anne's Revenge*, during a sailing trip to Beaufort, North Carolina. Living the entries not only made *Jack Tar* a joy to write, it also brought to life the seafarers and events recounted within during my travels.

There are plenty of nautical trivia books that give the definition of a chock or tell how many feet are in a fathom, but that's where *Jack Tar* is different. Imagine a nautical equivalent of *Ripley's Believe It or Not!* and its slogan of "everything odd, weird, and unbelievable" and you'll have a good feel for the book you now hold in your hands.

Jack Tar was written for the reader who wants to know the rest of the story—like how the Amazon River came to be named after the one-breasted warrior women of Greek mythology or maybe why *Titanic* was possibly the worst name ever for a ship (even before the disaster).

Curious as to how Captain Fudge (as in "to fudge something") earned his nickname or interested in the life and times of Louis Le Golif (a.k.a. Captain Half-Butt), a real life pirate of the Caribbean who received his nickname after an accident involving a wayward cannonball? It's in here.

Before starting your own journey, a few words on how the book is organized. Entries are listed in alphabetical order. A head in quotation marks indicates a what is now a (mostly) common phrase in our vocabulary, e.g., "A Cup of Joe." Terms or phrases in **bold italics** following an entry are related topics.

Now turn the page and enjoy!

A1

The highest ship classification as rated by
that venerable standard of marine insurance speculation, Lloyds of London. Its
Register of Ships rates the overall quality of
a vessel alphanumerically according to her
seaworthiness: letters denote the condition
of the hull, while fittings (anchors, rigging,
and the like) are graded numerically.

As described in the *Register*, "The character A denotes New ships, or Ships
Renewed or Restored. The Stores of
Vessels are designated by the figures
1 and 2; 1 signifying that the Vessel is
well and sufficiently found."

In the original *Lloyd's List* (a weekly
shipping paper of the early 1700s and
precursor to the *Register*) ships were
designated by the letters A, E, I, O,
and U, which referred to a vessel's
hulls, while the letters G,
M, and B ("good," "mid-
dling," and "bad") rated
the vessel's equipment.
A rating of AG denoted
a first-class ship
with good outfitting,
while UB described
the lowest class of ship
with bad outfitting.

I

It was the 1776 edition of the *Register* that first used the numerals 1, 2, 3, and 4 to describe a vessel's outfitting, thus giving rise to the designation "A1" as something of the highest quality. *(Chamber of Horrors, Lloyds of London)*

A.B.

Able-bodied, a seaman who has proven he possesses and is familiar with the sailing skills necessary to ship as a man before the mast. An O.S. (ordinary sailor) would be one with the rudimentary ability to reef, steer, or lend a hand as required.

Those still lower on the shipboard food chain were simply labeled "sailor" or the more derogatory "common sailor." Even a common sailor possessed a quick retort when cornered, however, that being that so and so was "a dirty dog and no sailor." *(Hand, Sail before the Mast)*

"ABLE TO WALK A CHALK"

Sober, after the bosun's trick of making crewmembers walk a chalked line on deck in an effort to ferret out those suspected of being drunk. *(Toe the Line)*

ABLE-WHACKETS

A nautical card game where the loser is given a sound whack with a knotted handkerchief for every point or game lost.

ABRAM MEN

Eighteenth century beggars who, while feigning madness, passed themselves off as old British naval ratings cast into the streets once their services were no longer needed. The term itself dates back to the sixteenth century and is most likely an allusion to the Biblical Abraham associated with the beggar Lazarus. It was the Abraham Ward of Bedlam (the Hospital of St. Mary of Bethlehem) that quartered the insane, who on specific days were turned loose on the streets in order to go a-begging.

Nice place, that Bethlehem Hospital. Originally established in London around 1330 to address the needs of impoverished folks, by 1377 it began admitting lunatics, a term used to describe those whose insanity was believed affected by the lunar phases of the moon.

Beginning in the early seventeenth century, visitors were allowed (for a small fee, of course) the privilege of touring the institution in order to view the inmates. Radford (see Bibliography) cites the following account given by one such visitor, which was later printed in the *London Spy*.

> "Accordingly we were admitted through an iron gate, within which sat a brawny Cerberus of an indigo colour, leaning upon a money box. We turned in through another iron barricade, where we heard such a rattling

of chains, drumming of doors, ranting, holloaing, singing and rattling, that I could think of nothing but Don Quevado's vision, where the damned broke loose, and put Hell in an uproar."

Add to that the rowdies seeking entertainment among "the frantic humours and rambling ejaculations of the mad folks" and one could scarce imagine a more raucous, disorderly setting. It was these chaotic scenes that established the modern use of the word bedlam as "a scene of wild uproar and confusion."

One seamen describes seeing a meager, gray-haired hag, continually chanting "The wind is . . . blow, devil, blow; the wind is . . . blow, devil, blow." Seems sailorman inquisitiveness kicked in, compelling him to ask, "Where is the wind, mother?"—to which she quickly replied with a cackle, "The wind is at my stern! [that'd be breaking wind to you and me] Blow, fool, blow!"

"Shamming Abram" aboard ship was feigning sickness in order to avoid work (i.e., a malingerer). *(Ballyhoo of Blazes)*

"A CAP FULL OF WIND"

A sudden light breeze or "cat's paw." The phrase itself is derived from a legend surrounding King Eric of Sweden (1560–1568) and his alleged mastery over the impish demons of the air. It was said he could control the wind by merely pointing his cap in the desired direction, which is where the cap full of wind thing comes from.

"A CLEAN SWEEP"

A phrase describing the experience of shipping a large wave at sea, an event often resulting in a vessel's deck being swept clear of all gear or cargo. Another possible origin can be traced to a naval engagement between English and Dutch fleets during the seventeenth century. The story goes Dutch Admiral Maarten Harpertzoon Tromp ordered a broom hoisted to his masthead following the Dutch victory at the Battle of Dungeness (1652), signifying he had swept the British from the sea. The tides of war turned the following year, however, and the British commenced to open a can of *Ye olde whoop-arse* upon the Dutch fleet in a number of naval engagements. In a retort to Admiral Tromp's broom British Admiral William Blake hoisted a horsewhip aloft, signifying it was now the British who had whipped the Dutch off the sea. His gesture set the precedent for what even now remains the distinctive symbol of fighting ships the world over—a long, narrow, commissioning pennant, said to be modeled after that original horsewhip.

A-COCKBILL

A sign of mourning aboard a square rigger that involved hauling or sloping one side of the yardarms and securing them at odd angles to the deck, so that when viewed from ahead or astern they were seen as a series of Xs. First light was the proper time for cockbilling, whereas sunset was the official end of mourning, at which time the yards were then "squared away" (placed parallel) to the deck.

Ships whose crews were predominantly Catholic often wore yardarms a-cockbill on Good Friday as a show of sorrow, with some even keelhauling an effigy of Judas as well.

A more mundane reason for placing the yards a-cockbill, however, was to allow square riggers to lie alongside a warehouse or another vessel without fouling its spars. The phrase also describes an anchor hanging from the cathead prior to being dropped. *(Half-Masting of Ensigns, Mourning Line)*

"A CUP OF JOE"

This nickname for coffee came about due to the reforms initiated in 1913 by Josephus Daniels, then Secretary of the United States Navy under President Woodrow Wilson. One such reform was the elimination of the officer's wine mess, a policy received less than enthusiastically by many.

Since that time, a cup of the strongest drink allowed onboard U.S. naval ships has been referred to as "a cup of Joe."

ADMIRAL

Thank our Arabic friends for this one, which comes to us from the word *amir*, meaning a ruler or commander.

Abu-Bekr, Muhammad's faithful follower, relinquished his title of "The Truthful" upon succeeding him and assumed the new title of *Caliph* or successor. Omar, the man slated to replace Abu-Bekr, promptly labeled himself *Amir-al-muminin* or "Commander of the Faithful." The title sounded pretty snazzy to the rest of the posse as well, who soon followed suit with such titles as *Amir-al-Ahgal* (for the minister of finance) and *Amir-al-Hajj* (Commander of Caravans to Mecca). Even the Caliph himself got his groove on, assuming the title of *Amir-al-Umara*, or "Ruler of Rulers."

Amir-el-bahr, or "ruler of the sea," was carried northward by returning eleventh-century Crusaders, where it was often Latinized as *ad-miralius maris* by Christian writers, who just assumed the "am" was how the Arabs spelled Latin words beginning with "adm."

Amir-al was also spelled as one word, *amiral*, and it was King Edward I who is often credited with Anglicizing the word in 1297 with his appointment of William de Leyburn as "Amyrel of the sea of the King of England." (Italy, France, and Spain already had similar ranks, and the English didn't want to be left out.) The word itself continued to endure a number of spelling changes until the sixteenth century, when the current spelling of admiral was reached.

The rank of Lord High Admiral (as the title eventually came to be known)

was initially a shoreside position, one more concerned with administrating naval policy than actual command at sea. The rank did eventually put to sea, however, with admirals assuming command afloat as early as the sixteenth century.

Comparing the original Arabic expression with the modern term produces some interesting results, especially when considering that Admiral Lanier or *Amir-al-Lanier* would literally be "Commander of the Lanier," a title more fitting for my wife.

"ADMIRAL OF THE BLUE"

Probably the most sought-after flag officer in any fleet; a publican, so called due to the blue apron once worn by gentlemen of that profession. It's a reference to the time when English admirals were classed according to the color of their flag, with the *Admiral of the Red* holding the center during a battle, *Admiral of the White* holding the van, and *Admiral of the Blue* bringing up the rear. The distinction has since been eliminated, with all admirals carrying the white flag since 1864. *(Yellow Jack)*

"ADMIRAL OF THE NARROW SEAS"

Lofty title bestowed upon a drunken sailor who vomits into his companion's lap.

Not to be confused with "Vice Admiral of the Narrow Seas," describing an inebriated tar who urinates under the table into his shipmate's shoe.

Regardless of their rank, sage advice is avoiding either as a possible dining companion.

ADMIRAL'S WATCH

A full night's rest, one uninterrupted by watches, drills, cannibal attacks, or other such nuisances.

"AHOY"

Derived from the ancient Viking battle cry *Aoi*, "Ahoy!" is the traditional hail or greeting used between ships. It was also suggested by Alexander Graham Bell as the proper form of salutation when answering his newfangled invention, the telephone.

New Haven, Connecticut, which is located along the bustling shores of Long Island Sound, was the first area provided with regular telephone service and ahoy seemed appropriate in keeping with the area's rich nautical heritage.

"ALL BEER AND SKITTLES"

A phrase invariably used by misty-eyed sailors while fondly describing the last ship they sailed on. It was there, in the hazy recollection of Jack Tar, that everything was a paradise when compared to the current scow he was sentenced to. Grub served was fit for a king, the mates knew what they were about, the old man was lenient, and every member of the crew was a shipmate you could count on.

The term references two of a sailor's favorite pastimes, drinking beer and playing skittles, or ninepins. *(Jack Tar)*

"ALL HANDS AND THE COOK"

An emergency in which the entire crew was needed on deck, even the cook. The phrase became synonymous with the most desperate of situations, as the cook was not typically known for his seamanship.

"ALL HOLIDAY"

A *holiday* aboard ship was an undertaking set about or completed in a less-than-seamanlike fashion. From missing a portion of the ship's bottom while caulking to sloppiness in the areas of cleaning, sweeping, or painting, the bosun's melodious bellow of "Didja hear tha news? Ya took a holiday here!" served as a gentle reminder that runs in a freshly painted bulkhead and unshined brass were bad things.

"ALWAYS HANGING OUT THE BLUE LIGHT"

An admonishment to the continued dire predictions of the ship's self-appointed doomsayer, that one guy on board who was always able to find the worst in any particular situation. Such sailors were said to be "always on the lookout for Davy Jones."

Displaying blue lights at night or firing blue rockets was once the universal sign of a ship in distress. It's also interesting to note the term "Blue light ship" was used during the mid-1700s to describe a British Royal Navy vessel with a chaplain stationed aboard. Many sailors thought shipping a priest brought bad luck, although this could be ascribed to the fact that their primary goal was bringing religion to those who felt they had quite enough of it ashore. *(Davy Jones' Locker)*

AMAZON RIVER

Homer's epic tales speak of a fierce tribe of large, powerful, female warriors who dwelled near the Caucasus Mountains in the days before the Trojan War. They were said to have stood against the invading Greeks until their queen, Penthesilea, was killed by Achilles. They were called *Amazons*, derived from the Greek words *a* (without) and *mazoa* (breast)—from the belief each warrior had her right breast removed to facilitate shooting of bow and arrow.

Fast forward to 1541 when the Spanish seafarer Orellana, while exploring a large river in South America, was attacked by a tribe of natives whose women fought as fiercely as the men. Thinking them a tribe similar in nature to that known by the Greeks, he named them Amazons—and that's what a tribe of large, one-breasted women and the largest river in the world have in common.

AMERICA'S CUP

Originally called the "100 guinea cup," the Holy Grail of yachting (that being the America's Cup trophy) was fashioned at a cost of $500 in 1851, the same year it was won by the schooner *America* while sailing against the Royal Yacht Squadron. Quite a small sum compared to the millions currently spent trying to obtain it.

AMERICA'S FIRST MILLIONAIRE

Although smaller than Boston, New York, or Philadelphia, the New England town of Salem, Massachusetts, was once famous throughout the world for its ships, sailors, and prosperous merchants. Of the wealthy traders located there none was more famous than Elias Hasket Derby, America's first millionaire, who became rich financing privateers during the American Revolution (1775–1783).

AN ACQUISITION

Said of a newly shipped seaman deemed an asset by the crew, meaning he was a good sailor, quick to lend a hand, could sing, dance, and spin a good yarn to boot.

AN AMY

Nickname given all noncitizens who served aboard British warships. It's derived from *ami*, the French word for friend.

ANCHORS AWEIGH

This common bit of salty lingo comes from the nautical definition of the word *weigh*, meaning to raise, heave, or hoist. *Aweigh* simple means that the act of raising an anchor clear of the bottom has been completed.

ANCHOR WATCH

In modern seafaring terminology an anchor watch is stood to ensure the ship's anchor remains firmly set. Such watches were originally posted in port, "Lest," as Captain John Smith penned, "some miscreants from ye other ships about steal ye anchors whole theye [the happy crew] sleepe."

AND HE COULDN'T HULA EITHER

Seems Captain Cook, along with the majority of his fellow European explorers, had difficulty reproducing the musical language of his Hawaiian hosts (it contains only seven consonants, by the way). That's why when something's forbidden, us *Haoles* think of it as being *taboo* rather than the correct pronunciation of the word, *kapu*.

AND RICH FOLK STILL GO THERE

Captain Peter Easton was the terror of Newfoundland and as early as 1610 was widely known as the "Arch Pyrate" to herring fisherman frequenting the area. Pirates of the day considered Newfoundland an excellent place to refit and victual their ships. In addition to the abundance of food, drink, and supplies available during the fishing season, the 20,000 or so fishermen manning the boats were an invaluable source of fresh recruits, who were induced to join the pirates either by promises of riches or force. Law and order was nonexistent in the rough and tumble fishing camps, meaning a strong pirate could pretty much loot and pillage as he pleased, all without fear of reprisal from civil or military forces.

Such was the case when Easton raided Harbour Grace in 1612, stealing five ships, 100 pieces of ordinance, and sundry items to the tune of ten thousand pounds. He also "enlisted" an additional 500 crewmembers and took various and assorted prisoners as well, one being Sir Richard Whitbourne, who was at the time busily engaged in losing his considerable fortune in efforts to colonize the island.

Whitbourne proved to be unlike any other prisoner Easton had ever encountered, however, for he so severely vilified the pirate's life during his eleven weeks of captivity that Easton finally cracked, begging him to return to England "to some friends of his and solicit them to become humble petitioners to the King for his pardon."

To this Whitbourne agreed, waiving aside an offer of great wealth by the pirate. It was decided Easton would take his time in returning to England, thus giving Whitbourne ample opportunity to secure Easton's pardon.

Easton decided to put this waiting to good use by easing over to the Azores and intercepting a Spanish plate (treasure) fleet. His fourteen ships now bulging with plunder, he then cruised the coast of Barbary, waiting for news of his pardon. Finally deciding the pardon thing wasn't working out, he proceeded to another favorite pirate haunt, Villefranche. Moving his booty ashore (an estimated two million in gold), he purchased a magnificent palace and lived the remainder of his life in wealth and luxury, the first of many rich folk to retire on the French Riviera.

"AND THE DUTCH HAVE TAKEN HOLLAND!"

Sailorman retort to a shipmate's proclamation of old or stale news. Another would be "and the ark has rested on Mount Ararat!"

ANGEL'S FOOTSTOOL

Also known as *Cloud Cleaners*, these were imaginary sails said to be carried by Yankee ships, both names referring to the extraordinary height of the masts found aboard extreme clippers of the nineteenth century.

A POX ON YE!

Surgeons aboard British naval vessels of the eighteenth century could double their monthly salary of five pounds with every hundred cases of venereal disease treated. Funding for this additional compensation was derived from fines imposed by crewmembers contracting *gleet* (gonorrhea) or *pox* (syphilis).

Additional moneys were to be had, however, by unscrupulous practitioners who treated the symptoms rather than the disease. In such cases the patient was pronounced "clear" once the symptoms subsided. It wasn't until the inevitable reappearance of the disease later on that proper treatment was administered (with an additional fine, of course), along with sage advice to avoid a Fire Ship when "making the beast with two backs." **(Dock, Fire Ship, Take in One's Coals, To Go into Dock)**

A SAD DOG, YER LORDSHIP, A SAD, SAD, DOG

While the lure of riches definitely made the initial decision easier, the majority of seamen who turned pirate during the seventeenth and eighteenth centuries did so for quite a different reason: freedom. In a society where only the rich or nobly born knew personal liberty (the lot of the common man being limited to abject poverty and oppression), the life of a pirate offered a way to freedom, self-respect, and true democracy.

Pirates never forgot the hated figures of authority they fled, even during times of leisure. Amusements such as singing, dancing, and playacting were certainly enjoyed, but their favorite diversion by far was a mock trial, where each pirate took turn as judge, jury, and prisoner.

It was a morbid form of entertainment, doubly so when one realizes that each participant knew full well their chances of one day standing accused before a real judge and court of law. Perhaps that's why they were so serious about it—there are accounts of defendants and onlookers becoming so impassioned during these make-believe trials they had to be physically restrained in order to prevent them from shooting the judge and prosecutor.

Johnson in his *A General History . . . of the Pirates* describes the following mock trial. I include it here not only for the insight it provides into a pirate's life, but because it so nearly mirrors my own experience at traffic court in Chesapeake, Virginia. I can fully relate to my oppressed brothers . . .

> The Court and Criminals being both appointed, and also Council to plead, the Judge got up a Tree and had a dirty Taurpaulin hung over his shoulder; this was done by Way of a Robe, with a Thrum cap on his Head, and a large Pair of Spectacles upon his Nose. Thus equipp'd he settled himself in his Place; and abundance of Officers attending him below with Crows, Handspikes, etc., instead of Wands, Tipstaves, and such like—The Criminals were brought out, making a thousand sour faces; and one who acted as Attorney-general opened the Charge against them; their Speeches were very laconick, and their whole Proceedings concise. We shall give it by Way of Dialogue.
>
> **Attor. Gen.:** An't please Your Lordship, and you Gentlemen of the Jury, here is a Fellow before you that is a sad Dog, a sad, sad, Dog; and I humbly hope your Lordship will order him to be hang'd out of the Way immediately–He has committed Pyracy upon the High Seas, and we shall prove, an't please your Lordship, that this Fellow, this sad Dog before you, has escaped a thousand Storms, nay, has got safe ashore when the Ship has been cast away, which was a certain Sign he was not born to be drown'd; yet not having the Fear of hanging before his Eyes, he went on robbing and ravishing Man, Woman, and Child, plundering Ships Cargoes fore and aft, burning and sinking Ship, Bark and Boat, as if the Devil had been in him. But this is not all, my Lord, he has committed worse Villanies than all these, for we shall prove, that he has been guilty of drinking

Small-Beer; and your Lordship knows, there never was a sober Fellow but what was a Rogue. My Lord, I should have spoken much finer than I do now, but that as your Lordship knows our rum is all out, and how should a Man speak good Law that has not drunk a Dram—However, I hope your Lordship will order the Fellow to be hang'd.

Judge: Heark'ee me, Sirrah—you lousy, pitiful, ill-look'd Dog; what have you to say why you should not be tuck'd up immediately and set a sun-drying like a Scare-crow?

—Are you guilty or not guilty?

Pris.: Not guilty, an't please your Worship.

Judge: Not guilty! say so again, Sirrah, and I'll have you hang'd without any Trial.

Pris.: An't please your Worship's Honour, my Lord, I am as honest a poor fellow as ever went between stem and stern of a Ship, and can hand, reef, steer and clap tow ends of a Rope together, as well as e'er a He that ever cross'd salt Water; but I was taken by one George Bradley (the name of him that sat as Judge) a notorious Pyrate, a sad Rogue as ever was un-hang'd, and he forc'd me, an't please your Honour.

Judge: Answer me, Sirrah—How will you be try'd?

Pris.: By God and my Country.

Judge: The Devil you will—Why then, Gentlemen of the Jury, I think we have nothing to do but to proceed to Judgment.

Attor. Gen.: Right, my Lord; for if the Fellow should be suffered to speak, he may clear himself and that's an Affront to the Court.

Pris.: Pray, my Lord, I hope your Lordship will consider . . .

Judge: Consider!—How dare you talk of considering?—Sirrah, Sirrah, I never considered in all my Life—I'll make it Treason to consider.

Pris.: But, I hope your Lordship will hear some reason!

Judge: D'ye hear how the Scoundrel prates?—What I'd have you to know, Raskal, we don't sit here to hear Reason—we go according to Law—Is our Dinner ready?

Attor. Gen.: Yes, my Lord.

Judge: Then heark'ee, you Raskal at the Bar; hear me, Sirrah, hear me—You must suffer, for three reason; first, because it is not fit I should sit here as Judge and no Body be hanged. Secondly, you must be hanged, because you have a damn'd hanging Look—and thirdly, you must be hanged, because I am hungry for you know, Sirrah, that 'tis a Custom, that whenever the Judge's Dinner is ready before the Tryal is over, the Prisoner is to be hanged of Course—There's Law for you, ye Dog,—So take him away, Gaoler.

"AT LOGGERHEADS"

At odds; fighting. A *loggerhead* or *loggerheat* was a fist of iron attached to a long wooden handle; it was heated and then used to melt tar or pitch for caulking the ship's seams. It was also the name for a fireplace poker, which

most tavern hearths were equipped with in order that patrons could heat and then stick into their mugs of liquor to warm them. Both made pretty handy weapons for shipmates to swing at each other during those inevitable personality conflicts, which is where the phrase originates.

A loggerhead was also a dullard or stupid fellow. A running joke aboard ship was writing the phrase "We three loggerheads be" beneath a drawing of two heads, the third loggerhead being made once the reader repeated the sentence.

"AVAST"

Nautical command meaning *Stop! Hold on!* or *Be Quiet!* Most of us know how to throw it into a conversation to make salty talk, but where does it actually come from? Best guess is the Dutch *hou'vast* or "hold fast."

BABOON WATCH

For a sailor, the only thing worse than enduring a miserable watch at sea was the privilege of standing one during the ship's port call. It was there the "Baboon Watch" (those unfortunates so tasked) enjoyed fourth-class liberty, sampling a port's charm via the ship's telescope.

BALLAST

The unwritten law concerning ballast (and common sense as far as most sailors were concerned) was that a ship's master never allowed ballast onboard that had been taken from the seabed. Logic dictated this was the property of Davy Jones (i.e., the devil) and if he ever wanted it back, ship and crew would likely be claimed as well. Along the same lines, white ballast was considered unlucky as well—treating what was considered a sacred color in such a manner was viewed as an affront to God.

Probably the most unusual ballast of recent times was that carried by the U.S. Navy submarine *Trout* during World War II. In February 1941 she finished unloading her cargo of munitions and supplies at Corregidor, a strategic island located at the entrance to Manila Bay. Like all submarines the *Trout* required ballast once her cargo was discharged and would typically have taken on a load of gravel prior to departure (to make up for lost weight); however, all gravel was desperately needed for construction of fortifications in anticipation of a Japanese assault.

As the Philippine government and private mining companies were eager to move assets out of the country for safe keeping, the *Trout* left the islands with a load of ballast fit for a Spanish galleon—583 gold bars and eighteen tons of silver pesos, a cargo valued at over nine million dollars, all of which was transported through the war-torn Pacific and delivered safely to authorities in San Francisco, California, without loss of a single coin. *(Davy Jones' Locker)*

BALLOCKY BILL THE SAILOR

"It's only me from over the sea," said Ballocky Bill the Sailor.

Partridge (see Bibliography) describes him as "A mythical person commemorated in a late century 19-20 low ballad and often mentioned by way of evasion . . . he is reputed to have been most generously testicled."

"BALLYHOO OF BLAZES"

Ballyhoo (also spelled *ballahou*) is a term of contempt describing a ship of slovenly or unseaman-like appearance. Worse still would be one labeled a "ballyhoo of blazes," which indicated a veritable bedlam of disorganization and confusion. A *ballahou* was a type of fast, two-masted sailing vessel having the foremast raked forward and the mainmast raked aft.

BAMBOOZLE

The practice of deceiving another vessel as to your own ship's nationality by hoisting false colors, a ploy commonly used by pirates. According to Nathan Bailey's *Universal Etymological English Dictionary* (1721), which contains "A Collection of Canting Words . . . used by Beggars, Gypsies, Cheats, House-Breakers, Shop-lifters, Foot-pads, Highway-men, et al.," *bam* is defined as " . . . a Sham or Cheat: a knavish Contrivance to amuse or deceive."

BANYAN DAYS

In efforts to stretch supplies aboard British naval ships, certain days of the week were often deemed meatless or *Banyan Days*. On these days (normally Monday, Wednesday, and Friday) each man's ration of salt pork, beef, or fish was substituted with twenty ounces of butter and forty ounces of cheese. The practice was instituted during the reign of England's Queen Elizabeth I, who initially called for the issuance of fish or cheese in lieu of beef and pork as a cost-saving measure. Banyan was in reference to a Hindu trading caste of that name, whose members ate nothing that once had life.

BARGE-MAN

A large, black-headed maggot that often infested ship's biscuits. It was pretty much impossible to get all of them out, which is one reason eating in the dark was popular with many sailors.

BARNACLES

Old nautical slang for spectacles or goggles, this based on their resemblance to the shape of said critter's conical shell.

BARREL FEVER

"He died of barrel fever" was said of a shipmate who drank himself to death, in reference to the casks or barrels used to transport spirits back in the day.

BASED . . .

. . . on data from the British crown at the time, the average age of a pirate in the early eighteenth century was 27, which just so happened to be the average age of merchant mariners at the time. Theories anyone?

BATTLE OF THE CORAL SEA

The Battle of the Coral Sea (which took place off the northeast coast of Australia in May 1942) was the first naval engagement in history fought exclusively with planes. It was also the first action in which aircraft carriers engaged each other, as well as the first naval battle in which ships of the opposing sides never sighted or fired directly upon each other.

BEACHCOMBER

I meet lots of folks who aspire to become one of these upon retirement (sooner in some cases), so I've included the following for their benefit, just in case they lack a proper job description.

Beachcomber was originally a term used to describe a runaway sailor, specifically one who had jumped ship from a whaling vessel cruising the South Pacific grounds. The *Random House College Dictionary* defines it as "a person who lives by gathering salable articles of jetsam, refuse, etc., from beaches . . . a vagrant who lives on the seashore, especially a white man on a South Pacific Island."

Hotten (see Bibliography) identifies them in *The Slang Dictionary* (1887) as "a fellow who prowls about the sea-shore to plunder wrecks, and pick up waifs and strays of any kind." *(Flotsam and Jetsam)*

"BEATING UP AGAINST AN ALE-HEAD WIND"

A phrase used during port calls to describe the efforts of a drunken sailor as he weaved his way down the dock, tacking first to port, then starboard, often with a few knockdowns in between. *(Three Sheets to the Wind)*

BEING AT THE SEAS IN A MAN-OF-WAR

Whereas a medieval pirate would have called himself a *rover* and buccaneers during the seventeenth century spoke of "going on the account," those who sailed in search of plunder during the Elizabethan period preferred to use the term "being at the seas" (as opposed to using that mean old word *piracy*).

Another interesting note is that during the reign of Queen Elizabeth I the term *man-of-war* was used exclusively to describe a pirate ship, naval vessels being referred to as "the Queen's ships." *(Buccaneer, On the Account)*

BELAYING-PIN SOUP

Harsh treatment served out to crewmembers by the ship's officers, particularly aboard sailing vessels. Other disciplinary delights included heavy and full portions of "handspike hash" or "tiller soup" (the severe drubbing threatened by the coxswain to encourage his boat's crew to a higher state of enthusiasm while rowing). *(Bucko, Coxswain)*

BELL-BOTTOMS (STYLISH BEFORE THE SIXTIES)

Bell-bottoms were initially believed to have been issued to sailors around 1817. Why, you ask? Other than for the obvious fashion statement, they were easier for swabbies to roll above their knees while scrubbing the decks.

Another benefit was the speed with which they could be removed (and not just in port, either). If washed overboard, a sailor could fabricate a makeshift life preserver by knotting the legs and trapping air in them.

BELLY TIMBER

Why, victuals and grog of course, for it can rightly be said, "As a man eateth, so is he."

Beef, pork, and rum were considered by Jack to be the only proper forms of belly timber. *(Jack Tar)*

BELLY VENGEANCE

A term used to describe weak or *small beer* often issued aboard ship. Other names included whip-belly vengeance, pinch-gut vengeance, rotgut, and beer-a-bumble, of which it was said "will burst one's gut before 'twill make one tumble" (i.e., drunk).

The worst of the lot was known as "arms and legs" because, of course, it had no *body*.

The beer itself (little more than water in which a few hops had been bathed) did keep longer than plain water, but its only other benefit was exercising one's bladder. It came about by crooked contractors and was most often associated with dishonest brewing practices.

BIBLE-THUMPER

An excessively pious seaman, especially one prone to ranting or excitability.

BIGWIGS

Strangely enough, this is one bit of seafaring lingo that pretty much means what it says. Senior officers of Britain's Royal Navy at one time actually did wear bodaciously large wigs after the style of the day. That's where we get the term "Bigwig" as slang for those in positions of power, though it was just as often used in a derogatory fashion, indicating the size of the wig and the wearer's brain were often inversely proportional.

These hairy monstrosities (complete with white hands, rouged cheeks, and perhaps a fake beauty mark or two) were embraced by certain foppish Englishmen of the eighteenth century wishing to achieve the Continental style predominate in Italy at the time. The fashion itself was instituted by a gathering of dandies called the Macaroni Club, whose members consisted primarily of chic, well-traveled sissy men. As such, any effeminate gentleman perceived to be garish of clothing and light of step was duly dubbed a *Macaroni*.

Sound familiar? Think *Yankee Doodle* dandy, that English song used to slam those redneck wannabes over in the colonies. The Macaroni style of dress advocated wearing a large feather in one's cap, and the song itself was a stiff-fingered little poke at those uppity colonists, who were considered such country bumpkins by the British as to believe mere possession of a feathered hat entitled the wearer to call himself a Macaroni.

This custom of wearing wigs by the eighteenth century wealthy generated another well-known phrase. The wigs themselves were sometimes constructed of wool, rather than human hair. This was especially true during times of plague, when a buyer couldn't be sure his new headgear wasn't shaved from one of the corpses he'd seen lying in the street the previous day. Upon spying a likely target, muggers of the day first pulled these large woolen wigs down over their victim's eyes to temporarily blind them, which is where we get the phrase "to pull the wool over" one's eyes.

BILGEWATER!

The earliest known mechanical device constructed to remove water from a vessel's hold was the hydraulic screw, which was invented by the Greek mathematician Archimedes of Syracuse in the year 217 BCE. When that city was besieged during the Roman conquest of Sicily, he offered some of his other mechanical devices in its defense, such as the catapult and a fabled system of mirrors capable of focusing the sun's rays on invading boats, thus igniting them.

Archimedes was killed by a Roman soldier, who was apparently offended when the great mathematician, deep in thought while sketching in the dirt, ignored his questions and absent-mindedly told him not to step on the drawings.

BINNACLE LIST

A roster or sick list of crewmembers not fit for duty. A binnacle is the stand or housing where a vessel's compass is mounted. The ship's physician or surgeon generated a daily list of hands unable to report for duty due to sickness or injury. The list was then given to the officer or mate of the watch for use throughout the day during muster, drafting of work details, or other such evolutions. Deck officers normally kept the list beside the binnacle for ease of reference, hence binnacle list.

"BITE THE BULLET"

This familiar phrase can be traced to the surgeon's practice of borrowing a lead pistol shot ball from the gunner for patients to bite down on during surgery.

"BLACK AS THE EARL OF HELL'S RIDING BOOTS!"

Sailor's term used to describe an exceptionally dark, moonless night.

BLACKBEARD

It's certainly amazing the impression Blackbeard's legacy has stamped on popular culture concerning how your typical pirate of yesteryear looked and carried on, especially when considering his piratical endeavors lasted less than two years. He wasn't particularly daring or successful as pirates go, but what he lacked there he made up for in showmanship.

A huge man, Edward Drummond (who later changed his named to Teach or the various spellings of Thatch or Tatch) was capable of consuming prodigious amounts of food and drink; he also viewed his excesses of brutality, vicious temper, and foul language as assets rather than liabilities. Just read the description below and you'll understand why the folks who didn't believe he was the devil incarnate thought him at the very least a close relation.

> "He was of most bloody disposition and cruel to barbarity . . . [his black beard] he suffered to grow of an extravagant length; as to breadth, it came up to his eyes. He was accustomed to twist it with ribbons, in small tails, after the manner of our Ramillies wigs, and turn them about his ears. In time of action he wore a sling over his shoulders, with three brace of pistols, hanging in holsters, like bandoliers; and stuck lighted matches under his hat, which, appearing on each side of his face, his eyes naturally looking fierce and wild, made him altogether such a figure that imagination cannot form an idea of a Fury from Hell to look more frightful."

After being killed by Lieutenant Maynard and his crew near Ocracoke, North Carolina, on November 22, 1718, it was discovered Teach had sustained no less than thirty-seven major wounds, any one of which would have incapacitated a man of lesser strength. Maynard subsequently cut the pirate's head off, affixing it to the bowsprit of his sloop as proof of his capture.

As powerful as he was in life, seems he was pretty damn tough in death too—legend has it once the headless body was cast overboard, it swam around the ship three times before sinking.

BLACK MARIA

Seaman's term for a police van or other such conveyance used to transport prisoners. Story goes the original was named after Maria Lee, a giant black woman who ran a boarding house for sailors in early nineteenth century Boston.

Seems Black Maria (as she was known by her tenants) once rescued a police officer being overpowered during an arrest, while subsequently collaring the miscreant until help arrived. Due to this and the numerous occasions afterward in which she assisted authorities in arresting tenants who became a trifle too rowdy, policemen jokingly sent out an SOS for "Black Maria" whenever backup in the form of extra muscle was needed.

BLACK TOT DAY

July 31, 1970. It's the last day a *tot* (the daily ration of rum) was officially issued to sailors aboard ships in the British Royal Navy. *(Grog, Grog-Blossom, More Northing!, Six-Water Grog, Splice the Main Brace)*

"BLOODING AND SWEATING"

One of the many creative ways a pirate crew encouraged prisoners to remember where they had hidden gold and other valuables. The pirates first placed lighted candles in a circular pattern around the mizzenmast, normally at a juncture between decks. The victim was stripped of all clothing and placed within, while his antagonists formed another circle outside the candles, each armed with a sail needle, penknife, fork, broken bottle, or other such instruments.

The prisoner was then forced to run the gauntlet in the space so provided around the mast (often to the accompaniment of the ship's musicians) while the fun-loving crew pricked and poked him as long as he remained standing. Thus blooded, he was sealed within an empty sugar cask teeming with cockroaches, which feasted on the hapless victim's blood. He remained so imprisoned until confessing the location of his valuables (or until the pirates got bored and started the whole process over again).

Another favorite torture was placing lighted matches between the prisoner's fingers and toes, or perhaps one behind each ear for variety. *(Running the Gauntlet, Wooding)*

"BLOW THE MAN DOWN"

A well-known sea shanty most everyone's heard of; however, few know the meaning of the title or refrain, which is to knock down with the fist (a reference to the brutal Yankee "Bucko" mates prevalent in the heyday of clipper ships). *(Bucko)*

BLUE MONDAY

A reference to Monday, the day traditionally reserved for dispensing the week's accumulation of whippings among ships' boys found delinquent in their duties.

Black Monday was another common term for the day during the seventeenth century. *(Making Wind, Tailwinds)*

BLUE PETER

Sailors' nickname for the international "P" or "Papa" flag. It was flown as a recall signal from the yardarm in order to inform those on liberty ashore that the ship was preparing to get underway. I've found only one rather racy explanation as to the origin of the term. Suffice it to say the reference dealt with sailors and leaving behind newly made acquaintances of the female persuasion.

British seamen also knew it as the "salt horse" flag, in reference to what they could expect food-wise once underway. *(Flogging a Dead Horse, Harness Cask)*

BOATS DON'T ROCK—THEY ROLL

Use of the word *rock* to describe the motion of a boat, such as in "don't rock the boat" is strictly a landlubber's term. Boats don't rock—they roll, pitch, cant, capsize, heel, or list, but never rock. *Tip* (as applied to vessel movement) is also strictly a lubber's word.

BOATSWAIN'S PIPE

The boatswain's badge of office, this shrill-toned whistle shaped in the form of a dog's penis was and still is used to signal various evolutions or commands aboard ship. Until the mid-seventh century it was often cast of some precious, bejeweled metal and worn around the neck on a gold or silver chain.

Purists insist it be correctly referred to as a *boatswain's call* or *pipe*, but never a whistle. It was also the only wind instrument allowed aboard early ships, as others (flutes, horns, and the like) were thought to cause storms. *(Bos'n)*

BODY AND SOUL LASHINGS

Lashings applied to the wrists and ankles of foul-weather gear in order to keep water out.

BODY SNATCHERS

Nautical slang for members of the ship's police force.

BOMBAY OYSTER

Old salt's laxative consisting of two shots of castor oil in a glass of milk. Sailors aboard whaling ships used a concoction called *Spanker-boom tea*, which was made of herbs gathered from the South Seas islands.

BOMB-BOATING

The business of providing credit and accommodations to sailors ashore, while at the same time finding them berths on outbound vessels. It was an especially profitable sideline for madams engaged in running "houses of entertainment," such lodgings being eagerly sought by sailors for some reason.

BOMBS AWAY!

The word *bomb* originated from naval rather than air warfare. It comes from the sound early shipboard munitions made when fired from a cannon, *bomb* being a corruption of the Latin word *bombus*, the sound of a bee.

BONE BOX

The mouth, as in "Pipe down and give your bone box a rest!" Another quaint retort for a shipmate who talked too much would be "Shut your bone box and keep your guts warm; the devil loves hot tripes!"

BONE POLISHER

The cat of nine tails, or just as often the person wielding it. *(Cat O' Nine Tails)*

BOOBY HATCH

Alternately a sliding hatchway (or hoistway) providing access to storage spaces beneath the poop deck or a small, hooded compartment located in the bows of a ship.

Booby (as in a dunce, dullard, or nincompoop) has been used in the English language since 1599 and is probably derived from the Spanish word *boho* (a fool), which in turn most likely comes from the Latin word *balbus*, or stammering.

As to how it came to mean an insane asylum or nut house (for the less politically correct of us), a few theories crop up. One put forth is that booby hatches aboard ship were large and easily entered (as opposed to scuttles and other smaller, more difficult openings) and therefore more suited for use by landlubbers, who were often referred to as Boobies.

Booby is also common slang for a slow, stupid fellow, this from any of several tropical sea birds so named by sailors due to their disregard for danger and ease of capture upon landing on ship. It doesn't take much imagination to see the entertainment value they undoubtedly provided bored sailors as they captured the dimwitted birds by hand, confining them to a small, hooded coop or "hutch" (a word easily degraded to "hatch").

Others theorize the asylum reference derived from the practice of confining sailors in the cramped, stifling confines of the booby hatch (that small, hooded hatch mentioned earlier)—a punishment that elicited screams similar to those of an insane asylum from the unfortunates within. *(Scuttlebutt)*

BOOM BOAT

A boat boom (a.k.a. riding boom) was a spar riding on a hinge or gooseneck riveted to the ship's hull. At anchor, it was lowered to a horizontal position (at right angles to the hull) and used for holding small boats off from the ship's sides. "Boom boats" were small craft authorized to lie at the boat boom while in port to sell trinkets and sundries to the ship's crew. *(Bumboat)*

BOOM-PASSENGER

Shipboard slang for a convict, from the practice of chaining said individuals to the ship's boom for punishment aboard convict transports.

BOOTLEG

This term for the smuggling of illegal liquor was derived from the old sailors' ruse of bringing in contraband by hiding it in the tops of their sea boots.

BOOT TOPPING

A quick, temporary measure to remove marine growth from a ship's *boot top* (the area of the hull between the waterlines when fully loaded and when unloaded) in lieu of a complete haul out or careening. Boot topping involved running the ship into shallow water and causing a list by shifting guns, cargo, ballast, or even running tackle from the ship's mast to sturdy trees ashore, all in an effort to expose as much of the hull below the waterline as possible. The fouled area was then scraped clean of growth, and the process repeated for the other side.

Careening was basically the same thing; however, it normally involved a more thorough cleaning and repair of the ship's bottom. Crews often brought guns, cargo, and supplies ashore (to further lighten the ship) while setting up temporary camps or forts to offer protection during such a vulnerable phase of ship repair.

Ships traversing areas lacking proper haul-out facilities utilized both methods, especially those such as privateers or pirates that were hard pressed to find friendly ports to work in.

BOOTY CALL!

Privateers were legalized men-of-war granted commissions and *Letters of Marque* from a patron nation authorizing them to attack and plunder enemy shipping. Such ships were normally fitted out by a syndicate of merchants or other private backers, who invested capital in hopes of realizing substantial returns.

Although the government issuing such commissions normally received a percentage of any profits, the real advantage went beyond said moneys. Not only did privateers disrupt the flow of goods and supplies bound for enemy ports, they essentially furnished the crown with fighting ships at no more cost than a piece of parchment and a royal John Hancock. The practice can be traced to as far back as 1273, when Edward I of England employed privateers against the French.

Once a ship or *prize* was taken, it was secured and then disposed of as circumstances dictated. She could be sailed to the privateer's port of origin and placed into the eager hands of the backing merchants—a viable choice if she was particularly rich or captured near the end of a voyage—or she could be stripped of cargo and anything else of value, then scuttled or released (depending on the mood of the captors). Another alternative was rigging the prize to serve as a privateer herself.

The final option was making for the nearest friendly port and selling her. Goods were normally so scarce in outlying colonies that local merchants (even in enemy ports) thought nothing of buying privateer merchandise, regardless of the knowledge it was probably stolen from their fellow countrymen in the first place.

Once a prize was boarded, the "general rules of plunder" usually governed how the ship was supposed to be, well, plundered. Everything above the main deck level was considered fair game for the ship's company and as such not accountable to those who had financed and outfitted the expedition. Needless to say this was a system widely open to abuse, as sailors would often secure items from the hold, later to be dropped and "found" on the main deck.

The booty itself was normally divided into either *ship's plunder* or *cabin plunder*, the former being designated as fair game for the crew, while the latter was reserved for the privateer's captain. He usually came out ahead, however, as the cabin was where most items of value were normally located, including the all-important charts and navigational information concerning enemy waters. Many's the captain who, upon standing accused of crossing the thin line between privateer and pirate, saved his hide by presenting such documents to a grateful, forgiving monarch.

BOOZE

Booze (strong alcoholic drink or the act of drinking until drunk) is derived from the now defunct phrase "bowse (or bouse) the can" meaning to drink heartily or to cinch a rope tight with block and tackle.

BORGNE-FESSE

Chances are good you've heard of Captain Kidd or Blackbeard, but how about the daring exploits of Captain Half-Butt?

Most pirates preferred living under pseudonyms while carving out their fortunes, both to avoid bringing shame upon their family name and (hopefully) evade future prosecution. Such was the case of one Louis Le Golif, a pirate who roamed the West Indies between 1660 and 1675.

Seems Le Golif acquired the nickname Borgne-Fesse (literally *Half-Bottom*) after an embarrassing wound required the removal of his left buttock. He received the injury while raiding a Spanish settlement when a cannon ball (that's right, a cannon ball) passed between his legs and ricocheted off a rock behind him, causing the derrière damage.

History shows him a mediocre pirate at best, and if his memoirs are to be believed, his chosen profession wasn't the only (brace yourself) half-arsed decision he made in life.

They tell of his marriage to a prostitute, one of thousands sent from England to populate the new colonies, and his killing of a rival named Babord-Amure or *Port Tack* (in reference to his skewed nose) on their wedding night.

It must have been a happy home, one filled with love and trust; too bad he had to murder the lady in bed (along with another new lover) a few days after the wedding. *(Blackbeard, Captain William Kidd)*

BOS'N

A corruption of the word *boatswain* or *bosun, swain* being an Anglo-Saxon term for attendant or controller. Thus, the bosun is a keeper of boats. In the early days of sail the swain was simply a lad charged with maintaining the ship's small boats, including its oars, steering paddle, sails, and rigging. He also summoned its crew as required, a task most likely done initially by whistling, a method replaced by the bosun's pipe around the fifteenth century. *(Boatswain's Pipe, Coxswain)*

BOSUN! KEELHAUL HIM!

Punishments in the days of sail were brutal and severe, as those in command believed a strong hand and harsh discipline were the deciding factors that kept a well-run ship from descending into mutiny and chaos.

Keelhauling originated in the Dutch navy and was one of the more barbarous forms of punishment awarded to those brought "before the mast"

(trials, punishments, etc., were often carried out on the main deck at the base of the ship's mainmast). A sailor so convicted was bound hand and foot, weighted, and hauled up to the ship's highest yardarm. He was then dropped into the sea and dragged beneath the ship by prearranged ropes around chest and feet, finally being hauled up to the yardarm on the opposite side. This was continued until death (which was usually the case due to drowning or wounds received from the razor sharp barnacles encrusting the hull) or until sufficient punishment was deemed to have been suffered.

An even more brutal variation was *keelraking*, in which the victim was dragged fore and aft along the entire length of the keel. Both forms of punishment pretty much went out of vogue during the early eighteenth century, when the cat o' nine tails became the disciplinary aid of choice. *(Cat O' Nine Tails, Sail before the Mast, Strappado)*

BOTTOMS UP

As far as sailors are concerned, some things on board were just asking for trouble. A hatch carelessly left upturned or an upside-down chart might induce the ship to assume a likewise position. Chinese seamen disliked upside-down shoes on deck, whereas an overturned calabash gourd did it for West Indian sailors.

Having flowers aboard was to be avoided as well (they suggested wreaths and death), while black trunks or suitcases were shunned due to their similarity to coffins.

BOX THE COMPASS

The ability of a sailor not only to repeat the thirty-two points of the mariner's compass both forward and backward, but to answer all questions concerning its divisions as well.

It's said the mariner's compass (in almost its exact present form) was invented by the Chinese Emperor Ho-Ang-Ti in 2634 BCE, over 3,700 years before its appearance in Europe. Clever folks, the Chinese—they also invented the sternpost rudder, watertight compartments, and produced the world's first printed charts.

BRASS-BOUNDER

Midshipmen in the British Royal Navy, the term itself being derived from the numerous brass buttons on their uniforms. Ever wonder why military uniforms sport brass buttons on their sleeves? I mean, they don't really do anything, do they? I've found one explanation, with credit being attributed to either Admiral Horatio Nelson or Napoleon, depending on your allegiance.

Napoleon was said to have ordered buttons from the jackets of dead men sewn onto the sleeves of his soldiers during a winter campaign in Russia.

Seems the soldiers had the disgusting habit of wiping their noses on the sleeves of their jackets and this was the emperor's solution to the problem.

Admiral Nelson was also credited with the button idea, using it to combat the same habit among the younger, homesick midshipmen of his fleet (who were also known as *snotties*). *(Snotty)*

BRICKLAYER'S CLERK

Old salt's term for someone who goes to sea, but dislikes his occupation.

BRIG

Seems during one of his naval campaigns, Admiral Nelson ordered captives sequestered aboard a small brigantine, or brig. That, as well as the later practice of converting stripped down ships (often brigs as well) into floating prisons, pretty much assured its place in salty lingo as nautical slang for jail. *(Stone Frigate)*

BUCCANEER

Buccaneer comes from the French word *boucaner*, meaning to cure or preserve by smoking. It was used to describe the half-wild men residing on the isle of Hispaniola (now Haiti and the Dominican Republic) during the seventeenth century. Mostly of French stock, they subsisted by hunting the abundant herds of wild cattle and pigs first brought to the island by the Spanish, who seeded every such island they came across in hopes of providing a food source for any future Spanish settlers or castaways.

The buccaneers became renowned throughout the region as excellent marksmen, utilizing a peculiar rifle with a spade-shaped stock and a barrel whose length often reached over four a half feet in length. *Buccaneer* was derived from their practice of preserving meat by cutting it into thin strips and smoking it over open fires on wooden grills, an idea stolen from the Carib Indians (you know, those folks who gave us the name for the Caribbean Sea—gave us the word cannibal, too).

Boucan was an Indian word meaning dried meat and campfire, while the wooden grill used during smoking (or any elevated framework, for that matter) was *barbacoa*, a word eventually corrupted by the Spanish into *barbecue*.

Buccaneer acquired its more familiar meaning when the island's residents began raiding the merchant ships and Spanish galleons transporting the plundered wealth of Mexico and Peru to the coffers of Spain. *(Know Your Pirates, Pierre Le Grand)*

BUCKO

Name given the brutal Yankee mates often found aboard extreme clipper ships. Favorites of captains who lived by the creed "carry on or carry under" (in reference to carrying so much sail as to endanger the ship), theirs was the job of "motivating" the crew via a sadistic combination of curses, threats, hazing, and belaying-pin soup (i.e., a good old-fashioned drubbing).

How bad were they? One such mate forced his men to eat cockroaches as punishment, while another was said to have been particularly fond of breaking off teeth with an iron bolt to keep his crew in line. Common knowledge said they "ate a sailor every morning and picked their teeth with the frayed end of a wire hawser." *(Belaying-Pin Soup)*

BUGS

Nickname for a dirty, slovenly seaman, who was himself considered a "bug trap."

BULL DANCE

Nautical term for a manly dance of manliness with manly men only in presence. Avast there, Long John! Keep your distance from me captain's quarters!

BULLY-BOYS

Eighteenth-century sailors, the nickname arising not from antisocial tendencies on their part, but rather from *bully beef*, a leather-like staple served aboard ship at the time.

BUMBOAT

Small boats engaged in supplying ships with foodstuffs, provisions, mercantile items, prostitutes, or anything else deemed likely by their owners to turn a profit. The term itself is derived from *boom boat*, which at one time signified boats permitted to lie at the ship's booms in order to display and sell their wares. *(Boom Boat)*

"BUNG UP AND BILGE FREE"

Nautical phrase describing a vessel in perfect order, after the proper stowage of casks in the hold, which called for the "bung," or hole, to be up and the barrel itself to be stowed above the ship's bilge water.

BUOY

OK, so you know what it is, but how'd it get its name? Simple—just drop the last three letters from the word buoyant.

BURGOO

A thick oatmeal porridge often popular with a ship's cook for its ease of preparation and hated by the crew for the same reason.

BURIAL AT SEA

Loss of life is always a sobering reality check on one's own mortality; however, such tragedy was especially poignant in the close confines aboard ship. Jack needed to look no further than the vacant spot in the mess or the short-handed watch section to see the hazards of following a life at sea.

Those who died at sea were normally committed to Davy Jones' locker, a euphemism for burial at sea. As there was no means of preservation, it was imperative to dispose of the body as quickly as possible. Superstition played a role in the matter too, as corpses onboard were thought to be *windraisers*, causing storms and other such misfortunes.

The sailmaker sewed the body inside sailcloth or the sailor's own hammock, often placing a cannon ball at the dead man's head and feet to ensure it would sink. He was also charged by the old salts on board to ensure the last two stitches of this makeshift shroud passed through the nose of the deceased, this to prevent the spirit from returning to haunt vessel and crew, while ensuring there was absolutely no life left in the body.

Senior hands also warned those of the ship's company uneducated in the ways of the sea not to watch the corpse sink, lest they invite the same fate upon themselves. If the deceased was deemed to be of a restless nature, it was those same shellbacks who made certain once darkness fell that the cook floated a shingle astern containing a lighted candle, a cake of flour and water, and a pinch of salt to keep him quiet.

As the remaining sailors were in duress during a burial at sea (leaving them vulnerable to possession by demons), the ship's guns were often fired three times as a precaution to frighten away evil spirits. The number three was considered magical, in reference to the holy trinity, and also as a symbol of life (birth involving father, mother, and child).

Ship owners were acutely aware of how crews felt about shipping a body onboard as cargo and the bad luck it could bring. When contracted to ship one, they ensured the cadaver was placed in a nondescript container, often listing it on the ship's manifest as "natural history specimen." *(Davy Jones' Locker, Jack Tar, Hand, Shellback)*

BURNING THE WATER

Sailor slang for torch fishing from the ship's small boat or skiff. This form of getting fresh grub was usually carried out in the shallows using spears or makeshift harpoons.

BUT WHY IS IT CALLED THE HEAD?

The forward-most part of a ship was originally known as the *bows* or *beakhead*, after the ram on the bow of a fighting galley (think *beak* as in a bird of prey). During the medieval period, the bows evolved into a raised, castle-like structure from which archers (and later musketeers) could fire down upon the enemy during battle, which is where the name *forecastle* (or *fo'c'sle*) is derived.

Over time, the forecastle devolved into basically a work platform covered with open grating. Due to the continuous flushing action of the seas and its location (which allowed the wind to carry the smell forward, away from the ship) this is where the lavatories or "seats of ease" came to be located, these being nothing more than benches built over holes cut into the grating.

Those who used them were fully exposed to both the elements and ship's company, with at least one Spanish traveler describing with mock sentiment the lovely views afforded the crew of the moon and planets, as well as the tarred rope (which served the same purpose as the corncob in rural America) and those impromptu washings provided by the waves. Thoughtful captains often had safety netting strung around the entire area, as it was not uncommon for patrons caught off guard to be washed overboard by larger seas.

They could be busy places, too, as a typical eighteenth-century man-of-war possessed only six seats of ease for a crew of roughly eight hundred.

"BY AND LARGE"

In the days of sail a helmsman could expect this order or its opposite, *full and by*.

When sailing *full and by* the ship sailed as close to the wind as possible, a position requiring a more experienced hand at the helm in order to keep the ship from luffing and thus losing headway.

By and large meant sailing slightly off the wind with sails "large" or well eased, a condition that presented less opportunity for inexperienced sailors to get into trouble.

The term later washed ashore, where it came to mean *generally* or *overall*.

"BY WAY OF THE LUBBER'S HOLE"

The *lubber's hole* was an opening in the main-topmast platform through which the more timid of the crew could climb or descend. More experienced hands went aloft the manly man's way via the futtock shrouds (meaning they climbed over the outside of the platform). As such, "by way of the lubber's hole" came to be synonymous with anything cowardly or less than the hundred percent a true sailor would give. *(Lubber)*

CALIFORNIA BANK NOTE

Sailor's name for the partially cured cattle hides early Spanish inhabitants of California used to barter for goods brought in by visiting merchant ships.

CAMEL CORPS

Nineteenth-century term given those young seamen who, at every import, staggered home with a humplike load of dirty clothes and hammocks slung over their backs. Young couples often faced a tough prospect running a household on naval wages, so the wife frequently washed the clothes of her husband's shipmates to make ends meet.

CANNED WILLIE

Sailorman slang for canned corned beef, after a morbid style of short little poems popular during the latter part of the nineteenth century describing the murderous exploits of a young boy named "Little Willie," who butchered siblings and parents alike in a variety of grisly fashions. The poems also gave rise to another well-known phrase, that of something that "gives you the willies."

Let's take a stroll through the halcyon days of yesteryear for a taste of what was tickling the fancy of sailors and landsmen alike way back when . . .

Willie, I regret to state,
cut his sister into bait.
We miss her when it's time to dine,
but Willie's fish taste simply fine.

Little Willie hung his sister.
She was dead before we missed her.
Willie's always up to tricks.
Ain't he cute! He's only six.

And let's not forget that childhood classic we all know and love . . .

William with a thirst for gore,
Nailed the baby to the door.
Mother said, with humor quaint:
"Careful, Will, don't mar the paint."

CAPE OF STORMS

With the ascension of King John II in 1481, Portugal began a new era of exploration and expansion along the West African coast, the ultimate goal of which was trade with India and the spices so in demand throughout Europe. Until well into the seventeenth century, chronic shortages of winter fodder forced European farmers to slaughter large numbers of their cattle each fall, which in turn had to be salted, pickled, or otherwise preserved. Spices such as pepper, cinnamon, mace, and cloves from the Malabar Coast played a crucial role in this yearly cycle of preparing Europe for winter. The spices themselves arrived overland across Asia or through a torturous Red

Sea/Mediterranean route, both of which were Muslim controlled, a situation that didn't sit well with the Christian nations of Western Europe. Seeking an alternate route via the Atlantic seemed just the ticket to break the Arab-held monopoly, a choice that served not only to remove Portugal from much of the political backstabbing of European affairs at the time, but also enabled them to focus on their strength as a nation of shipbuilders and sailors (skills that eventually allowed them to outpace their much stronger neighbors).

Of the many distinguished captains King John employed, it was Bartholomeu Dias who finally solved the riddle of Africa's southern extremity and the key to establishing a trade route to India. While searching for the expected "great cape" Dias and his tiny fleet were caught in a gale and blown southward for thirteen days, after which a port tack brought them to land at Mossel Bay in the Indian Ocean.

It was actually during the return leg of the voyage that Dias sighted Cape Agulhas (the southernmost point of the continent) and the cape he was initially seeking, an area so marked by severe weather and difficult sailing he named it *Cabo Tormentosa,* or the Cape of Storms.

It was changed to the more familiar Cape of Good Hope upon his return to Portugal, a name selected by King John based on the future riches it was hoped the discovery would bring.

CAPTAIN

A title originally derived from the Latin word *caput,* meaning "head" or "top." Caput is the origin for a variety of English words, including capital, decapitate, and chief, among others.

CAPTAIN BOW-WOW

Nickname given the infamous Scottish captain of a Clyde passenger boat who once used a dog as an impromptu fender.

CAPTAIN CHALONER OGLE

While commanding the HMS *Swallow*, it was Captain Ogle and his crew who finally killed the infamous pirate Bartholomew Roberts (a.k.a. Black Bart) off the coast of Africa in 1722. Ogle returned to England a hero, and to this day remains the only man ever knighted for actions against pirates.

CAPTAIN COOKER

"A gaunt, ill-shaped, or sorry-looking pig," in reference to the swine introduced to New Zealand by Captain Cook.

"CAPTAIN COPPERTHORN'S CREW"

Said of a crew containing too many chiefs and not enough Indians, i.e., one consisting of all officers, each of whom wants to be captain.

CAPTAIN FUDGE

In his *Dictionary of Slang and Unconventional English* Partridge defines fudge as "a lie, nonsense; exaggeration." The origin of the term itself, however, can be traced to one Captain Fudge, a seventeenth-century sailor whose propensity for telling outrageous whoppers prompted his crew to meet any tale of dubious origin with a cry of "You Fudge It!"

Mention of the good captain is found in the writings of William Crouch, a Quaker whose memoirs relay the following anecdote told him by another Quaker, Degory Marshall:

> "In the year 1664 we were sentenced for banishment to Jamaica by Judges Hyde and Twisden, and our number was 55. We were put on board the ship *Black Eagle*; the master's name was Fudge, by some called Lying Fudge."

Finally, a bit of Quaker trivia—how did they come to be known as Quakers? Anyone? Anyone? The most plausible explanation is related by a follower named George Fox while commenting on his arrest, "This was Justice Bennet of Derby that first called us Quakers because we bid them tremble at the word of God, and this was in the year 1650."

CAPTAIN HOOK, I PRESUME?

Challenge your salty friends at the yacht club bar to come up with Captain Hook's first name (you know, the pirate of *Peter Pan* fame). Dazzle those smug landlubbers with gems from your storehouse of nautical knowledge by informing them it was Jacobus.

If that doesn't do it, ask them the name of the *Minnow*'s skipper (played by Alan Hale, Jr.) on *Gilligan's Island*. The name that should win you at least one free beer: Jonas Grumby.

CAPTAIN WILLIAM KIDD

Probably no name in history is more popularly associated with piracy than that of Captain William Kidd. The rest of the story, however, makes it easier to view Kidd as a victim of circumstance rather than the murderous rogue he's invariably portrayed as.

It all started in August 1695 with prominent New York businessman Thomas Livingston's arrival in London. His reason for traveling to England was twofold—he wanted to press his lawsuit against New York's current governor, Benjamin Fletcher (who was in the process of getting the royal boot by King William on charges of corruption and a liberal open-door policy concerning pirates and their booty), and he wanted to suck up to Fletcher's replacement, Richard Coote, the Earl of Bellomont.

When Livingston visited Coote on August 10, the two found they had much in common, not the least of which was an eye for business and a passion for intrigue.

At some point during the course of the evening, Coote mentioned an earlier conversation he'd had with the King himself. Seems the Madagascar pirates were making a nuisance of themselves and the East India Company was squealing for assistance from the Royal Navy. England, however, was involved in King William's War with France at the time. The crown refused to send even one ship to duty halfway around the world, especially to help a private enterprise, when all were needed for the war effort.

It was during this conversation between Coote and the king that the idea of sending a privately financed privateer to deal with the situation came up. This pirate-killing venture, granted full authority by the crown, would disperse the pirates and at the same time generate a tidy profit by relieving them of their ill-gotten plunder. The enterprise was to be initially financed by selling shares, and the list of interested backers was a veritable who's who of parliamentarians, with even the king initially planning to get in on the action.

Livingston embraced the idea wholeheartedly, as did Coote, and both discussed how best to bring the project to fruition (the morality of stealing stolen goods for profit didn't seem to concern them). The main stumbling block was finding a suitable captain who could be trusted to get the job done. He would have to be a respected man, not only a competent mariner but also one whose discretion could be counted on while dealing with rich folks in high places (such as the expedition's potential backers). It was while puzzling out this show stopper that Livingston bumped into another fellow New Yorker, who happened to be in London on a mission of his own: Captain William Kidd.

Kidd at the time was a well-respected man of means. He had done exceedingly well in the shipping business, where he was known as a simple yet honest captain. It was his marriage to the young, beautiful widow of another wealthy New Yorker, however, that catapulted him up the financial and social ladder.

Kidd not only owned a fine house overlooking New York's harbor and a large farm along the banks of the East River, but also several plots of land in Manhattan (along modern day Wall Street), which today is some of the most valuable real estate in the world.

In addition to being highly regarded by the community at large, Kidd was a pillar of the church as well; it was he who donated the block and tackle used to construct New York's famous Trinity Church. There was even a Kidd family pew located within the completed tabernacle.

Yet, despite the love of a beautiful wife and a life of wealth and ease, Kidd was an unhappy man. He had one dream unfulfilled—one life-long wish denied that became so unbearable it drove him to London during the summer of 1695 in efforts to achieve it.

Captain William Kidd "merchant master, who had barely enough education to write a comprehensible letter, longed to captain one of His Majesties men-of-war . . . hungered for the prestige and the dignity of a command in the Royal Navy."

Although possessing in reality the proverbial snowball's chance in hell, Kidd convinced himself he could overcome his lack of social graces, lack of background, lack of powerful connections, and a British society that had raised snobbery to an art form to achieve his goal.

To his credit, Kidd had fought valiantly as a privateer for the Royal Navy during the outbreak of King William's War aboard his ship the *Blessed William*. Sherry (see Bibliography) notes, "Perhaps it was this experience with the professional fleet in the West Indies, plus Hewson's praise [the fleet commander], that had convinced Kidd that for all his lack of schooling and background, he did possess sufficient natural merit to realize his dream of a Royal Navy command."

Armed with a letter of introduction and recommendation from New York's attorney general, Kidd traveled to London in search of William Blathwayt, a powerful man known for his ability to procure "favors" for friends. It was he Kidd hoped could persuade the Admiralty to grant him his request. Kidd's first stroke of bad luck upon arriving in London was missing Blathwayt, who at the time was with the king in Flanders. His second was bumping into Livingston.

Livingston saw Kidd as the ideal man to lead his new venture. He was not only a man of good character, but a highly skilled mariner and proven privateer captain to boot. Coote agreed and the two met with Kidd to put forth their glorious plans of pirate hunting. Where the two armchair quarterbacks saw nothing but opportunity and profit, however, Kidd saw a disaster in the making.

He pointed out that pirate ships were not only heavily manned with tough, seasoned fighters, but that it was also impossible to positively identify them as pirates unless you literally caught them in the act. He also mentioned the fact that even if you did manage to locate, identify, and take one, the chances of there being any booty aboard were almost nil. After securing a prize, pirates invariably headed to some safe, well-guarded location to sell or divide their treasure. It was after the loot was spent that they normally went on the prowl.

Coote and Livingston would hear none of it and really began putting on the pressure. After veiled threats concerning how the future governor of New York would view an unwilling Kidd, they sweetened the deal by saying that as he would be acting on a writ from the king himself and was serving as captain, he was kind of like an officer himself—yeah, that's the ticket—and who better to recommend him to the Admiralty upon his triumphant return than a grateful king?

It was that argument that finally placed Kidd's feet firmly on the deck of a venture that eventually led to the gallows—hanged as a pirate because he dreamed of being a Royal Navy officer. *(Booty Call!)*

"CARRY A BONE IN HER TEETH"

Phrase used to describe a ship sailing fast enough to foam the water in front of her bow.

"CARRY THREE RED LIGHTS"

Reeling drunk, from the maritime signal of three vertical lights in a row, indicating a vessel is not under control.

"CATCH A CRAB"

Said of a rower whose oar drags the water on his return stroke, the result of a "crab" grabbing it. Another source attributes the saying to a stroke that misses the water altogether, the crab part describing what the rower looks like after falling on his back and flailing about in the bottom of the boat.

CAT O' NINE TAILS

This is the big one—that must-have accessory for any captain wanting to dole out a little flogging among the happy crew. The *cat o' nine tails* (or *cat* for short) was the actual whip used in these floggings. Constructed from a short piece of thick rope with one end unravelled into nine strands or whips, each whip or tail was approximately a quarter of an inch in diameter, with the entire affair weighing around fourteen ounces.

On naval ships, a man was rarely flogged on the same day accused. He was first brought before the captain, who stated the charges, weighed the evidence, and then pronounced judgment. If the sentence was flogging, the punishment was normally carried out the following day.

There were a couple of reasons for this delay. First, it gave the bosun's mate time to make a new cat (they were never used twice aboard military vessels). This served double duty, as having the crew witness the grizzled old bosun carefully cutting the lines, doing the tucks, and adding the whippings no doubt served well the use of public flogging as a deterrent to crime, the main reason behind them in the first place. The delay between judgment and punishment also gave both captain and crew time to reflect upon the transgression, verdict, and penalty awarded.

Another interesting point is that among pirate crews it was the quartermaster, not the captain, who retained sole authority to administer floggings. As a duly elected representative of the crew, the quartermaster had the responsibility of looking after their well-being in all matters, from discipline to division of booty.

Floggings were a rarity among pirate crews, however, no doubt due to overuse of the lash on the naval vessels from which many had deserted. It was so despised that even the quartermaster couldn't flog an individual without a majority vote of the crew.

As to how the *cat* got its name, I've found a couple of practical explanations.

The ancient Egyptians worshipped cats (which even then were said to have nine lives) and believed nothing removed evil from a person quite so well as a good thrashing with a whip fashioned from the hide of said sacred critter. Another source claims the name was derived from the wounds it inflicted, which resembled the scratches of a cat. As to the nine tails, it was believed a trinity of trinities was just the thing needed to beat the devil out of someone.

The cat was often carried in a red baize bag (to hide bloodstains) and to "let the cat out of the bag" has since come to mean an action that invites disaster. "Not enough room to swing a cat" is popularly attributed to a space lacking sufficient room for a good flogging, believable when one considers the length of the lash was around 3 feet, plus the arm of the man wielding it.

I've also read the latter phrase was attributed to a Shakespearean play, which mentions the practice of using cats for archery practice. Seems they made a pretty good target when placed in a sack and swung from a limb of ye old oak tree. *(Checkered Shirt, Cold Burning, Cursing and the Cangue,*

Flogging Around the Fleet, Goose without Gravy, Killing the Cat, Marry the Gunner's Daughter, Nightingale, Salt Eel, To Flog or Not to Flog, Whipped and Pickled)

"CAULK OR YARN?"

A question likely asked of those who found themselves sharing a coach with a man of the sea. *Taking a caulk* was sailor's slang for a nap, so Jack was merely asking his fellow traveler if they wanted to talk or sleep. *(Take a Caulk)*

CHAMBER OF HORRORS

A room within Lloyds of London where notices pertaining to shipwrecks or other such maritime losses are posted. Use of the term stems from Madame Tussaud's Wax Museum, whose room of gruesome relics from the French Revolution was dubbed the "chamber of horrors" by a contributor of London's *Punch* magazine in 1845.

Interesting lady, that Madame Tussaud. She perfected the art of casting wax "death masks" by practicing on nobles and revolutionaries during the French Revolution (many of whom she knew from court), including King Louis XVI and Marie Antoinette, her former employers (she was an art tutor for the king's sister). *(A1, Lloyds of London)*

CHECKERED SHIRT

Term sailors jokingly used to describe the diamond-shaped pattern of scars left by the cat o' nine tails. *(Cat O' Nine Tails, Cold Burning, Cursing and the Cangue, Flogging Around the Fleet, Goose without Gravy, Killing the Cat, Marry the Gunner's Daughter, Nightingale, Salt Eel, To Flog or Not to Flog, Whipped and Pickled)*

CHEEKS THE MARINE

An imaginary crewmember found aboard English men-of-war who was pretty much blamed for whatever went wrong. He was created and popularized by one Captain Marryat, a writer of sea tales during the early nineteenth century (see the Bibliography). Giving cheek to one's superiors or acting cheeky is to be insolent or saucy, which is most likely how Marryat came to choose the name.

CHEESY VICTORY

After firing his last cannonball during a pitched naval battle with a Brazilian vessel in the mid-1800s, Uruguayan Captain Coe ordered the cannons loaded with stale Dutch cheeses, reasoning, "They were too old and hard to eat anyway."

The first two shots passed well above the Brazilian ship; however, one cheesy projectile smashed into her mainmast, producing a deadly shower of cheese shrapnel, killing two sailors standing next to the Brazilian admiral. After taking a few more rounds through the sails, the Brazilian admiral discovered a sudden aversion to cheese and ordered his ship to disengage.

"CHEWING THE FAT"

A popular shipboard refrain during the days of sail was "God made the vittles, but the devil made the cook." Giving the devil his due, I don't know if even St. Peter himself could have made the daily ration of brine-toughened salt pork any less a gastrointestinal nightmare.

One of the few food items that could withstand long voyages without spoiling, salt pork was so tough I've read accounts of crew members repairing the soles of their shoes with it or chewing it for hours like gum. The prolonged chewing required to make it edible was referred to as *chewing the fat*, a phrase that crossed over into landlubber lingo as gabbing or shooting the breeze.

"CHIMNEY'S AFIRE!"

A whaler's term used to describe the fountain of blood a dying whale spouted after being successfully lanced. Lances, considerably longer than harpoons, were used to pierce the whale's *life*, a large reservoir of oxygen-rich blood located near the lungs. Unlike a harpoon, a lance was pushed (rather than thrown) into the whale and churned upon entry to cut as much area as possible. Blood then filled the whale's lungs, turning the spout crimson and indicating a mortal wound.

CHIPS

Nickname for the ship's carpenter, from the chips and shavings he invariably produced while practicing his profession. His less-skilled mates or helpers were more often than not dubbed *woodspoilers*.

CHRISTOPHER COLUMBUS

Few know that prior to his exploitation of the New World, Columbus had another maritime career, as a notorious pirate and terror to the sea-born traffic of Western Europe. It was said that when his family moved to the coastal city of Savona, Italy, around 1470, Columbus sailed the seas preying on ships belonging to the Moors. Kind of ironic, when you consider his voyage to the New World was an effort to establish a trade route with the East in order to circumvent the fierce Moslem pirates of the Mediterranean.

Ever wonder why Queen Isabella of Spain financed Columbus when everyone else pretty much showed him the door? It could have been she felt him a kindred spirit, as they both shared an unusual trait among those of Latin descent—reddish-blond hair and freckles (a good enough reason for us redheads).

Another popular misconception is that the queen hocked her jewels to bankroll the voyage—in actuality it was financed by taxing the butcher shops of Seville, based on the amount of meat each sold.

And those statues and paintings of the great explorer? All fake. No likeness of Columbus while he was on this earthly plane of existence has ever been found, which means they're all "interpretations" of what the artists thought he might have/ought to have/should have/sort of looked like.

Finally, just to keep it all in perspective, here's another little-known fact concerning ships then and now. If you compared the *Santa Maria* with say, the *Titanic*, you'd find Columbus's pride and joy weighed considerably less than the other's rudder.

CLAPPING ABOARD

The piratical act of boarding a prize and the subsequent hand-to-hand combat that followed.

Exciting stuff, but it brings to mind another Hollywood-induced misconception concerning pirates and their preferred method of securing a captured vessel. Practically every pirate movie in the history of cinematography shows the cutthroats securing themselves alongside a victim with the use of grappling hooks and such. In reality, they preferred cutting across a victim's bow in an effort to tangle the bowsprit in the pirate's rigging. This not only deprived the ship being boarded use of its cannon, but also placed the pirates in position to deliver a point-blank broadside (and use the entangled bowsprit as a handy boarding ladder).

Clap aboard in sixteenth- and seventeenth-century nautical terminology meant to approach, lie alongside of, or board another vessel.

CLEAN BILL OF HEALTH

This popular phrase came about in reference to documents maintained by a ship's master stating his last port of call was free from plague or other such epidemics, an important consideration in clearing the vessel for entry. *(Quarantine, Yellow Jack)*

CLEAN TAILORED

Said of a vessel converted for use in the *sweet trade* (a.k.a. piracy). The term referred to the numerous modifications often made to such craft, such as raising the bulkheads (to conceal the crew and offer additional protection) or razing the deckhouses flush, in order to reduce silhouette and alleviate the danger of flying splinters during battle.

COBBING

A punishment often used aboard ship to address petty offenses. It normally involved twelve or so whacks to the posterior with a *cobbing stick* (a heavy, flat piece of wood resembling a yardstick) or pipe staff, although handsaws or anything else flat could also be used in a pinch. The first stroke was traditionally accompanied with the cry of "Watch!" at which time all crew in the vicinity removed their hats on pain of like punishment. The closing stroke, which was always delivered with as much force as possible, was called the *purse*.

COCKPIT

The cockpit was originally an area designated for use by the ship's surgeon during battle. On many British naval vessels it was the after part of the orlop deck, a dark, close area that ordinarily served as quarters for midshipmen and the like. Being the ship's lowest deck, it was well below the waterline and thought most protected against enemy cannon fire (which is why the powder magazine was located there as well).

Although the cockpit's exact location often varied between ships, it was normally a paneled area situated near a hatchway, which allowed the surgeon's mates and loblolly boys to more easily transport those wounded in battle. Surgeons hard-pressed to find suitable locations on some ships moved to one of the lower gun decks, in which case unused cannon and a few planks often served as make-shift operating tables.

Preparations for battle included placing buckets of sand and boiling pitch or tar at strategic places about the cockpit (one to catch blood from amputations, the other for dipping stumps to seal the wound and prevent further bleeding). Sand was also spread liberally about the deck to reduce slipperiness due to blood accumulation.

But how did the cockpit come about its name, you ask? While in port the area was often used to sequester visiting "wives" or other such lady friends of the crew during the workday. Consensus was the frequent fights and accompanying caterwauls from the doxies below reminded those on watch of a cock-fighting arena.

"COIL UP ONE'S CABLES"

Another salty euphemism for dying, similar to saying a sailor has "cut his painter" or "gone aloft for the last time." My favorite is "he went out with the tide and sunset," a phrase used to describe old salts who died under particularly peaceful conditions. It stems from the belief that a sailor's spirit "would wish to float out of the harbor with the ebb and once more survey familiar scenes—kelp-marked ledges, foaming tide rips, circling sea birds, friendly lighthouses—before it left for another world." *(Cut and Run)*

COLD BURNING

A petty offense-type shipboard punishment in which cold water is poured down the sleeves of an offender's upraised arms and allowed to run out of his trousers. *(Cat O'Nine Tails, Checkered Shirt, Cursing and the Cangue, Flogging Around the Fleet, Goose without Gravy, Killing the Cat, Marry the Gunner's Daughter, Nightingale, Salt Eel, To Flog or Not to Flog, Whipped and Pickled)*

COMMODORE MATTHEW CALBRAITH PERRY AND THE OPENING OF JAPAN

What was the main onus behind U.S. Commodore Matthew Calbraith Perry's 1853 expedition to drag Japan (kicking and screaming) into the modern world by forcing it open to Western trade? The answer is simple, yet one well concealed from public view at the time.

The United States needed a coaling station in the North Pacific. Perry, often called "the father of the steam navy," knew the recent acquisition of California coupled with the opening of China to trade presented excellent opportunities for the expansion of American interests in the North Pacific. A coaling station was critical if the U.S. were to realize its goals in the region (one being a steamship line between California, Hawaii, and China).

After the establishment of a station in Hawaii, Perry promoted an expedition to Japan, insisting on steamers once it was approved. His fleet consisted of two sloops (the *Plymouth* and *Saratoga*) and five steamers—the *Mississippi, Susquehanna, Powhatan, Allegheny,* and ship of the line *Vermont*. Perry felt they would generate "astonishment and consternation" amongst the Japanese, moving as they did "without sails, and without regard to wind and tide."

If the name Perry sounds familiar, you've probably heard it before—Matthew Perry's brother was none other than Oliver Hazard Perry of the Battle of Lake Erie fame (commanding officer on the American side). *(Hunki-Dori, Steam-Propelled Warships, Tycoon, Who Said "Don't Give up the Ship?")*

CONGREVE ROCKET

An early British military rocket invented by Sir William Congreve (1772–1828), it consisted of a carcass or casing propelled by a mixture of niter, charcoal, and sulfur topped with a warhead of various flammable mixtures designed to explode upon impact. The rockets themselves could be mounted on ship, boat, or carried ashore for use as a shock weapon. Guidance was accomplished by use of a long wooden stick built into the carcass, making it in essence the great-great granddaddy of the bottle rocket.

Congreves were used by British ships in an attack on the French at Boulogne 1805 and at the siege of Copenhagen a year later. Many historians believe their use by Britain during the War of 1812 inspired Francis Scott Key's reference to "rockets' red glare" in the "Star Spangled Banner."

COOK'S WARRANT

Naval slang for surgery resulting in an amputation, particularly that of a leg. It's a reference to the fact that the only rating officially open to amputees in the Royal Navy was the position of cook (think Long John Silver of *Treasure Island* fame). Had to be a leg, however, as applicants were required to possess both hands, though not necessarily the ability to cook.

COOTIE

Nautical slang for lice, the word itself being derived from the Polynesian word *kutu* meaning parasitic insect or mother-in-law (OK—I made that last one up).

COXSWAIN

The coxswain or cockswain was initially the boy or *swain* responsible for upkeep of the cockboat, a small boat maintained for the purpose of rowing the captain to and from shore or while visiting other vessels. Use of the term can be traced as far back as 1463; however, in its modern form it describes the helmsman of any boat. *(Bos'n)*

THE CROAKER

Nickname bestowed upon the ship's surgeon. It stemmed from the *crocus* (burlap) bag containing his "medical" instruments. Early shipboard practitioners of the medical arts were often considered less-than-adept at their calling, which is where we got the word croak as a euphemism for "to die."

CROSS-GIRL

Harlots who specialized in befriending lonely sailors, only to milk poor lovelorn Jack of his hard-earned ballast (money) prior to running away. The word *cross* is variously defined as having sexual congress with a woman, or to cheat, swindle, or otherwise act dishonestly. *(Jack Tar)*

CROW'S NEST

Name for the highest lookout station aloft, a term most likely derived from the old Norse practice of bringing cages of ravens aboard to assist in navigation. Story goes that if the navigator was in doubt as to the direction of the nearest landfall, the cage was hoisted aloft and a raven released. As the bird invariably headed for land, the navigator noted the direction of flight and plotted accordingly.

Best guess is the lookout stationed aloft likely shared his perch with the feathered members of the crew from time to time, thus the name.

CUMSHAW ARTIST

Sailors introduced this term into our nautical vernacular during the opening of trade with China. A *cumshaw* was a present, gift, or gratuity demanded by most every Chinese official encountered during the routine of trade. Sailors elevated its meaning to better align with what it in actuality was: bribery and outright theft.

Cumshaw is derived from a Chinese word meaning "grateful thanks" in the dialect of Xiamen, a port city in southeast China, which (per the Pinyin system of Romanizing Chinese words) was translated as "Kam Sia." It likely entered the English language by way of British Navy sailors during the Opium War (1839–1842) who reportedly heard it from beggars frequenting the ports and assumed it was a Chinese word for handout.

Another less-substantiated (but more entertaining) source was told to me by a grizzled old Coast Guard warrant officer. He stated the Chinese merchants, who paddled out to meet visiting ships after they'd dropped anchor, would pull alongside yelling "Cumshaw!" (come ashore) in efforts to initiate trade. Once there, sailors usually found themselves picked clean by the crafty Chinese traders.

Regardless of the origin, cumshaw has evolved in the modern naval services to be the unofficial liberation of government-owned resources (particularly via devious or ingenious means) from one ship or unit by government personnel of another. However, as these items are "borrowed" in order to complete a project, mission, or other good government cause, no theft really occurred, right? Artist, of course, denotes the high level of expertise attained by some individuals. *(The Opium War)*

CURSING AND THE CANGUE

Although sailors and swearing may be considered interchangeable to many, foul language could be considered an offense if the ship's captain were a suitably religious man. Punishment could range from *spiking* (forcing the offending crewmember to hold a marlinspike in his mouth until his tongue bled) to having the offending tongue cleansed via a good scrubbing with sand and canvas; burning it with a hot iron was another popular option during the mid-eighteenth century.

Another favorite was the *cangue* (from *canga*, the Portuguese word for yoke), a type of wooden collar consisting of two pieces of 3-inch planking upon which a nine- or twelve-pound cannon shot was attached. Lord Admiral Gambier (an officer known for his strict principles of religion and morality) favored one utilizing a 32-pound shot, but was forced to abandon its use after a sailor suffered injury while wearing it.

The offender was typically forced to wear this "portable pillory" (while attending to his normal duties, of course) for a predetermined amount of time, although in some cases he was forced to sport it until hearing another of his shipmates swear.

According to *The Seaman's Narrative* by William Spaven, an offender "would often stagger with design, and tread on the toes of some of the after guard or maintopmen, who would perhaps say, d—n your eyes, why don't you keep your feet to yourself . . . when the prisoner would cry out 'Sir, such a man swears!' then the collar was taken off him and fixed on the other." *(Cat O'Nine Tails, Checkered Shirt, Cold Burning, Flogging Around the Fleet, Goose without Gravy, Killing the Cat, Marry the Gunner's Daughter, Nightingale, Salt Eel, To Flog or Not to Flog, Whipped and Pickled)*

"CUT AND RUN"

Another common term with saltwater roots, "cut and run" originally meant to slip or cut a ship's anchor cable in order to make a quick or stealthy getaway, one free from the rattle of anchor chains or creak of a windlass. In the former case, where a ship might be forced to get underway quickly due to storms, hostilities, etc., the anchor was normally buoyed to aid in retrieval once the danger had passed. To "cut one's painter and go aloft" (a euphemism for dying) is derived from this as well.

"Cut out," as in to deprive someone of an advantage, comes from the old nautical practice of cutting out or stealing ships from an enemy's port. *(Coil up One's Cables)*

"CUT OF ONE'S JIB"

To judge someone or form an opinion based on their appearance. The term itself refers to a ship's jib, often a telltale indicator of its overall sailing performance or character.

"DANCE THE HEMPEN JIG"

Quaint old pirate term for swinging at the end of a hangman's rope. Those so released from earthly woes were said to have "walked up ladder lane and down hawser street" or maybe to have been "fitted with a hempen collar" (in reference to that material's widespread use in manufacturing most cordage of the day). *(The Deadly Nevergreen, Jack's Kitchen, Swinging from the Gibbet, Turning a Profit with the Upright Man, You'll Grin in a Glass Case)*

DANDY FUNK

A version of "hasty pudding" made of molasses or marmalade, fat, and broken hardtack biscuits (along with the weevils that often infested them). *(Strike Me Blind)*

DAVY JONES' LOCKER

Plenty of lore remain concerning the who's and what's of Davy Jones, that legendary evil spirit of sailors' lore, even after discounting those concerning that guy in *The Monkees*.

One explanation is that the name is a corruption of *Duffy Jonah*, a term used by West Indian sailors to describe an apparition of the biblical prophet Jonah, who was thrown overboard and swallowed by a whale in the Old Testament. *Duffy* is a West Indian word for ghost or devil.

Another contends Davy Jones was the owner of a sixteenth-century pub in London where unwary sailors were drugged, placed in lockers, and sold to navy press-gangs.

Some English sailors believe it is a mispronunciation of "Duffer Jones," a clumsy fellow of English tales whose misadventures often landed him overboard.

An altogether different frame of thought is that Davy is actually derived from St. David, the patron saint of Wales, who was often called upon by Welsh sailors in time of need.

That notwithstanding, the vast majority of tales peg ol' Davy as a more often than not evil spirit (often the Devil himself) whose malevolent tricks inflict nothing but pain and suffering upon sailors of all nations. They often referred to the ominous sound of a rising wind as "Davy putting the coppers

[tea] on for the parson" in reference to the bad luck brought when shipping a priest aboard.

Davy Jones' locker (a symbolic reference to a sailor's chest) is the sea, especially when used in the context of an ocean grave. *(The Man in Black, Press-Gangs)*

DAVY JONES' NATURAL CHILDREN

Why, pirates, smugglers, scamps, scalawags, rovers, and other such scurvy dogs of the sea, matey!

DEAD MARINE

Nautical slang for an empty wine bottle, a euphemism highlighting the sailor's opinion that one serves as much purpose as the other aboard ship (live marines being considered useless enough). King William IV once apologized to the marine officers present for telling the steward to "clear away the dead marines" during one wardroom visit by saying what he *really* meant was that, like their namesake, the bottles had performed their duty nobly and were ready to do it again. Yeah, right.

DEAD MEN

In nautical parlance "dead men" were loose reef points or gaskets carelessly left hanging from a yard. Also known as *Irish pennants*, it was unilaterally used to describe any loose end of a line that should be properly tucked in or stowed.

THE DEADLY NEVERGREEN

The gallows—a tree said to bear fruit all year-round. Another quaint little saying along these lines was, "You'll ride a horse foaled by an acorn!" in reference to swinging from the oaken gallows or "Wooden Mare," as it was also known. Pirates meeting such an end were said to have died from "hempen fever," a pun on the hemp rope used.

Rouges who bruised themselves on being properly outfitted prior to swinging into eternity ensured they carried a posy or nosegay for sniffing and a prayer book, regardless of the fact most were illiterate. *(Dance the Hempen Jig, Jack's Kitchen, Swinging from the Gibbet, Turning a Profit with the Upright Man, You'll Grin in a Glass Case)*

DERELICT

An abandoned ship that remains afloat, presenting a hazard to navigation. It's an old admiralty law term derived from the Latin word *derelictus*, meaning unfaithful or negligent in one's duty or obligations.

DERRICK

Initially a heavy crane used in salvaging sunken vessels, but now commonly used to describe any crane utilized in the loading and unloading of cargo. The term itself comes to us from a seventeenth-century hangman named Derrick, famous for his expertise with the noose.

"THE DIPPER IS HOISTED"

A shipboard phrase indicating that strict water rationing was in effect. It comes from the old sailing practice of hoisting the dipper for the scuttlebutt up the mast to prevent the crew from stealing more than their ration. *(Scuttlebutt)*

DITTY BAGS

A sack or bag used by sailors to hold small tools, toiletries, and other personal items—also called a sailor's "housewife." As to the origin of the name itself, a little disagreement exists. Some say it was derived from the Hindi word *dittis*, a type of duck or canvas cloth manufactured in Manchester, England, from which they were presumably made. Other sources suggest it comes from *dite*, the Anglo-Saxon word for tidy.

Still others claim the name is a corruption of *ditto bag*, so called because it contained at least two of everything (two needles, two buttons, two spools of thread, etc.).

DOCK

Dock has many connotations in maritime slang beyond reference to a pier or wharf.

To dock meant sexual intercourse (from the Gypsy *dukker*, to ravish or bewitch), while "docked smack smooth" described a sailor whose penis had been amputated due to contraction of a venereal disease.

Docking was also a punishment sailors inflicted on prostitutes who had infected them with said disease. It consisted of cutting the woman's clothes off and turning her naked into the street. *(A Pox on Ye!, Fire Ship, Take in One's Coals, To Go into Dock)*

THE DOCTOR

Universal nickname for the ship's cook, so called after the ministrations often required to make the ship's victuals edible. It comes from the old use of the word *doctor*, meaning "to adulterate or drug liquor; to poison, to hocus; also to falsify accounts."

DOCTOR QUICKSILVER

One Thomas Dover, a ship's surgeon during the early 1700s who earned the nickname through his practice of administering large doses of mercury for all ailments. He prescribed it in liberal amounts to his clients ashore as well, a practice that led to at least one unpleasant social occasion.

Seems after taking a rather large dose of Doctor Dover's curative, an unnamed lady of means "inadvertently and uncontrollably" discharged the load in a fit of wind-breaking virtuosity while dancing the minuet. Fortunately, chivalry proved itself alive and well (if a trifle odiferous) as a number of well-intentioned genteel men in attendance tried unsuccessfully to retrieve the shimmering mercury globes, each under the assumption the lady had broken her necklace.

Antonio Pigafetta, a chronicler who accompanied Magellan on his ill-fated voyage around the globe, mentions the practice of ingesting quicksilver for medicinal reasons was common among the Moors of Borneo as well.

Bad stuff, that mercury poisoning. Remember the Mad Hatter from *Alice in Wonderland*? Inclusion of the character was actually a biting social commentary concerning work-related health hazards of the day. Hat makers of the nineteenth century used mercury salt in the manufacture of felt hats. Continued exposure eventually led to insanity, which is where the phrase "mad as a hatter" originated.

DOG'S VOMIT

Every time I see this one it reminds me of a skit the original *Saturday Night Live* players did about Smucker's jam. "With a name like Dog's Vomit, it has to be good!"

What we're talking about here, however, is a moist hash of hardtack biscuits and meat cooked together.

DOGWATCH

Watches aboard ship are based on a schedule of four-hour rotations. However, to ensure crew members aren't forced to stand the same watches every day, the 4:00 p.m. to 8:00 p.m. watch was divided into two-hour watches, called the first dogwatch and second dogwatch. This division shifts the entire watch rotation every twenty-four hours, ensuring all sailors have ample opportunity to sample the particular joys associated with each (from polishing the ship's brass during the midwatch, to scrubbing the decks while standing the morning watch).

As to the name, one theory states the term is a corruption of "dodge watch," as sailors dodge standing the same watch every day or are viewed as dodging a full watch. Smyth's *Sailor's Word-book* (1867), however, offers that the name stems from the fact that the shorter dogwatch is "cur-tailed." Although no one can prove its origin with any certainty, reference to the word has been traced as far back as the seventeenth century.

Below is a schedule of standard watch rotations observed aboard ship.

8:00 a.m. to noon—Forenoon watch
Noon to 4:00 p.m.—Afternoon watch
4:00 p.m. to 6:00 p.m.—First dogwatch
6:00 p.m. to 8:00 p.m.—Second dogwatch
8:00 p.m. to midnight—First night watch
Midnight to 4:00 a.m.—Middle or midwatch
4:00 a.m. to 8 a.m.—Morning watch

(Eight Bells, Hotbed, Sweating the Glass)

DOLPHIN STRIKER

A short spar of wood or iron hanging down from the bowsprit of a sailing vessel that's used to spread the martingale stay. It was so named due to the occasional whack it gave dolphins riding the pressure wave in front of the bow as the ship rose and fell.

DONKEYMAN

The operator of early steam engines placed aboard large sailing vessels to handle halyards, mooring lines, cargo transfers, etc. *Donkey engine*, the nickname of the engine itself, was derived from the sailor's comparison to its labor-saving namesake.

DONKEY'S BREAKFAST AND CARPENTERS' FEATHERS

To the old salts of yesteryear accustomed to sleeping in hammocks or upon the bare bunk boards of the fo'c'sle, a mattress was the epitome of fancy frills and high living.

Why, ol' Jack could almost consider himself a dandy when issuance of such came into common practice. The first of these seagoing mattresses were filled with straw, hence the name *donkey's breakfast*. Others were stuffed with *carpenters' feathers*, that being sailor slang for wood chips. *(Jack Tar)*

DOUBLOONS AND PIECES OF EIGHT

What pirate treasure would be complete without a chest overflowing with doubloons and pieces of eight? Doubloons carried more worth than any other Spanish coin in circulation (being minted of gold); however, pieces of eight were arguably the most famous coin associated with Spain's exploitation of the New World.

Minted of silver and worth roughly $23, pieces of eight usually bore the Spanish coat of arms on one side and the Twin Pillars of Hercules on the other. Named by the ancient Greeks, these two spires of rock (the northernmost being the famed Rock of Gibraltar) flank the Strait of Gibraltar, the general area where Atlantis was supposedly located. The dollar sign of today evolved from these twin pillars found on said pieces of eight.

DRESSING DOWN

Thin or worn sails were often given a coating of wax or oil to renew their effectiveness. The treatment itself was called a "dressing down" and the term eventually came to mean a reprimand or admonishment given to a subordinate in hopes of effecting better service.

"DRINK TOAST SEATED"

Protocol aboard British ships once called for those present to stand when toasting the king. All that changed, however, when Charles II of England rose for such a toast while dining aboard a ship of the line and whacked the royal noggin on a cross beam. After a hearty laugh, he decreed henceforth officers drinking to the king's health could *drink toast seated* without fear of incurring regal displeasure.

DROWN-PROOFING

Sailors were exceptionally keen on acquiring the proper wards to prevent drowning, particularly as most never learned to swim. One popular belief was that having a pig tattooed on one foot and a cock (rooster) on the other prevented it, as both animals hate water. Another was possession of a *caul*, the membrane sometimes covering a child's head at birth. Sailors believed it prevented the unborn child from drowning while in the womb, and would similarly protect those who carried one from drowning at sea.

Coal taken from a beach's highest tide line provided similar protection when carried in old Jack Tar's pocket, assuring he too would be washed ashore, while others believed wearing a gold earring did the trick.

English sailors carried a wren feather to prevent drowning, while French sailors believed if a sailor did drown, his wife would hear the sound of dripping water near her bed at night.

The ultimate in drown-proofing, however, was afforded a sailor's child whose right hand was baptized in water gathered during a flood tide, a precaution yielding protection for life. *(Jack Tar, Tattoos)*

DRY NURSE

Term used to describe a subordinate officer who shoulders the captain's responsibilities aboard ship due to that worthy's lack of seamanship skills. A captain of such caliber was often known by his subordinates as a *Paper Jack*, due to his lack of substance in the maritime arts.

DUFF

A pudding (and I use the term loosely) consisting of flour and suet combined in a cloth sack, boiled in water, and served with molasses. Normally served to the crew on Sunday, it was considered a special treat (which in itself attests to the quality of shipboard food back in the day). It's been said many a rascally captain sweetened their disgruntled crews by authorizing twice-weekly rations of duff on the homeward-bound leg of a voyage.

Add prunes and violà!—the fancier variant *plum duff* is the result. Common practice was forcing the cook to whistle while pitting said prunes, just to reassure shipmates he wasn't eating the main ingredient.

Other treats for the crew included *burgoo* (a mixture of oatmeal and molasses) or even a mess of *doughboys*, which were dumplings of wet flour fried in pork fat.

As for the term itself, *duff* is merely a Northern English corruption of the word dough. *(Burgoo)*

DUFFLE

A sailor's personal belongings (normally referring to his clothing) as well as the seabag of coarse, woolen fabric used to carry and stow them in. The name most probably originated from the Flemish town of Duffel (near Antwerp) where the cloth was made.

DUNGAREE

Webster's once defined *dungaree* as "a coarse kind of fabric worn by the poorer class of people and also used for tents and sail." While we probably couldn't picture our favorite pair of jeans hanging from the yardarm, discarded sailcloth (which was not dyed blue or as well-woven as today's fabric) was often utilized by sailors to make items such as work clothes and hammocks. In fact, it was standard practice for captains in both the American and British navies to exaggerate the amount of sail lost during battle in order to provide the crew with material.

As the cloth was called dungaree (from the Hindi word *dungri*), the name became synonymous with the clothes themselves.

"As smart a young fellow as ever you'd see, in jacket and trousers of blue Dungaree."

DUTCHMAN'S ANCHOR

Nautical term used to describe anything needed that's been left at home. It stems from the tale of a Dutch captain, who commented after his ship had been wrecked that he had a most excellent anchor . . . he just left it at home.

EIGHT BELLS

Prior to 1735 (the year John Harrison introduced the first effective marine chronometer) ships kept time by use of sandglasses, whose accuracy they verified via noon sightings of the sun. From its crucial role in navigation to the more mundane chore of watch rotation, accurate time keeping was essential to many aspects of shipboard life.

Watches aboard ship were generally four hours in duration (barring the two-hour dogwatch thrown in for variation) with a half-hour glass being used to mark the watches in 30-minute increments. The all-important task of reversing the glass fell upon the ship's boy, who struck a bell at each rotation that all might know he was faithfully executing his duties; one stroke of the bell for each turn of the glass, for a total of eight bells per watch.

Standing watch was a long, often boring proposition, however, and sometimes a sailor or ship's boy stooped to unscrupulous practices such as *sweating the glass* (holding it against their belly in the belief the additional heat expanded the neck slightly, causing the sand to flow faster) or reversing it before all the sand had passed through in an effort to help old Father Time along.

Needless to say, such activities played the devil with intricate navigational calculations and those found guilty of such infractions faced being stripped, lashed to the capstan, and flogged. *(Dogwatch, Hot Bed, Ship's Bell, Sweating the Glass)*

ENSIGN

One of the lowest grades of commissioned officers in the U.S. Navy, the word itself dates back to medieval Europe, where senior squires carried into battle the banners of those they served. Eventually, such a squire became known as an *ensign*, after the banner itself.

According to the *Century Dictionary* the title of ensign was first introduced in 1862 to replace the unofficial rank of passed midshipman, a nineteenth-century term used to describe a midshipman who had passed his lieutenant's exam and was eligible for promotion, but was awaiting a vacancy to become available at that grade.

EXPENDED

Dead—finished, scuppered. It comes from the gunner's use of the word when entering spent rounds and munitions into his account books. *(Scuppered)*

THE EYES HAVE IT

The forward-most lookout station on board is universally known as the "eyes of the ship" after the ancient custom of painting eyes on either side of the bow. A ship's eyes were thought to avert the evil eye, intimidate hostile sea-gods, and generally enable the ship to better look after herself.

The bulging, staring eyes of a ship's figurehead were remnants of these painted eyes, which they eventually replaced. *(Family-Head, Fiddlehead, Go Figure, Women Onboard)*

FAMILY-HEAD

An intricately carved figurehead (often found on a warship) that has not one, but several full-length figures. *(Fiddlehead, Go Figure, The Eyes Have It, Women Onboard)*

FANNY ADAMS

British naval slang for tinned mutton. It arose from the 1810 murder of a young woman by that name, whose body had been chopped into tiny pieces and thrown into the river at Alton, Hants. Who says those Limeys have no sense of humor?

FAST SETTLEMENTS AND NO PESKY SALESMEN

Most pirate ship articles made provisions for an insurance policy of sorts, one that reimbursed members of the crew wounded during battle. The drafters addressed possible injuries and set amounts to be paid for each in addition to a crewmember's normal share of the loot.

Six hundred pieces of eight (or six slaves) was a common sum for loss of a right arm, with the left being worth around five hundred. Eyes and fingers topped out at around one hundred pieces of eight, while the loss of both eyes generated a hefty one thousand pieces, or perhaps a special vote from the crew to decide compensation.

It brings to mind a scene from an old pirate movie I once saw in which two grizzled old salts were mulling over the newly drafted articles for their ship.

"Blimey!" one exclaimed to his companion upon reading the insurance provisions. "A man could get rich if he were lucky enough."

FATHOM

Old English law decreed a fathom to be "the length of a man's arm around the object of his affections." Makes sense, as the word itself is derived from *faethm*, or "embracing arms." Body parts were commonly used as a unit of measurement, which is why horses to this day are said to be so many "hands" high.

Skipping over the possibility of navigational errors induced by the squeezing of fat wives as opposed to skinny ones, modern terminology defines fathom as a nautical unit of measurement equal to six feet in length.

Fathom was also the word used to describe the act of measuring, which is why a sailor who's puzzling over something is said to be trying to "fathom it."

FEARNOUGHT

A type of heavy woolen cloth used in the manufacture of foul-weather gear. Sailors who wore it were said to "fear nought" from the elements. *Dread-noughts*, a word often used interchangeably with the former, was said to be the actual garments fashioned from such cloth.

FIDDLEHEAD

A scroll or billethead rather than a proper figurehead. It's also the origin of a term that pretty much sums up Jack's feelings concerning a ship without a figurehead: *Fiddleheaded*, meaning plain or ugly. *(Family-Head, Go Figure, The Eyes Have It, Women Onboard)*

FIDDLER'S GREEN

A sailor's heaven for those with fifty years of sea service—less for those stout of heart and loyal to shipmates—it was the final destination for old shellbacks who'd "cut their painter" and "gone aloft for the last time."

It's described by the *Century Dictionary* as "a name given by sailors to their dancehouses and other places of frolic on shore; sailor's paradise."

It was said that upon death a sailor's soul entered a gull, in which form he flew to the South Pole and entered Fiddler's Green through an open hatch rotating in sync with the earth's movement. There he settled in peace, where

" . . . the drinks and smokes are logged but never paid, there are pubs on every corner and steaks and plum duff every day."

It was here all the good-looking women of the world were gathered to fill the pipes and glasses of sailors forever more.

It was all serious business to Jack, and he didn't particularly cotton to terrestrial naysayers sticking their oar in on the matter. Hotten (see Bibliography) relates the following:

> A story is told of a drunken sailor who heard a street preacher threatening all listeners with eternal damnation, and who went up and asked where he (the sailor) was going after death.
>
> "To hell, of course," replied the preacher.
>
> "No, you lubberly son of a sea-cook!" shouted the seaman, knocking the itinerant down; I'm going to FIDDLER'S GREEN; and if you say I'm not, I'll throttle you."
>
> Under compulsion, the preacher admitted the existence of FID-DLER'S GREEN, protempore.
>
> *(Coil Up One's Cables, Duff, Shellback)*

FIFTEEN MEN ON A DEAD MAN'S CHEST (OR HOW PIRATES CAME TO LOOK LIKE PIRATES)

Pirates! We all have a mental picture of what one did or should look like once fitted out with the prerequisite eye patch, wooden leg, earrings, and outlandish clothing. Let's break down your typical pirate and see why they had earrings versus nose rings, or pantaloons instead of an Elvis-type jumpsuit.

Earrings first—why did they wear them? Surprisingly enough, for health and wealth! When pirates (as well as sailors in general) began interacting with the far-eastern cultures of Asia, they "discovered" acupuncture, a popular therapeutic technique. According to acupuncturists, pressure points located in and above the ear lobe not only reduce hunger, but supposedly boost one's energy as well, attributes that would certainly have proven useful during long, arduous sea voyages. They were also believed to improve eyesight, an additional benefit as bonuses were normally given to those who first spied a potential prize on the horizon.

As to the eye patch, I've come across a couple of explanations, from wounds received in battle to drunken barroom brawls, but the one I like best deals with the more mundane art of navigation. Many navigators of the day used a monocular or other such instrument to take sun sights when determining their ship's position. Theory is this unfiltered sun gazing over time caused blindness in the eye used.

Peg legs and hand hooks? Probably the only thing a pirate (or any sailor for that matter) feared more than battle was a business call from the ship's surgeon, which was more often than not a collateral duty of the ship's carpenter, who was selected because he already possessed the necessary saws and such. Limbs smashed in battle had to be amputated quickly to reduce the risk of infection. Rum was given to dull the pain (no anesthetics were used) and the patient was given a gag made of leather or rope—or a bullet—to bite on. Best-case scenario was when the victim just fainted until it was over.

After amputation, the stump was dipped in boiling pitch (tar) to seal the wound and prevent bleeding. Afterward, wooden legs were carved and presented to allow a sailor to walk again. Many become cooks, one of the few jobs aboard ship a disabled seaman could still perform in the Royal Navy.

As for the clothes, pirates robbed their captives of any items that caught their fancy, the gaudier the better. Mismatched wardrobes were the norm. Green pants and a lavender shirt? No problem!

Lastly, the parrot-on-the-shoulder thing. Sailors often bought exotic animals (birds, monkeys, etc.) in foreign ports as presents for their lady friends back home or to sell.

So now, when Biff Spiffington down at the yacht club bar broaches the subject of pirates, you can kick him with your wooden leg, spill some rum on him, and tell him all about it. *(Bite the Bullet, Cockpit, Cooks Warrant)*

FINE BY ME

While sailors throughout the ages have never wasted time when it comes to sampling the pleasures a port has to offer, they have been known to overdo it on occasion. Below is what a sailor would find himself paying if too much of a good time was had during a port call in Honolulu during the mid-1800s:

Hanging, as a murderer, for knowingly and maliciously violating those laws whereby a contagious disease is communicated on shore

$10 for coming ashore with a knife, sword cane, or any other dangerous weapon

$2 for every seaman seized on shore, after the firing of the second gun from the fort, at half past nine o'clock p.m.

$10 on every person who aids, secretes, or entertains a seaman on shore after that hour; and the same fine on every person who by force opposes the police in their search for such seaman

$1 to $5 for hallooing or making a noise in the streets at night

$6 for striking another in a quarrel

$5 for racing or swift riding in the streets or frequented roads

$1 for desecrating the Sabbath for the first time

$2 for desecrating the Sabbath for the second time, and then the fine is doubled for every repetition of the offense

$6 for drunkenness

$5 for fornication

$30 for adultery

$50 for rape

$10 for lewd, seductive, lascivious conduct

$1,000 and a public flogging of two hundred lashes to be laid on "with a will" for any male found wearing a thong on Waikiki Beach. (OK—I made this one up, but I sure wish it had been in effect when I lived there.)

"FIRE IN THE HOLE!"

Cannon were once fired using an external touchhole containing primer. Once the command to fire was given, the gunner, by way of reply to the order and as a warning to the gun crew, cried "Fire in the hole!" while touching his slow match (a smoldering fuse or cord attached to a pole) to the hole.

FIRE SHIP

An expendable vessel that was filled with explosives and all manner of combustible material at hand, set on fire, then cut free so as to drift down upon an enemy fleet in order to destroy them. It was also a sailor's term for a prostitute afflicted with venereal disease. *(A Pox on Ye!, Dock, Take in One's Coals, To Go into Dock)*

FIRST ALPHABET

The first alphabet was created by the Phoenicians, who developed it as an aid to help keep track of their maritime trading empire.

FIRST CIRCUMNAVIGATION

Few realize Sir Francis Drake, the greatest privateer of the Elizabethan Age, was the first commander to complete a circumnavigation of the globe (1577–1578). His ship *The Golden Hind,* however, was the second vessel in history to complete the voyage. Come again?

Magellan's expedition (1519–1522) is generally credited with the first circumnavigation; however, he was killed while participating in a petty tribal skirmish in the Philippines prior to completing his voyage. This would place Drake as the first captain to actually complete a circumnavigation, unless of course you count Sebastian del Cano, the Spanish navigator who commanded the *Victoria*, the only ship of Magellan's fleet to return to Spain.

Most refute this line of thinking, however, as del Cano was only in command during the return leg and not the entire expedition—still others contend Magellan rightfully holds the title as first circumnavigator as he supposedly had reached the same longitude in the Philippines on an earlier voyage to the east while employed by Portugal. Regardless, Drake was the first English captain to complete the journey, as well as the first Englishman to sight the Pacific.

As to the first person to make the circumnavigation, Magellan was said to have brought with him an eastern slave named Enrique of Malacca, who acted as interpreter upon his arrival in the Philippines. If Enrique was originally a native of the Philippine colony located in Malacca (as some believe) then he would have been the first person to circumnavigate the globe.

FIRST IRONCLAD BATTLESHIP

The first true ocean-going, ironclad battleship was the French ship *La Gloire*. Launched in 1859, she boasted iron plating 12 cm (4.7 inches) thick backed by 43 cm (17 inches) of timber and was designed in response to advances in naval warfare used during the Crimean War (1853–1856). These new technologies included rifled guns (which significantly improved both firing range and accuracy) and the Paixhans gun (the first naval gun designed to fire explosive shells), both of which dramatically increased the destructive power available for use against wooden warships. The successful use of ironclad floating batteries by the British and French to bombard Russian forts during the Crimean War made development of a true ironclad battleship a logical progression.

The launch of the *La Gloire* immediately rendered all unarmored wooden ships-of-the-line obsolete; however, it was a short-lived reign. The *La Gloire* herself was supplanted the following year with the British Navy's launch of the HMS *Warrior*, the world's first iron-hulled warship.

FIRST MATE?

In order to ensure bountiful catches, Breton fishermen once believed the captain's wife was required to sleep with a crewmember on the night prior to the season's start.

FIRST SHIPS TO CROSS THE ANTARCTIC CIRCLE

These would be the *Resolution* and *Adventure,* the two ships used by Captain James Cook during his second voyage of discovery to the Antarctic in search of *Terra Australis Incognita* ("the great southern continent"), an "unknown" continent he proved to be a myth.

Purchased by the British Navy Board and originally named the *Marquis of Granby* and the *Marquis of Rockingham* (respectively) both ships were similar to *Endeavour* (the ship used on Cook's first voyage), although neither was really barque-rigged like the *Endeavour*, falling more in the classification of ship-rigged sloops-of-war.

Originally commissioned as the *Drake* and *Raleigh*, their names were subsequently changed to *Resolution* and *Adventure* over fears the names would have offended the Spanish.

With a lower deck length of 110 feet and a displacement of 462 tons (100 more than the *Endeavour*) Cook called the *Resolution* "the ship of my choice, the fittest for service of any I have seen."

A few more interesting notes concerning this, the second voyage of arguably the greatest navigator in maritime history:

Cook crossed the circle on January 17, 1773.

The expedition was completed in July 1775, having lasted a total of three years and eighteen days.

During the course of the voyage Cook sailed in excess of 20,000 leagues (a distance greater than three times the earth's circumference) with the loss of only four crewmen—only one of whom died from disease (scurvy)—an astounding accomplishment for the day and a direct result of the strict antiscorbutic diets prescribed by Cook. Strangely enough, the one crewman who succumbed to scurvy was Mortimer Mahoney (a.k.a. Murduck Mahoney), ship's cook for the *Adventure*.

The first steamship to cross the Antarctic Circle was the British ship *Challenger* during its 1872–1876 voyage, the first truly scientific expedition to Antarctica that yielded (among other things) the earliest photos of icebergs. *(Limeys, The Petty Talley, Scurvy)*

FIRST STEAM-POWERED VESSEL

That would be the *Pyroscaphe*, a vessel designed by Claude-François-Dorothée, marquis de Jouffroy d'Abbans featuring an engine and two small paddlewheels. The good marquis held his first shakedown cruise in eastern France on the River Saône in 1783, and although the engine failed after fifteen minutes, the boat nonetheless moved forward under its own power.

FIRST SUBMARINE

Although ideas for an under-the-sea boat had been talked of as early as the 1500s, the first inventor known to have actually built one was Cornelius van Drebel, a Dutchman in the service of King James I of England. His "submarine" was unveiled during a demonstration on the Thames River in 1620, where the king watched the strange craft make the trip from Westminster to Greenwich either barely awash or submerged to a depth of fifteen feet, depending on which account you believe. It was powered by twelve rowers.

FIRST U.S. LIGHTHOUSE

The first lighthouse constructed in America was the Boston Light. Located on Boston Harbor's Little Brewster Island, it was placed into service on September 14, 1716, and burned sperm whale oil, as did all early American lights. Destroyed during the Revolutionary War, it was rebuilt in 1783 and still stands today.

THE FIVE L'S

Commenting that a sailor knows "the five L's" indicates he's mastered latitude and longitude (plotting), lights (as in the proper navigation lights a ship must display), log, and lead (the heaving of the knot log and lead line, respectively). *(Knots)*

"FLOGGING A DEAD HORSE"

Sailors were customarily advanced their first month's earnings when signing on for the duration of a ship's voyage. Needless to say, what with buying food for his poor old mother, shoes for the orphanage, and contributions to the Marblehead Home for Unwed Mothers (with maybe just a few trips to the local tavern in between) ol' Jack normally found he'd spent his advanced wages prior to even setting sail.

It was during that first month, traditionally called the *dead horse month*, sailors fancied themselves working for nothing but salt horse (their meals of salted beef or pork) while paying back the ship's master. The name itself was derived from the above-mentioned salt horse and the fact that most English ports were roughly one month's sail from the horse latitudes.

As the work ethic of a Tar who felt he labored for nothing was less than enthusiastic to say the least, most officers agreed one was more likely to flog a dead horse into activity than get a wholehearted work effort from the crew during their first month at sea.

British sailors marked its end by "killing" the dead horse (an event signifying they'd finally worked off their advanced wages) by constructing an effigy of a horse from canvas, straw, or other such scrap material. This they then paraded around the decks amid huzzahs and shouts of "Old man [captain] your horse must die!" The hated horse was then set on fire and cast over the side. *(Harness Cask, Horse Latitudes, Jack Tar)*

"FLOGGING AROUND THE FLEET"

"Flogging around the fleet" was one of the most severe forms of punishment awarded in Britain's Royal Navy. Such punishment could only be awarded by convening a special court martial consisting of at least five captains, meaning at a minimum five ships of the line would be riding at anchorage during the trial. Any trial placing upwards of five thousand men on hand to witness the results was a situation not wasted on the Admiralty, which was concerned more with flogging as a deterrent to future crimes rather than the punishment of one individual.

Upon being awarded the sentence of flogging around the fleet, the offender was secured in his ship's largest boat and rowed with much fanfare to each of the anchored man-of-war present. Once alongside, with the ship's drummer beating out the Rogue's March, the crew was called to quarters to witness punishment, as boatswain mates from their own vessel climbed down into the small boat to administer lashes.

As this type of punishment meant a man could receive upwards of 300 lashes, a ship's doctor stood by to ensure the lashings didn't kill the man (immediately anyway). If he fainted, punishment was postponed until he was sufficiently recovered to receive the remainder of his sentence. *(Cat O'Nine Tails, Checkered Shirt, Cold Burning, Cursing and the Cangue, Goose without Gravy, Killing the Cat, Marry the Gunner's Daughter, Nightingale, Rogue's March, Salt Eel, To Flog or Not to Flog, Whipped and Pickled)*

FLOTSAM AND JETSAM

OK, we know it's that stuff floating in the water, but which is which? *Jetsam* is material thrown overboard in order to save a foundering ship, whereas *flotsam* is used to describe the floating cargo or debris washed overboard or remaining after she sinks. In the same vein, *lagan* is the heavier items aboard ship allowed to sink to the bottom, but marked with a buoy or float for later salvage.

FOOTLOOSE

Uninhibited or spontaneous. The bottom of a triangular sail is called the foot, and a "loose-footed" sail is one attached fore and aft but unsecured along the boom itself and able to dance freely in the wind if the clew (aft end) is freed.

FRIENDS, ROMANS, COUNTRYMEN . . .

In 78 BCE a merchant ship was taken by pirates while sailing past the island of Pharmacusa, located off the coast of Turkey. As the chief of the pirates boarded the craft, he immediately noticed amid the frightened passengers a young aristocrat, one clothed in the latest of Roman finery, who sat reading nonchalantly among his servants and slaves.

Standing before the young man and demanding his name, the pirate received only the briefest look of disdain from his captive, who otherwise turned back to his reading, ignoring the infuriated bandit. After learning his captive's name from the young Roman's personal physician, the pirate conferred with his second in command, asking how much ransom he thought should be asked for the party.

Sizing up the somewhat effeminate Roman and his group, ten talents was voiced to the captain as a realistic sum.

"Then I'll double it! Twenty talents is my price!" snarled the captain, irritated at the aristocrat's imperious airs.

At this, the young man finally spoke.

"Twenty?" he asked with arched eyebrow, "If you knew your business you'd realize I was worth at least fifty."

The stunned pirate chose to take the man at his word. Sending messengers to relay terms for ransom, he transported the prisoners to his stronghold to await reply. During that time, the somewhat foppish young Roman entertained his captors with tales of his plans to return upon being released and crucify the lot of them. They, of course, listened to the threats with much laughter.

Once the ransom was received and his party freed, the young man proceeded to Miletus, where he borrowed four war galleys and five hundred soldiers. Returning to the stronghold of his former captors, he not only recovered his fifty talents, but apprehended some three hundred and fifty of his former hosts as well.

Arriving at Pergamum, he summarily executed the entire gang, reserving the promised fate of crucifixion for thirty of the principal leaders. As a show of compassion for their previous hospitality, however, he granted them the favor of cutting their throats before crucifixion.

The young man's name, you ask? Caius Julius Caesar.

FULL MOON

Italian sailors once believed tempestuous weather could be calmed if some of the crew bared their bottoms to the storm.

GALAPAGOS TORTOISE

Weighing upwards of 600 pounds, these giant tortoises were for centuries a chief source of fresh meat for early sailors transiting the area of the Galapagos Islands. Ideal for shipboard use, they could be kept alive for months by simply turning them on their backs until needed.

Old salts believed they housed the souls of shipwrecked officers sentenced to crawl and hiss for centuries in the massive shelled bodies. Kind of a creepy thought, considering they can live up to two hundred years.

GALLEY

Your standard nautical name for a ship's kitchen. One source has it being a corruption of the word *gallery*, a simple affair of stone or brick upon which ancient sea-folk cooked their meals. I prefer the other explanation, which states those forced to toil at the oft-times thankless task of fixing grub for the crew considered themselves galley slaves.

GALLEY PEPPER

Sailor's slang for smut and ash from the galley stove blown into the cook's pots during rough weather.

GALLEY RANGERS

Title bestowed upon the "grub hounds" of the ship's company who "appeared in everybody's mess but in nobody's watch."

GALLEY YARN

Why, nothing less than a good old-fashioned sea story. If, after rigging his yarn tackle, Jack's tale was deemed too big a whopper to swallow by those present, cries of "G.Y.!" were normally sufficient to convey their audience's feelings on the matter.

GAMMING

A *gam* was a mutual visit between the crews of whaling ships when they happened to meet abroad. It was there the latest news was exchanged, gossip was shared, and yarns were spun amid plenty of song, dance, food, and drink.

As far as the origin of the term itself, the word *gam* was whalemen slang for a pod of whales.

GANGPLANK

Whether you call it a gangplank, gangboard, or gangway, this term for the platform utilized in boarding or exiting a ship comes from the old English word *gang*, literally "a going."

GARBLING

Garbling was a term used by customs and dock officials to describe the process of removing inferior or damaged portions of a commodity (tobacco, spices, drugs, etc.) to legally avoid paying duties (taxes) on them. Conversely, it was also used to describe the unscrupulous act of mixing dunnage or other such rubbish into a ship's cargo in order to cheat an owner or merchant. That's why to this day we can't understand a *garbled* message.

GATE OF TEARS

Babelmandeb (alternately translated as the *Gate of Tears* or *Gate of Scars*) is the passage leading into the Red Sea from the Gulf of Aden. It was so named by Arab sailors due to the many shipwrecks that occurred there.

GEEDUNK

To those of the modern sea-going services, *geedunk* is synonymous with candy, chips, and other such snacks, or just as often the machine or place where one can purchase them aboard ship. No one can say for sure just where the term originated, but I've listed below my favorite theories.

The *Geedunk* was a candy store featured in a 1920s comic strip, where a character named Harold Teen and friends hung out. No explanation was ever given for the store's name.

Gee dung is a Chinese word meaning "a place of idleness," a term that sounds like geedunk and is certainly appropriate description-wise.

And finally my favorite explanation, that being *geedunk!* is the sound the machine makes when it dispenses your snack.

"GILDING THE LION"

Also known as "building the galley," Captain Grose (see Bibliography) described it as follows:

> "A game formerly used at sea, in order to put a trick upon a landsman, or fresh-water sailor. It being agreed to play at that game, one sailor personates the builder, and another the merchant or contractor; the builder first begins by laying the keel, which consists of a number of men laid all along on their backs, one after another, that is, head to foot; he next puts in the ribs or knees, by making a number of men sit feet to feet, at right angles to, and on each side of, the keel; he now fixing on the person intended to be the object of the joke, observes he is a fierce-looking fellow, and fit for the lion [the figurehead]; he accordingly places him at the head, his arms being held or locked in by the two persons next to him, representing the ribs.
>
> "After several other dispositions, the builder delivers over the galley to the contractor as complete; but he, among other faults and objection, observes the lion is not gilt; on which the builder, or one of his assistants, runs to the head, and dipping a mop in excrement, thrusts it into the face of the lion."

(King Arthur, Paint the Lion)

GIVE 'EM THE BIRD

European sailors widely believed the soul of a drowned sailor resided within every albatross, hence the belief it's extremely bad luck to kill one. Others were a little more specific, stating shipmates came back as seagulls, whereas an albatross housed the soul of a dead sea captain.

Regardless of just who's in there, albatrosses are the largest of all sea birds, with some attaining a wingspan of over 15 feet. *(Water, Water Everywhere, Nor Any Drop to Drink)*

"GIVE NO QUARTER"

Upon surrender, a captured officer was customarily given the option of saving his life by paying a ransom equal to one quarter of a year's pay. In this manner, they were "given quarter," or mercy. In a fight to the death, however, combatants were said to "give" or "take no quarter."

GIVING THE DEVIL HIS DUE

"The devil to pay" was a phrase originally coined to describe the odious task of caulking seams on a wooden ship. The *devil* was the ship's longest seam, usually taken to mean the outboard seam where deck and ship's sides meet, whereas *paying* (from the French word *payer*, to pitch) referred to the process of sealing a newly caulked seam by pouring hot tar or pitch along its length.

"Paying the devil" was a task universally despised due to the seam's size and the awkward contortions usually required to *chinse* (caulk) its entire length.

"The devil to pay, and no pitch hot or ready!" was another phrase coined in reference to this hateful task, it being used to describe a challenging situation one is ill-prepared to cope with.

As standing room was nonexistent for the most part, repairs to the devil were normally performed while hanging over the ship's side from a bosun's chair, often while underway. In fact, being in the unenviable position of swinging around below the devil in said chair while attempting to caulk *and* pour hot pitch gave rise to another phrase, that describing one "caught between the devil and the deep blue sea."

GO FIGURE . . .

Ancient sailors patronized a host of deities in order to guarantee safe passage through tempestuous ocean realms—sacrifices played a crucial role in securing these blessings from the fickle gods of wind and sea. Human sacrifice was viewed as the ultimate gesture of devotion and the practice itself led to the evolution of figureheads.

The first figureheads were actually human heads attached to a vessel's bow prior to her first voyage. As these sacrifices were often beautiful maidens (common sense dictating the ratio of safe passages versus those using an ugly sacrifice would be inversely proportional) this is most likely where the term *maiden voyage* originated.

When the head (eventually) fell into the sea, it indicated the gods had accepted the sacrifice and that the soul of the maiden had entered the ship—another reason why sailors always refer to a ship as *she*.

As society became a bit more squeamish, red wine (and later champagne) replaced the traditionally required blood offering during a ship's christening, with figureheads coming to represent the human sacrifices. As such, it was believed figureheads should always be human in shape (never animal) to remind the likes of Neptune and Aeolus of our devotion in the good old days. *(The Eyes Have It, Family-Head, Fiddlehead, Women Onboard)*

GOLD COAST?

Below is an excerpt from the journal of one Captain George Shelvocke, an English privateer of the early 1700s. It describes an area where he landed briefly while cruising the Pacific coast of North America to take on water.

> "The soil is a rich black mould which, as you turn it fresh up to the sun, appears as if intermingled with gold dust, some of which we endeavoured to crush and purify from the dirt. But though we were little prejudiced against the thoughts that it could be possible that this metal should be so promiscuously and universally mingled with common earth, yet we endeavoured to cleanse and wash the earth from some of it, and the more we did the more it appeared like gold. But in order to be farther satisfied, I brought some of it away which we lost in our confusions in China."

Sounds too good to be true, doesn't it? Unfortunately, the rest of Shelvocke's journal pretty much cast him as a habitual liar and all-around sneak. Too bad—if he could have kept either his sample or credulity, he may have been able to anticipate the California gold rush of 1849 by over a hundred and twenty years.

THE GOLDEN FLEECE

Who didn't watch the 1963 movie classic *Jason and the Argonauts* as a kid and think *"Man! These fighting skeletons kick ass!"* The whole Golden Fleece thing had me stumped, however, until I came across the following tidbit of information.

As the Greeks came into their own as a seafaring nation, they expanded outside the Mediterranean, establishing and trading with colonial settlements as far as France, North Africa, and the Black Sea. The Black Sea colonies supplied much of the wheat for Greece at one time, but the gold found in its many rivers was the real treasure. The Greek settlers staked sheepskins to the bottoms of the fast-flowing rivers to catch gold nuggets washed down by the current, and there we have the basis for the legendary *Golden Fleece* the Argonauts were seeking.

GOOD VIBRATIONS

Used to be many of the sailing community swore waterspouts could be dispersed by firing at them with a rifle. It was thought vibrations created by the shot did the trick; however, you had to be within two hundred yards of the waterspout for it to work (got to be scientific about this type of stuff).

"GOOSE WITHOUT GRAVY"

Humorous attempt by sailors to describe a flogging that drew no blood. *(Cat O'Nine Tails, Checkered Shirt, Cold Burning, Cursing and the Cangue, Flogging around the Fleet, Killing the Cat, Marry the Gunner's Daughter, Nightingale, Salt Eel, To Flog or Not to Flog, Whipped and Pickled)*

"GRAVY-EYE WATCH"

Sailor's original term for the midwatch (midnight to 4:00 a.m.) when eyes were sticky and heads were prone to nod. Corrupted by later sailors to graveyard watch, it eventually washed ashore to become the graveyard shift. *(Dogwatch)*

GREAT GUNS

With the development of heavy cannon in the sixteenth century, ships found themselves possessing the ability to actually sink each other in battle, as opposed to the previous goals of boarding or crippling an enemy. Use of these *great guns* spurred radical changes not only in ship design, but also naval warfare tactics. Reaching their zenith in the man-of-war of the eighteenth and nineteenth century, these guns ruled the seas for the better part of three centuries—not too shabby, considering they remained basically unchanged in design the entire period.

Regardless of their effectiveness, they weren't without their little idiosyncrasies. Undetectable flaws during manufacture meant they might blow up on the first, fifth, or five-hundredth round fired (or anytime in between). Fact of the matter was, no one knew with certainty just what would happen each time the gunner placed burning linstock to touchhole.

During extended use overheating became an issue as well, despite the crew's best efforts at cooling via buckets of water or constant sponging with a solution of vinegar and water. All cannon (brass or iron) bucked violently if fired when hot, and nothing was more dangerous to ship and crew than a loose cannon on deck. Breaking free of their carriage and restraining tackle, they could recoil into bulkheads, overturn, leap up and smash into the beams overhead, or simply explode. *(Fire in the Hole, Loose Cannon on Deck, Of War Galleys and Ships of the Line)*

GROG

Thank Admiral Edward Vernon of Britain's Royal Navy, the hero of Porto Bello and Commander in Chief, West Indies, for this one. It came about in response to sailors hoarding their daily rum ration in order to get hammered, a practice especially popular on the night before a major battle. The daily drink ration for British sailors during the seventeenth century was one gallon of beer. Due to the space required to store such large quantities of beer, in 1655 it was converted to a daily rum ration (a.k.a. a *tot*) of one-half pint.

The good admiral, concerned with what he called "the swinish vice of drunkenness" hit upon the idea of diluting the daily rum ration with water as a measure to prevent drunkenness aboard ship. He believed rum diluted with water would have less effect on the senses, even though the men continued to receive the same ration (which was true, as their tot would no longer be straight rum). It would also be more difficult to store the larger quantities of watered-down rum needed to get suitably hammered.

His Order to Captains No. 349 issued on August 21, 1740, stated in part

" . . . unanimous opinion of both Captains and Surgeons that the pernicious custom of the seaman drinking their allowance of rum in drams, and often at once, is attended with many fatal effects to their morals as well as their health . . . besides the ill consequences of stupifying [sic] their rational qualities . . . You are hereby required and directed . . . that the respective daily allowance . . . be every day mixed with the proportion of a quart of water to a half pint of rum, to be mixed in a scuttled butt kept for that purpose, and to be done upon the deck, and in the presence of the Lieutenant of the Watch who is to take particular care to see that the men are not defrauded in having their full allowance of rum . . . and let those that are good husbanders receive extra lime juice and sugar that it be made more palatable to them."

Needless to say, the concoction was less than enthusiastically received by the crew. They promptly dubbed it *grog*, after the admiral's nickname *Old Grogram*, from the grogram cloak (a roughhewn fabric of mohair and silk) he invariably wore in all types of weather. It's also said to be a reference to the color green, the color of both the cloak and (more often than not) of the ship's water as well. So if you've ever felt *groggy*, now you know why. *(Black Tot Day, Grog-Blossom, More Northing!, Six-Water Grog, Scuttlebutt, Splice the Main Brace)*

GROG-BLOSSOM

Slang for a facial carbuncle or red nose associated with excessive drinking. It's defined in the *Century Dictionary* as "a redress or eruption of inflamed pimples on the nose or face of a man who drinks ardent spirits to excess." Other names include *rum-blossom* and *toddy blossom*. *(Black Tot Day, Grog, More Northing!, Six-Water Grog, Splice the Main Brace)*

GUN SALUTES

Gun salutes were initially fired as an act of good faith, rather than a show of respect.

In the days when it took a considerable length of time to reload and prep a ship's cannon, discharging them when approaching another vessel or upon entering port ensured good intentions.

Gun salutes were always odd in number based on the timeless belief that odd, not even, numbers were lucky in nature, particularly one, three, five, seven, and nine. It's a belief prevalent in both Christian and pagan doctrine as well. Radford (see Bibliography) cites the following examples: "One represents the Diety, three the Trinity, five the chief division, seven the sacred number, and nine is three times three, the great climacteric."

Seven weighs in pretty heavy, too, as far as Christianity and the Bible are concerned. There were seven days of creation, seven graces, seven deadly sins, and seven divisions of the Lord's Prayer. Revelation is particularly rich in regard to this: the seven churches of Asia, the seven seals, the seven-headed dragon (Satan), as well as the seven angels and their seven golden bowls filled with the wrath of God (and don't even get me started on the Seven Wonders of the World, the seven Japanese gods of luck, or the Seventh Heaven of the Mohammedans).

As for mythology, three was a favored number of the ancients. From the three fates, the three Furies, and Hecate's threefold powers, to Cerberus and Neptune's three-pronged trident, symbols relative to that number abound in the classics.

HALF-MASTING OF ENSIGNS

Custom once dictated the loss of a loved one be marked by the wearing of disheveled clothing or other such signs of disarray. Mourning was observed in a similar fashion aboard ship as well. Rope ends were left to fray; booms or yardarms were secured at odd angles to the deck (a-cockbill, as opposed to being squared away), lines left uncoiled, etc. The half-masting of flags as a show of mourning is an extension of this ancient sign of grief. (*A-Cockbill, Mourning Line*)

HAND

Crewmembers were often referred to as *hands*, as in "all hands on deck" and similar salty talk. It comes from the fact that when an able or common seaman was signed on, the only items he brought aboard were the tools of his trade, that being knowledge and his two hands. (*A.B., Sail before the Mast*)

HANDS OFF

Old admiralty law once dictated that any sailor guilty of pulling a knife on a shipmate was to have his hand cut off as punishment. (*Knives*)

HARDTACK

Sea or ship's biscuit, as opposed to regular bread, which was dubbed (you guessed it) *soft tack*. Along the same lines, loaf bread was called *soft tommy*.

The term itself is said to be a reference to eating during heavy weather, a time when the galley was secured as it was too rough to cook. Sailors required to be on deck during such weather often kept ship's biscuits in their pockets to eat between each "hard tack" of the ship.

HARD UP

Destitute; fallen on hard or trying times. It's derived from "hard up the helm," an order to place the tiller as far to windward as possible during difficult weather, thus turning the ship's head away from the wind that she might ride easier.

HARNESS CASK

Slang for the "salt horse" barrel, a tub or cask containing the salted meat currently being used by the cook. Old salts swore the ship's purser purchased horsemeat instead of beef or pork for the crew's table, pocketing the difference. They held the extra tough pieces as proof, saying they were part of the horse's harness. Probably didn't help matters that the cask itself was often secured to the deck using horseshoes. *(Making a Dead Man Chew, Nip Cheese)*

HAVE IT DONE BY FRIDAY

When English privateers under the command of Captain Woodes Rogers arrived at the Juan Fernandez Islands in 1709, they discovered "a man clothed in goatskins, who looked wilder than the first owners of them." The man, Alexander Selkirk, had marooned himself after a heated exchange with the captain of the *Cinque Ports* (another privateer) over four years earlier.

Seems Selkirk, who was serving in the capacity of sailing master at the time, had long ago deemed the leaking ship unsafe due to improper maintenance and repairs. He finally addressed his complaints to the captain, who pretty much told him to shut his pie hole. Almost as pugnacious and ill-tempered as the captain himself, Selkirk rashly declared if proper repairs weren't completed immediately the ship could go to the bottom without him. The Captain for once proved accommodating, promptly marooning him on the nearby island of Más a Tierra, the largest of the chain (which by the way is located some 363 nautical miles off the coast of Chile).

Selkirk spent his self-imposed exile dancing with the islands' only other inhabitants, goats (he ate over 500 of them) and praying. Rogers commented in his journal that "the Gouvernour" (as Selkirk was christened by the sailors) was so fleet of foot he captured the goats by hand, a task in which he bested not only crewmembers, but the ship's dogs as well.

Although joyous over rescue, of his adventure Selkirk wistfully remarked that "he was a better Christian than ever he was before or than, he was afraid, he should ever be again."

His adventure was the basis for Daniel Defoe's 1719 bestseller, *Robinson Crusoe*. *(Booty Call!)*

HEADS WILL ROLL!

When the infamous German pirate Klaus Störtebeker and his vicious band of *Vitalienbrüder* were finally captured off the North Sea archipelago of Helgoland in 1401, folk of the day were hardly surprised at the verdict awarded the "Terror of the Baltic" and his crew: death by beheading.

For years Störtebeker's depredations against Hanseatic shipping had caused much wailing and gnashing of teeth among the powerful Hamburg merchants. In fact, piracy was the driving impetus behind Hamburg's forced annexation of the mouth of the Elbe River in 1394, as city officials felt the local aristocracy (the von Lappe) had failed to take proper steps to counter the growing threat.

In October of the year he was captured, Störtebeker and his crew were taken to the Grasbrook area of Hamburg for execution. Beheading at the time called for the condemned to assume a kneeling position, with the swordsman approaching from behind to dispense justice. Although a single, clean stroke was the goal, this method of execution was far from perfect. Mis-cuts due to a poor swing or movement on the prisoner's part were commonplace and caused some pretty gruesome cleanup work, a state of affairs that eventually led to the invention of the guillotine . . . but hey, that's another story.

Chroniclers of the day reported that Störtebeker, upon being offered his customary last request, asked to have his former shipmates assembled before him and that he in turn be decapitated while standing. Once this was granted, Störtebeker asked that each crew his headless corpse walked past—post execution—be set free.

Based on which account you believe, Störtebeker's wildly spurting trunk purportedly staggered past fourteen lucky crewmen until someone (variously recorded as a soldier, old woman, or even the executioner himself) grew overly concerned at the rate of progress being made by the headless, upright, corpse and tripped it with a spear hasp, clod of dirt, or brick (respectively) thrown in front of its feet, thus proving the assumption that a walking, headless corpse would be unable to rise once fallen.

Pretty neat, huh? Gets even more interesting when you consider Washington Irving's "Headless Horseman" of Sleepy Hollow fame was thought to be derived from an old Germanic legend concerning a walking, headless corpse. The tale even describes him as " . . . the ghost of a Hessian trooper, whose head had been carried away by a cannon-ball, in some nameless battle during the Revolutionary War, and who is ever and anon seen by the country folk hurrying along in the gloom of night, as if on the wings of the wind."

Of course I can't say for certain the above actually happened at Störtebeker's execution, but after seeing how a chicken moves subsequent to getting the axe, I wouldn't put it past a determined man. Even if he just kind of flopped around a bit and fell forward far enough to save just a few, you've got to admire a headman (how's that for a pun) willing to go the distance (there's another one) for his crew; I'm willing to give Herr Störtebeker credit based on intestinal fortitude alone.

And now, the rest of the story . . .

Störtebeker's head was put on a stake on an island in the Elbe River to ward off other would-be buccaneers. It was discovered there in 1867 (the metal spike still protruding from its top) and had been displayed at the Hamburg Museum since 1922—until it was stolen on January 9, 2010. It was finally recovered in March 2011 and was again placed on display later that month (this time with improved security).

Other Störtebeker fun facts (or otherwise):

- *Störtebeker* (old German for "empty the mug with one gulp") was actually an alias the pirate assumed, supposedly in reference to his ability to drain a gallon mug in one gulp.

- Störtebeker reportedly offered his captors a chain of gold long enough to circle the whole of Hamburg in exchange for his freedom.

- Although regarded as a Robin Hood/Che Guevara-est type figure by many northern Germans due to his atrocities against the rich merchants of the Hanseatic League, there's little evidence he shared his booty with the poor. Legend has it that while dismantling Störtebeker's ship, it was found the masts contained separate cores of gold, silver, and copper.

- After chopping off the heads of Störtebeker and his 30 crew, the executioner was asked if he was not a little tired. His candid reply was that he had enough energy remaining to execute the senate elders as well, a jest apparently not well received by that august body, as they then ordered the executioner beheaded as well, by the youngest member of the senate. *(Buccaneers)*

THE HEAVY MANTLE OF RESPONSIBILITY

Side boys have been a part of naval tradition since the early days of sail. Necessity dictated the transporting of officers between ships, whether in port or on the high seas, to attend conferences or perhaps accept an invitation to dine. If the sea state was less than ideal, visitors were hoisted aboard in baskets or bosun's chairs by the ship's crew, who were said to be attending the "sides" of the ship.

Although the number of side boys attending an officer's arrival today conveniently mirrors rank (the more senior the officer, the more side boys used), the larger number was initially required out of necessity rather than respect. As an individual's rank and girth often increased proportionately, more side boys were needed to haul such worthies over the rail.

HEN FRIGATE

Around the mid-1800s many whaling captains began taking their wives to sea in order to avoid the separation of a three- to four-year voyage. A *hen frigate* was the label given a ship in which the captain's overbearing better half constantly bickered with officers and crew.

One such wife was described by a mate as "the meanest, most hoggish and the greediest female that ever existed . . . the whistle of a gale of wind through the rigging is much more musical than the sound of her voice."

HIGH SEAS

Ahhhh, what manly man of manliness hasn't dreamed at some point of setting a course for adventure on the high seas? But where exactly are these high seas and what are they high on? Rather than the physical elevation of the sea (or road for that matter—you take the high road and I'll take the low road, etc., etc.) *high* in this context is Old English and describes some feature or quality that placed whatever it was referring to above the rest. *High seas* described the vast magnificence of the open ocean (the freeway of all nations, seas that are not within any nation's jurisdiction) while the *highroad* and *highway* were major or primary roadways and streets. Other instances would be *High Mass* (celebrated with full pomp and ceremony) and *high tea*, a full-blown evening meal serving hot meat (as opposed to tea and light snacks).

HIJACK

A *Jack* was the nickname given smugglers who drove the boats trying to bring in illegal alcohol during prohibition. When stopped by law enforcement officers, the Jacks (so named for the way they tried to scurry away prior to capture, like jackrabbits) were ordered to raise their hands.

"How high?" was the standard retort, which the officers invariably countered with "High, Jacks." The phrase was eventually shortened to *hijack* and came to mean something seized or stolen in transit. *(Jack Tar)*

HMMMM . . . NEEDS MORE SALT

Nineteenth-century shipping magnate and railroad tycoon Cornelius Vanderbilt, who was both an insomniac and believer in the occult, was unable to sleep

unless the four legs of his bed each rested in a plate of salt (to keep evil spirits from attacking him during the night). The rich *are* different, aren't they!

HOLD THE STARCH

Soap was first issued in the Royal Navy in 1796; however, the practice didn't become standard until 1825. Prior to that, crewmen cleaned their clothes by a good soaking in urine followed by a brief rinse in seawater. The urine itself was stored in two large tubs on either side of the bowsprit (where the head was located) for use in the washing of clothes as well as hair, where its high ammonia content aided in both bleaching and head-lice control.

After the wash, rinse, and condition cycle, sailors then tied their laundry up to dry with their *clothes stops*, a 12-inch length of small-diameter cord provided for just that purpose. They were standard issue in the U.S. Navy until 1973. *(But Why Is It Called the Head?)*

HOLYSTONING THE DECKS

The wooden decks of a sailing ship were scrubbed using blocks of sandstone (called *holystones*) along with a scouring mixture of sand and water. Why the name holystone? Four plausible explanations come up.

The first has it the name arose from the British Navy's purported practice of "borrowing" broken gravestones from St. Nicholas Church in Great Yarmouth, England, for the purpose of scouring the decks. A second theory is that they were used to clean the decks on a Sunday.

The third explanation stems from the sandstone blocks themselves, which ranged in size from smaller stones called *prayer books* (used to scrub the tighter, hard-to-reach places) to larger ones called *hand Bibles*, which were roughly the size and shape of a big family Bible.

Finally, Rear Admiral Gerard Wells, R.N., stated that holystones were "so called because when using them an attitude of prayer is taken," as a sailor got on his knees to use them. Judging from the conflicts that often arose between the religious leaders ashore and sailors seeking pleasures denied at sea, one can imagine calls to holystone the deck or attend church were looked upon with equal enthusiasm.

HOMEWARD BOUND SPLICES

Splices and other such repairs to the ship's lines and rigging that were shoddy or of a decidedly inferior nature to what Jack would normally produce. As the name implies they became more frequent on the last legs of a voyage, when they were viewed more as a temporary repair required only to last until reaching homeport. "Homeward bound stitches" was a similar phrase used by sailmakers to describe a temporary repair intended to last only long enough to reach the next port.

HORSE LATITUDES

An area of tedious calm and contrary winds lying north of the northeast trades in the North Atlantic. The story goes that sailing ships were sometimes becalmed there for so long that livestock (horses for example) were forced to walk the plank to conserve fresh water for the crew. *(Flogging a Dead Horse, Harness Cask)*

HOT BED

Watches aboard ship in the early 1700s revolved around a four-hour rotation. When the first night watch commenced at eight, those off watch slogged below to get what sleep could be had before stumbling back on deck to relieve their shipmates at midnight. And so it went, a monotonous cycle of four-hour watches, spiced with the occasional dogwatch thrown in for variety.

Queen Elizabeth, astutely noticing that only half of the ship's company could be below decks at any given time, instituted the practice of carrying only enough hammocks for half the crew. Thus, each man coming off watch retired to what would later be known as a "hot bed" (in reference to it recently being vacated by another sleeper).

It was more often than not a cold bed, however, being most likely soaked by the previous sleeper's wet clothes and the continuous leaking of water from above decks. *(Dogwatch, Eight Bells, Sweating the Glass)*

THE HUNGER LINES

Old salt's nickname for shipping lines whose vessels were synonymous with bad grub, harsh working conditions, and meager wages. Common sayings among the hungry Tars manning such ships were "I could take up the slack of my belly and wipe my eyes with it!" or perhaps "My belly thinks my throat is cut!"

THE HUNGRY HUNDRED

Label applied to Britain's first group of Royal Navy Reserve (RNR) officers assigned to the fleet, the term itself indicative of the amount of compensation received for their services. Originally founded under the Naval Reserve Act of 1859, the RNR was a reserve of professional seamen from the British Merchant Navy and civilian fishing fleets who were called up during times of war to serve in the regular navy.

HUNKI-DORI

Commodore Matthew Perry's historic visit to Japan in July 1853 began an era of openness and commercial intercourse between east and west. Yokohama was one of Japan's busiest ports at the time and the main street of the waterfront district, Honki-dori, became famous for its ability to provide in abundance those pleasures of wicked ease so eagerly sought by sailors while in port.

While Honki-dori was relatively straightforward and easy to navigate, the winding side streets and back roads were not only confusing but potentially dangerous to unwary sailors (particularly those of the inebriated persuasion) who often fell victim to robbery or worse. Advice was if you stayed on Honki-dori, you could find everything you desired in relative safety, hence the street name's association with everything being OK. *(Commodore Matthew Calbraith Perry and the Opening of Japan, Steam-Propelled Warships, Tycoon, Who Said "Don't Give up the Ship?")*

THE HUSH-HUSH FLEET

The nickname given Britain's first battle cruisers (the *Courageous* class) in reference to the secrecy surrounding the revolutionary concepts utilized in their construction during World War I.

Known as "large light cruisers" they were nominally designed to support the Baltic Project, a plan championed by Admiral of the Fleet Lord Fisher (the second most important figure in British naval history after Lord Nelson) to land troops on the German Baltic Coast. Designed with shallow draft (to facilitate operation in the shallow waters of the Baltic) the three ships of this class (HMS *Furious*, HMS *Glorious*, and HMS *Courageous*) were fast but very lightly armored, and carried only a few heavy guns. They were also the first capital ships of the British Royal navy to use geared steam turbines and small-tube boilers.

I FEEL AH'HEALING COMIN' ON!

Boatswains often carried a rattan cane or short length of hard line called a *starter*, which they applied liberally and with a will to those viewed as lazy or not moving fast enough. With its help, the bosun was said to have effected more miraculous cures than the ship's surgeon, making the crippled whole and the lame to skip. *(Bos'n)*

ICU

Ships normally kept a telescope or "bring 'em near" in a drawer near the binnacle for use in espying the horizon. They also had a night glass, which was used in lieu of the regular day telescope, although users had to be careful, as it presented an inverted view.

IDIOTS

Old salts once believed meeting a mentally unbalanced person while heading toward their ship bespoke of a safe, prosperous voyage.

"I'LL EAT MY HAT"

Sailors often chewed tobacco in an effort to offset the bland, monotonous diet they were forced to endure. They chewed rather than smoked (as the fear of fire was so great aboard ship), and a good plug of cut tobacco could be chewed a few hours one day, safely stowed overnight, and then enjoyed the next.

Jack normally kept a "quid of baccy" in his hat, and upon running out often removed its tobacco-stained lining to chew on, which is where the expression "I'll eat my hat" originated. *(The New World, Quid of Tobacco)*

"IN THE DOLDRUMS"

This nautical equivalent of "down in the dumps" references the experience of sailing within the doldrums (an area of little or no wind located near the equator) and the depressingly slow progress often encountered while traversing the region.

"IN THROUGH THE HAWSEPIPE"

When an officer professes he entered the maritime service by climbing in through the hawsepipe, it's merely a statement that he's worked his way up from the rank of ordinary seaman. Hawsepipes (also known as *hawseholes*) are openings in a ship's bow through which the anchor chain or rode runs, a location forward of the mast that correlates to the area where the enlisted men were quartered.

This in contrast to "through the stern cabin window," a phrase used to describe those granted an officer's rank or other such promotion based on family connections rather than actual merit (the after cabin usually housing the captain and his officers).

As silver plate was used during meals by both officers afloat and the wealthy ashore, another phrase became popular for describing those lucky

enough to find themselves so promoted, that of being "born with a silver spoon in his mouth."

IRON JIB

Sailor slang for early steam propulsion engines.

IRON WATER

Back when the use of iron aboard ship was more of a novelty than the rule, salty geezers in the know kept a barrel of *iron water* available to drink from (rusty iron steeped in rain water). They claimed it was good for what might ail a sailor—full of vitamins and minerals, it was.

ISLE OF THIEVES

Name bestowed upon Guam by Magellan during his voyage around the world. It was made in reference to the islanders' habit of boarding the ships and snatching pretty much everything they could get their hands on. *(Yarn of the* Nancy Bell*)*

"IT BLOWS GREAT GUNS"

Old sailor's adage used to describe the explosive, booming winds of a particularly violent storm. "It's blowing marlinspikes" would be another, indicating a gale strong enough to lift marlinspikes off the deck.

"IT'S AN ILL WIND THAT BLOWS NO ONE ANY GOOD"

Old nautical saying indicating every wind, no matter what the direction, will surely benefit someone.

"IT'S A WASHOUT"

Yet another phrase descended from our rich nautical heritage. It comes from an order to wipe clean the slates once used aboard ship to record flag signals or messages.

JACK-OF-THE-DUST

Name given the purser's assistant, who was responsible for the ship's stores. His other nicknames included *Dusty Boy* (in reference to the flour dust he was inevitably coated with when handling the ship's bread), *Breadroom Jack, Dips,* and *Jack Dusty,* any of which were better than *Jack Nastyface,* nom de plume for the cook's helper. *(Jack Tar, Jumping Jacks)*

JACK'S KITCHEN

Publicly displaying the bodies of convicted pirates was an indispensable tool in educating the unwashed masses about that whole "crime doesn't pay" thing. As the sight of a corpse swinging in chains did wonders to keep the feet of many on the straight and narrow, English authorities were loath to lose such efficient deterrents to time and decay.

Jack's Kitchen was the cookery located in London's infamous Newgate Prison where the mortal remains of executed pirates and other such miscreants were boiled and treated as the first steps toward preserving them.

Entire bodies were often displayed in prominent locations for the maritime community to view (such as those unfortunates hanging from the gibbet at Execution Dock on the Thames), but in earlier days pieces or parts sufficed. You know—arms, heads, legs, and the like. At any given time hundreds could be seen impaled on rows of spikes atop the massive stone gate at the southern end of London Bridge. (*Dance the Hempen Jig, The Deadly Nevergreen, Swinging from the Gibbet, Turning a Profit with the Upright Man, You'll Grin in a Glass Case*)

JACK TAR

A sailor. One of the most common masculine names of the English language, Jack has been a popular euphemism for the common man since early on, particularly those of the working class—it's where we get jackhammer, Jack-in-the-box, Jack-of-all-trades, jackass, jack-o'-lantern, Jack-be-Nimble, jumping jacks, jackknife, Jack . . . well, you get the idea. Sailors applied the name liberally to a wide variety of descriptive terms, from *Jack Adams* (a stubborn seaman) to *Jack Whore*, meaning a masculine, overgrown wench.

As for the latter part, seamen have been known as *Tars* for centuries in reference to their use of that material to waterproof clothing and caulk hull seams. Interesting and good-to-know type stuff, 'cause you certainly wouldn't want anyone commenting that "you don't know Jack." (*Jack-of-the-Dust, Jumping Jacks*)

"JAWING UP"

Whaler's term for a sperm whale's trick of rolling over on its back and crushing any—and everything—within reach of its jaw. (*Nantucket Sleigh Ride, Right Whale*)

JAW TACKLE

The mouth. "To cast off one's jaw tackle" meant to talk too much.

JEAN LAFITTE

The governor of Louisiana once offered a reward of five thousand dollars for the head of gentleman pirate (or privateer, depending on your take of history) Jean Lafitte, who in turn promptly offered fifty thousand for the governor's head.

JEMMY (JIMMY) DUCKS

The lucky Tar whose duty it was to take care of the chickens, ducks, and other such poultry carried aboard a warship. His shipmates also jokingly referred to him as the "duck-f**ker," a fowl name if ever there was one.

JIG

A spare set of pulleys or watch tackle kept handy for use whenever extra pulling power was needed about the decks. Once the blocks were cheek to cheek (pulled together) no more could be done, giving us the phrase "the jig is up."

JIMMY BUNGS (OR BUNGS)

The ship's cooper, who was responsible for the repair and stowage of the various barrels and casks used onboard.

JIMMY THE ONE

Lower deck slang term for the first lieutenant of a British naval vessel. The first lieutenant (also referred to as the "First Luff" or simply "Number One") was the senior lieutenant onboard who was responsible for the organization and administration of the ship (navigation, organizing watches, maintaining discipline, training of the junior officers, etc.) under guidance of the captain. In modern navies it's a term for the executive officer, who is second in command and typically holds the rank of commander.

JOHNNY CAKES

Also called *journey cakes*, they consisted of flour shaped into loaves or cakes and boiled. That's it—boiled flour. Must have been an art to cooking them . . . eating 'em too, I imagine.

JOHNNY HAWBUCK

An officer who dressed the part of a dandy at sea, i.e., with lace and other such foppish accompaniments.

JOLLY BOAT

A workboat (typically a small yawl) carried by sailing vessels to run errands and such about the harbor while the ship was at anchor. The term itself is an English corruption of *jolle*, the Danish word for yawl.

JUMPING JACKS

Ever wonder where that staple instrument of torture used in every high school physical education class got its name? Thank Captain Cook's crew—

it's what they called penguins during his voyage of exploration to Antarctica, in reference to the way they jumped from the ice floes (*jack* being a euphemism for the common man). *(Jack-of-the-Dust, Jack Tar)*

JUNK

Another salty word washed ashore. *Junk* is the name given old rope ends that were unraveled or picked apart for later use in caulking seams aboard ship. It comes from *juncos*, the Latin word for bulrush (a source of cordage in ancient times).

The bosun of a vessel had the option of selling junk accumulated during a voyage to the "junkman" once in port, which is how that name came about.

Junk was also sailor's slang for salt beef or pork in reference to its toughness, which was said to be on par with old rope ends. *(Chewing the Fat, Salt Junk)*

KHAKI UNIFORMS

The khaki uniforms of today's navy actually originated from India. British soldiers stationed there in 1845 soaked their "whites" in a mixture of mud, coffee, and curry powder in an effort to better blend in with India's landscape.

KILLING THE CAT

Popular sentiment against flogging in the U.S. Navy crested in 1850 with the release of *White-Jacket*, a novel depicting life aboard the frigate *United States*. Written by a young whaleman who served as a seaman aboard her, the graphic, eye-witness descriptions of over 163 floggings (the ship averaged 6 per week) supplemented the Navy's report to Congress that same year concerning use of the *cat* (cat o' nine tails) as well as the *kitten* or *colt*, a single-strand whip used on boys.

Congress abolished flogging aboard U.S. warships and merchantmen that same year. It was suspended by the Royal Navy in the 1870s and finally abolished in 1881.

Oh—and the young seaman who wrote the novel? None other than Herman Melville. *(Cat O' Nine Tails, Checkered Shirt, Cold Burning, Cursing and the*

Cangue, Flogging Around the Fleet, Goose without Gravy, Marry the Gunner's Daughter, Nightingale, Salt Eel, To Flog or Not to Flog, Whipped and Pickled)

KING ARTHUR

A game played by sailors at sea when near the line or while traversing some equally hot clime, the particulars of which Captain Francis Grose describes in *A Classical Dictionary of the Vulgar Tongue.*

"A man who is to represent King Arthur, ridiculously dressed, having a large wig made out of oakum, or of some old swabs, is seated on the side, or over a large vessel of water, every person in his turn is to be ceremoniously introduced to him, and to pour a bucket of water over him, crying hail, King Arthur! If during this ceremony the person introduced laughs or smiles (to which his majesty endeavours to excite him, by all sorts of ridiculous gesticulations), he changes place with, and then becomes, King Arthur, till relieved by some brother tar, who has as little command over his muscles as himself."

(Gilding the Lion, Paint the Lion)

THE KING'S SHILLING

Recruiters for Britain's Royal Navy always carried "the King's shilling" for use when the opportunity arose. Recruiting laws of the seventeenth and eighteenth centuries decreed that if the coin was successfully passed to some unwary civilian, it could then be claimed the unlucky fellow had entered into a contract of service to God and king.

A favorite ploy was placing the coin in a tankard of ale, which was then offered to a likely acquisition. With the first drink he was considered to have accepted the coin and therefore worthy of congratulations for joining His Majesty's service. It happened more often than you'd think—recruiters weren't required to be in uniform, and on the contrary often appeared to be part of a group of jolly fellows out celebrating some erstwhile event.

Needless to say this didn't set too well with publicans, who were less than thrilled at having their best customers carted halfway around the world to serve in the good king's navy. As such, many supplied patrons with glass-bottomed tankards, thus enabling their more cautious drinkers a chance to peer into its depths to ensure no unwanted surprises awaited them.

Glass-bottomed mugs also allowed a drinker to keep an eye on cutpurses or other such scallywags at the bar while hoisting a brew, which is said to have given rise to the phrase "here's looking at you."

The expressions "press-gang" or "pressed into service" can be traced to this practice as well, *press* being a corruption of the word *imprest*, a term denoting money paid in advance for some later service to a government entity. *(Press-Gangs, Shanghaied by the Crimps, Son of a Gun)*

"KISSED BY MOTHER CAREY"

Said of those whose destiny seemed forever tied to the sea. Young boys so afflicted were said to have been kissed in the cradle by Mother Carey, the sailor's guardian angel. *(Mother Carey's Chickens)*

KNIVES

Standard was the practice of ordering the tips of all the crew's knives broken off, in an effort to reduce fatalities from deck fights. If blood was shed during a quarrel, the sailor responsible was often nailed by the hand to the mast with the knife he used in the brawl, there to remain until he could pull himself free.

For arguments ending in death, Richard the Lion Heart issued the following guidelines: "Who kills a man on shipboard, shall be bound to the dead body and thrown in the sea."

Waiting till the ship pulled in to settle a score wasn't much better in view of King Richard's decree that "if a man is killed on shore, the slayer shall be bound to the dead body and buried with it." *(Hands Off)*

KNOTS

While it may be correct on inland waters to state a vessel's speed in miles per hour, no sailor worthy of Fiddler's Green would ever give speed over saltwater as anything but knots. The term knot (or nautical mile) comes from the use of an ingenious device called a log or chip line, which was used to determine a ship's speed. It consisted of a long length of light line or twine marked at regular intervals with knots. The *chip* or *log* was a piece of wood similar in shape to a slice of pie and weighted slightly at the rounded bottom so as to float vertically and relatively stationary.

Use of the log was a two-person job, one normally accomplished by an officer and an assistant. After heaving the log over the stern, roughly fifteen

fathoms of line were allowed to pay out before the officer taking the reading cried, "Turn!" signaling his assistant to turn a half-minute glass. As the glass ran out, the assistant in turn shouted "Hold!" at which point the officer seized the line, noting the number of knots that had passed.

From there simple arithmetic could be used to determine the ship's speed in knots.

It only sounded simple, however, as errors could and often were introduced by mistakes in heaving the log, turning the glass, sloppy steering, or through anomalies induced through wind, tides, currents, or waves. *(Fiddler's Green, The Five L's)*

KNOTTED ENSIGN

Sea captains of old once knotted their ship's ensign to the mast as a sign of bankruptcy. According to the laws of ancient Rome, creditors could actually divide a captain's body into pieces proportionate to monies owed them if unable to repay his debts.

"KNOW THE ROPES"

One requirement of shipping aboard as able seaman (versus an ordinary hand) was a thorough knowledge of all ropes pertaining to the vessel's operation, which on a square-rigger could equate to miles of cordage. Crewmembers achieving that level of skill were said to "know the ropes." *(A.B.)*

KNOW YOUR PIRATES

Corsairs were pirates based in the Mediterranean, such as those found along the coasts of the "Barbary States," a band of Islamic nations that included Algeria, Tunisia, Tripoli, and oft times Morocco. *Landrones*, on the other hand, infested the South China Sea—the Landrone Islands originally being a place of banishment for Chinese thieves.

It was the *Buccaneers*, however, that were based on the Isle of Hispaniola (modern day Haiti and the Dominican Republic) and operated within the Caribbean during the seventeenth century. Most were initially French Huguenots, who fled to the island after the St. Bartholomew's Day Massacre (1572).

Freebooter was the English term applied to these pirates, as well as any other preying upon shipping without the proper letters or commissions. The French inhabitants of Hispaniola found the word impossible to pronounce, substituting the word *Flibustier* instead, a term used to describe military adventurers in search of plunder; it re-entered the English language two centuries later as *filibuster*.

The Spanish just played it safe and labeled all those not of Spanish blood who were raping the New World *piratas*. *(Buccaneer, Pierre Le Grand)*

LA CUCARACHA

Captain John Smith describes, in his 1624 journals, "A Certaine India Bug, called by the Spaniards a Cacarootch, the which creeping into Chests they eat and defile with their ill-sented dung." The Spanish actually called them cucaracha, but in light of the above description, the *caca-rootch* sounds much more appropriate.

LANDLUBBER

As far back as the fifteenth century, *lubber* was a term used to describe someone exceedingly clumsy or loutish. Sailors merely added the "land" part in order to describe those green seamen aboard who didn't know plum duff from a bosun's arse.

Lubberly is still used as a derogatory term to describe something with a definite unseamanlike aspect about it.

LANDSHARK

Sailor's term for a lawyer (an association that should insult both fish and barrister) or proprietor of a boarding house where sailors were often fleeced of their hard-earned money prior to being shipped out. The term is defined in the *Century Dictionary* as "A person who subsists by cheating or robbing sailors on shore; a land-pirate."

LANGRAGE

Cannon fire consisting of nails, nuts, bolts, or any other miscellaneous bits of scrap iron a gunner could get his hands on. It was used to damage the sails and rigging of an adversary (wasn't too healthy for those about the decks either). *(Two-Headed Angel)*

LARGEST SHIP MODEL

The largest ship model in the world is of the whaling vessel *Lagoda*, currently on display at the New Bedford Whaling Museum. At 59 feet from figurehead to stern, it's an exact half-scale replica of its namesake, which was built in 1826. The *Lagoda* was originally meant to be named after Lake Ladoga in Russia, however the "d" and "g" were mistakenly transposed while being applied to the transom. As sailors believed correcting the name would bring bad luck, she sailed as the *Lagoda*. They must have been right, as she was considered a "greasy" (profitable) ship during her time as a whaler.

Here's a little more ship model trivia for you to throw about. In 1813 Captain Isaac Hull, then commanding officer of the USS *Constitution* presented a model of his ship to the East India Marine Society of Salem (later known as the Peabody Museum). At a gala later given by the Society, the model was placed in a tub of water and used as a centerpiece. All sails were set and her tiny guns primed and fired. The resulting broadside shattered her rigging, which was later painstakingly repaired by British prisoners of war. The model was so accurate in detail it was later used as a guide when the real *Constitution* underwent restoration.

LAUNCHING

As with all other aspects of a ship's construction, proper rites had to be observed while launching to ensure a "lucky ship."

Launching before noon (when the sun is rising) on a rising tide ensured a ship of rising fortune and opportunities. Launch skids were always well greased prior to launch to prevent hesitation (as this spoke of setbacks during a ship's career), while skids catching fire as the ship slid over them indicated she would sail "lively as the leaping flame." Lard was never used to grease the skids, however, as pigs were considered unlucky in the nautical realm of things.

The traditional hoopla associated with a ship's launching (bands, blowing of nearby ship's whistles, etc.) stems from the belief that loud noise frightens away evil spirits. *(Laying the Keel)*

LAYING THE KEEL

As it was considered the heart of a ship, shipwrights took particular pains to follow the prescribed rituals while laying the keel to guarantee a prosperous, lucky ship. Such rites might include driving the first nail through a horseshoe or drinking to the ship's health before any work was begun. Red (the color of blood and therefore that of life) was the proper deterrent for witches or those possessing the dreaded *Evil Eye*.

Keels were to be laid in a north/south alignment whenever possible. Shipwrights believed this aligned the inherent magnetism of a ship with the poles, thereby reducing compass deviation (it also allowed the ship to weather evenly on both sides during construction).

No keels were laid on Thursday (named for Thor, the god of thunder and storm) or Friday, which was named after Frigg, wife of the Old Norse god Odin known both for her beauty and fiery temper.

Good omens during this delicate phase were the presence of seagulls (the reincarnated spirits of old sailors), a west wind coupled with a rising tide, or a full moon visible during the day, all of which ensured abundant catches or cargo to be hauled.

Omens that would portend an ill-fated ship included sparks generated by the hammering of the first spike (indicating the ship would meet its doom by fire) or the accidental spilling of blood, signifying it would become a "Death Ship."

Shipwrights never cursed around the keel, testimony in itself to the power of superstition, and the traditional banes of maritime good fortune such as pigs, hares, members of the clergy, women (especially red-haired virgins, whores, and brides), flat-footed people, and cross-eyed men were banned from the shipyard. *(Launching)*

LAZARET

The origins of nautical lingo never cease to amaze me. Take lazaret for example (also spelled lazarette) a derivative of *lazaretto*, an Italian word describing a hospital's quarantine or isolation ward. How that came to describe what modern terminology labels an out-of-the-way storage locker back aft is an interesting tale in itself.

It was common practice for those afflicted with leprosy during the Middle Ages to undertake a pilgrimage to the Holy Land in hopes of effecting a cure. Many booked passage by ship, where they were normally quartered aft by the captain in an effort to protect the remaining passengers and crew from the disease, an arrangement that also helped contain the stench to one small portion of the vessel.

Lepers were often called *Lazars*, after the diseased almsman spoken of in the parable found in Luke 16 concerning the rich man and the beggar. Over time, the area they were confined to aboard ship came to be known as the lazaret.

LEATHERNECK

While one explanation of this term refers to leather being sewn into their uniform collar as protection against sword blows, sailors maintain that this nickname for a marine originally referred to the dark, leathery appearance of a long-unwashed neck. According to sailors (who we know are always right), marines of yore were typically kind of nasty, even by yesteryear's standards.

When sailors washed, they typically did so by stripping to the waist and washing face, neck, and arms. A *leatherneck* or *marine wash,* however, involved simply removing one's coat, rolling shirt sleeves up to the elbow, and washing hands to the wrist and face to the neck.

LEND A HAND?

Since Grecian times many of the seafaring community have issued dire warnings against removing a body from the sea, or even assisting those who were drowning for that matter. It was seen as "cheating the sea," and where better to procure a replacement than from among the rescuers?

"LET GO AN ANCHOR TO THE WINDWARD OF THE LAW"

Nautical slang for conducting business within the letter of the law, but not necessarily the spirit of it.

LIBERTATIA

A pirate republic said to have been founded on Madagascar by Captain Misson, a French pirate of the late seventeenth century. Johnson (see Bibliography) describes his life in the second volume of *A General History . . . of the Pirates*, and while his accounts of other pirates are considered on the whole to be true, little in the way of hard evidence remains to corroborate his story of Misson or Libertatia.

The colony, said to be founded on the noblest ideals of freedom and equality, boasted its own laws, a communal system of property ownership, and a national language of sorts comprised of the multiple languages spoken by its citizens. No pirate he, Misson considered himself and his men followers of a higher cause. While pirates were uncivilized brutes lacking in principle or ideals, his would be the clarion call of truth, justice, innocence, and liberty. Not surprisingly, he chose for his flag a white ensign bearing the motto "For God and Liberty" rather than the more typical black flag.

Unfortunately, the whole affair failed to impress the island's original inhabitants. Two huge groups attacked the fledging nation one dark night, slaughtering the Libertatians almost to a man. Captain Misson managed to escape the massacre; however, he and the few remaining survivors were later lost in a violent storm off Cape Infantes, South Africa, while trying to reach America.

Ok, a little more trivia concerning Madagascar, an extremely popular pirate supply point and hangout during the seventeenth and eighteenth centuries. The island itself, which in total area is roughly five times the size of England, is situated some 500 miles off the southeast coast of Africa. A place of mystery to civilizations of the east, Arabic sailors claimed it was the nesting place of the Roc, a legendary bird so immense it could carry away an elephant. Sinbad fans will remember one attacking the famous sailor's ship during the tales of his voyages.

LIGHTNING RODS

The biggest hubbub over Ben Franklin's newest invention in 1757 was raised from the maritime community, rather than those ashore. At last, shipping could be protected from one of nature's most lethal occurrences: storm-induced fire at sea.

"LIKE A DOG WETTING THE SNOW"

Said of the wandering, snake-like wake left by an inexperienced helmsman.

LIMEYS

By 1795 the British Admiralty had ordered issuance of lemon juice as a preventative against scurvy (a disease brought on by lack of vitamin C), making it a required ration for all hands. They later switched to a cheaper, though less effective, ration of lime juice, hence the nickname *Limey* or *Limejuicer* for a British sailor. **(First Ships to Cross the Antarctic Circle, The Petty Tally, Scurvy)**

LLOYDS OF LONDON

The flagship company of marine insurance speculation was actually named after one Edward Lloyd, proprietor of a coffeehouse on Tower Street, London, during the 1700s. Coffeehouses at the time were a garish mixture of café, gentleman's club, and brothel (take that, Starbucks) and his was a favorite gathering place for early marine insurance *underwriters*, a term derived from their practice of signing a policy beneath or *under* the signature of their clients.

For the price of a cup of coffee or chocolate, insurance brokers, merchants, and sea captains could rub elbows at Lloyd's while discussing newly arrived ships, known wrecks, and vessels presumed lost at sea. In time, it became recognized as the unofficial headquarters for maritime insurance speculation of the day. The name itself became official in 1774, when the loosely organized group of insurance merchants moved bodily into the Royal Exchange under the name "Lloyds of London."

In keeping with the worries of modern society, Lloyds has risen beyond its humble beginnings in the maritime industry, offering peace of mind in the form of policies protecting customers against such inevitabilities as the Loch Ness monster being captured and Elvis Presley being found alive and well. They even insured one group of comedians against the possibility their audience would laugh themselves to death. **(A1, Chamber of Horrors)**

LOBLOLLY BOY

Ships' boys who served as sick-berth attendants and assistants to the surgeon and his mates. Duties of the loblolly boy included feeding, bathing, and
shaving patients confined to sickbay, as well as the announcement of sick
call. Every morning at eight o'clock (after the gun deck was cleaned and the
morning watch relieved) the loblolly boy traveled throughout the ship ringing
his bell, summoning to sick call crewmembers with minor ailments or those
being treated for venereal diseases. Sick call itself was held before the main
mast by the ship's surgeon, who was often "assisted" by the captain or mate
(to ensure against shirkers or malingerers).

The term itself was derived from loblolly, the thin, watery gruel of choice
most commonly served to the invalids in sickbay. It was also a pet name for
the ship's surgeon and in the old merchant marine service topped the short
list of printable nicknames the steward was known by. *(Sick Bay)*

THE LOCKED SEA CHEST

Honesty and trust among shipmates was paramount and something all sailors
prided as their own. Should a new recruit cautiously lock his sea chest when
leaving the fo'c'sle, he was quietly taken aside and counseled by one of the
old salts onboard, as a locked sea chest was an affront to all who sailed before
the mast. *(Sail before the Mast)*

LOGWOOD

Logwood cutting was one of the few legitimate occupations to be had in the
early days of England's West Indian colonies. Logwood (so called because it
was not cut into boards, but was shipped "in the log") was a dense, heavy
wood yielding brown, black, or red dye, depending on the tree. The dye itself
was highly prized by the Spanish and other Europeans, who utilized it in the
manufacture of calico cloth.

Logwood cutters could earn a fairly decent living. So good, in fact, the Spaniards (who laid claim to the entire hemisphere) often raided the non-Spanish
camps in efforts to drive them out. It was this policy that drove scores of English, French, and other such "squatters" into the ranks of piracy, they being
the very men who began preying upon Spanish shipping in the Caribbean.

Although profitable, the work possessed its own particular brand of risks.
William Dampier, explorer, pirate, and privateer, described an incident that
occurred during his brief tenure among the cutters. Seems he discovered a
festering sore on one leg and visited the local Indian medicine man for treatment. Upon examination, the old Indian cut into the wound, exposing the tail of
a large parasitic worm (known as a *Guineaworm*). Fastening the tail to a small
wooden stick, he instructed Dampier to roll it up at the rate of roughly an inch
each day (in order that the parasite could be removed without breaking it).

It took twenty-four days to remove the worm, which was over 2 feet in length.

LONG-TAILED BEGGAR

Nautical slang for a cat. Hotten (see Bibliography) describes the origin of the tale attached to the name as follows:

> "A boy, during his first very short voyage to sea, had become so entirely a seaman, that on his return he had forgotten the name of the cat, and was obliged, pointing to puss, to ask his mother 'what she called that 'ere LONG-TAILED BEGGAR?'
>
> "Accordingly, sailors, when they hear a freshwater tar discoursing too largely on nautical matters, are very apt to say, 'But how, mate, about that 'ere Long-Tailed Beggar?'"

"LOOSE CANNON ON DECK"

Any large, heavy object not secured properly for sea posed an exceptional threat to ship and crew.

Should a cannon break free from its securing tackle, it would roll with the motion of the ship, wreaking havoc and in general just plain crushing anything or anyone in its path. A loose cannon could cause more damage than enemy fire, crashing through wooden bulkheads and on occasion placing the ship in danger of foundering. The term washed ashore as a description of someone who was dangerous or unpredictable. *(Of Galleys and Ships of the Line, Great Guns)*

LORDS OF THE FOUL AND THE BRUTE

The city of Port Royal, Jamaica, was at one time considered to be not only the richest, but the most wicked city in the Western world. London newspapers of 1655 labeled it "the outhouse of the world," further stating it was "the dump of all creation, unhealthy and more dangerous than the Black Death plague . . . as wicked and mean as Satan and hotter than Hell."

It was to this city seventeenth-century buccaneers preying on Spanish shipping flocked to spend their ill-gotten gains in a furious orgy of food, drink, brawls, and wenching.

The actions of these pirates seemed crafted to shock and dismay what few decent folk the city possessed, and in contemplating the possible debaucheries a crew of randy sea rovers could commit, one would be hard pressed to think of an act deemed socially unacceptable in such a setting. One such incident did occur, however, and it stunned even the moralistically challenged citizens of Port Royal into labeling it the ultimate in depravity and lewdness.

Seems a buccaneer captain, much inflamed with drink and wickedness, paid a longshore trollop *three thousand dollars* to do it (and we're talking seventeenth-century money here, when a man could take this much loot and live at ease for life).

It was written by the God-fearing chroniclers of the day that "even fellow roisters were shocked sober at the unmitigated sinfulness of such immodesty."

What was it that so shocked those who witnessed or heard of it? She danced before the captain "clad only in her shift." Yep, that's right—danced in public wearing only her undershirt.

Not especially shocking? Well, one has to take into consideration the Nordic-style morality of the day. While lust, gluttony, and lopping brother Olaf's head off during a drunken brawl were considered good wholesome fun, public exhibitionism was considered ground just too damning for even the most hardened to trod.

When the city itself was swallowed by the sea during a huge earthquake in 1692 (along with over two thousand of its inhabitants) it was considered to be nothing less than an act of divine punishment against the wicked buccaneers. *(Buccaneers)*

"LOST THE HANDLE TO HIS NAME"

Said of minor officers aboard merchant ships who were relieved of their duties by the captain and sent "from the land of knives, forks, and teacups" (i.e., the officers' mess) to the forecastle as a common sailor. The phrase refers to the loss of *Mr.* preceding their names.

"LOST THE NUMBER OF HIS MESS"

Term used to indicate a shipmate's death. For the purpose of distributing rations aboard ship, crews were normally divided into small groups of four to eight men called a *mess*. Each mess was assigned a number, which was used administratively by the ship's purser in the issuance of food and grog.

As a sailor tended to remain in the same mess throughout the ship's commission, his mess number became an almost inseparable part of his identity. So strong was this association, the phrase "he lost the number of his mess" was used as a euphemism for dying or being killed. *(Coil Up One's Cable, Cut and Run)*

LUBBER

A heavy, clumsy fellow; a sturdy, awkward dolt: applied especially by sailors to any of the crew who is deficient in seamanship. *(By Way of the Lubber's Hole, Landlubber)*

LUBBER LINE

A line marked on a ship's compass that's aligned with the vessel's centerline and used as a reference point showing the direction straight ahead. Even the greenest hand onboard could be instructed on how to steer a course by simply keeping the lubber line on the correct heading.

MAGALLANES

Last of the fabled Manila galleons, the *Magallanes* sailed from Acapulco (the jump-off point for the Spanish Pacific fleet) to the Philippines in 1815, marking an end to over two centuries of regular transits. She was not only the last Manila galleon, but the last of all Spanish galleons for that matter.

Trivia buffs may thump their scrawny chests with pride at this point if they recall another famous Manila galleon, one captured by England's Captain Drake in 1577. The answer? Why the good ship *Cacafeugo*, a name that translates literally as "shit fire." Gotta love those Spaniards.

MAKE A BULL

"Bulling a cask" was the quartermaster's trick of sneaking a freshly emptied keg of rum from the purser and filling it with water. Smart fellers, them quartermasters—they knew if left for a few days, the keg would produce a drink almost as strong as its original contents. The term *bull* refers to a second pot of tea boiled from the same leaves.

"MAKE THE CROSSING BY RAIL"

A mode of travel none sought or enjoyed. No train this, but a play on words describing a transatlantic crossing in which "by rail" refers to the rail seasick passengers manned topside.

Seasickness—to describe its symptoms to those who have never experienced it is impossible. The first hour brings fear of death—the second, fear it'll never come.

Probably nothing has brought so much mirth to sailors as the time spent watching the lubbers aboard trying to tough it out while passing chameleon-like through the various shades of yellow and green heralding an attack of mal de mer. While captaining dive boats in Hawaii I likened it to watching an opera or maybe someone turning into a werewolf, both being similar in terms of vocal pitch, range, and facial contortions.

If you're among those so afflicted, you're in good company. Admiral Horatio Nelson, England's greatest naval hero, also suffered from chronic seasickness and was said to have been experiencing a severe bout during the Battle of Trafalgar. As to a surefire remedy, Nelson advised finding a tree to sit under. *(Lubber)*

"MAKING A DEAD MAN CHEW"

Pursers were clerical officers aboard ship whose duties included managing the crew's pay, provisions, and clothing. They were essentially contractors who purchased such necessaries in advance and were then reimbursed based on each item issued. As they were paid to scale, pursers were continually accused by the crew (and in many cases rightly so) of purchasing inferior items for shipboard distribution and lining their pockets with the savings.

Another avenue of profit was issuance and collection of pay, rations, and tobacco to sailors who had died or deserted, thus making a "dead man chew." *(Harness Cask, Nip Cheese)*

MAKING CHALKS

A form of punishment aboard ship in which boys in need of discipline were first told to draw two widely spaced, parallel chalk lines on deck. Afterward, they were ordered to place one foot on each and bend over, thereby presenting a stern aspect to the bosun and his whip. *(Put to the Hoop)*

MAKING WIND

If becalmed, captains always had the option of launching the ship's boats (filled with multitudes of happy crewmen, no doubt) and using them to tow his vessel in search of wind. Rowing applied in this manner was called a "white ash breeze," after the wood that oars were typically made from. The crew of the USS *Constitution* utilized this tactic while becalmed during a skirmish with a squadron of five British ships during the War of 1812, enabling it to gain enough distance to escape when a breeze arose the next morning.

Of course a captain could always visit a witch to purchase an assurance of fair winds for an upcoming voyage. Such conjurers would often give him a length of cord with three knots. Loosening the first gave fair winds, the second a storm, and the third a hurricane. Sailors of Finnish stock were also attributed to have power over the winds, sometimes to the point of being accused by other members of the crew of raising storms or worse.

Many European sailors believed a breeze could be raised by scratching a nail on the foremast or by sticking a knife in the mainmast while whistling. Scottish sailors believed hoisting a he-goat to the masthead ensured favorable winds.

The French, however, were a little more scientific concerning the matter. They routinely whipped the bare bottoms of young cabin boys before the mast each Monday (the traditional day punishments were awarded) with many swearing the tender little buttocks had to be thrashed in order to ensure favorable winds. Vive la différence! *(Blue Monday, Tailwinds)*

MAN-EATER

Label given those ships that seemingly hated their crews. Be it in the form of storms, equipment failure, or a fall from the rigging, death, injury, and misfortune seemed to plague every voyage.

Such a reputation spread quickly among waterfront taverns and boarding houses and as old Jack Tar never sailed on a hoodoo if he could help it, captains of such vessels often had trouble keeping a full crew aboard. *(Jack Tar)*

THE MAN IN BLACK

Viewed from the eyes of a sailor, shipping with a priest onboard was a sure sign bad luck would plague the entire voyage. Even saying the words *priest* or *parson* could bring doom, with the wise sailor substituting *gentleman in black, upstander, sky pilot, devil-dodger,* or *Holy Joe.*

This fear of clergy aboard ship could have stemmed from many observations: his black attire linking him with funerals and death, or perhaps the fear that conveying the representative of a rival across their domain might anger some of the thinner-skinned sea gods. *(Davy Jones' Locker, Sky Pilot)*

MANXMAN

Legend has it inhabitants of the Isle of Man are descendants of a union between man and mermaid and as such are blessed with immunity from drowning. Sailors considered it lucky to ship a Manxman aboard, as it foretold a successful voyage. Captains were equally enthused about their presence—what master wouldn't want a crewman who could nonchalantly attend to his duties in the foulest of weather, free from fear of the sea?

MARITIME DISASTERS

While the *Titanic* remains the worst peacetime disaster, the greatest maritime loss of life occurred with the explosion of the Mississippi River packet *Sultana* on April 27, 1865. While carrying 1,886 Union soldiers home as part of a prisoner exchange (the legal maximum was 376 persons including the crew), the badly overloaded paddle wheeler's boilers exploded 2 miles north of Memphis, Tennessee. Although no exact death toll is known, estimates ranged from 1,300 to 1,900. Casualties were placed by the U.S. Customs Report in Memphis at 1,547.

The catastrophe was all but ignored by newspapers of the day, however. They were still devoting all available space to other news of national importance: the death of President Lincoln and the shooting of his assassin, John Wilkes Booth.

MAROONERS

One pirate atrocity that's a matter of record is the practice of marooning. In fact, so frequent was this form of punishment employed among the Brethren of the Coast, they themselves were often referred to as *Marooners.*

The victim, often enough a backslider from among the pirates guilty of some repeat offense, was placed upon some deserted spit of sand where neither food nor water was available. It was on this barren isle, often so small as to be completely submerged by the incoming tide, the offender was marooned, traditionally with a bottle of water, a sea biscuit, and a pistol carrying a single charge and one ball. The Caribbean abounds with tales of discovery involving lonely cays and the remains of such unfortunates, one skeletal hand still clutching the pistol used to end the unbearable pain and blackness of despair.

Others didn't go so meekly.

One Dutchman marooned on St. Helena (the same isle Napoleon was later to be exiled upon) became so horrified at his situation that he "fell into a despair that made him attempt the strangest action that was ever heard of."

With hysterical frenzy he unearthed the coffin of a recently buried companion and utilized it as a makeshift vessel to reach his ship, which lay becalmed some leagues from shore. He was at first mistaken for a specter of some sort, but upon identification by his former companions "they were not a little startled at the resolution of the man, who durst hazard himself upon that element in three boards slightly nailed together, which a small wave might have overturned, though he had no confidence [of] being received by those who had so lately sentenc'd him to death."

Though the crew was divided, he was eventually brought back on board.

Maroon is an English derivative of *Cimarrones* (dwellers in the mountains), the name given escaped African slaves who fled their cruel Spanish masters into the mountainous, isolated forests between Dutch and French Guiana. *(Walking the Plank)*

"MARRY THE GUNNER'S DAUGHTER"

A lady no sailor wanted to get intimate with, it was the term used to describe a sailor who was lashed over one of the ship's cannon and flogged.

Grose (see Bibliography) cites "Kiss the gunner's daughter" as a similar punishment in which ships' boys were placed in the aforementioned position to have their heineys whipped. *(Cat O' Nine Tails, Checkered Shirt, Cold Burning, Cursing and the Cangue, Flogging Around the Fleet, Goose without Gravy, Killing the Cat, Nightingale, Salt Eel, To Flog or Not to Flog, Whipped and Pickled)*

MEDICINE CHEST

Ships sailing without benefit of a physician onboard often carried a medicine chest managed by the captain, who doled out whatever curatives were deemed necessary while at sea. Most medicine chests included a "doctor's book" to assist the captain in his role as physician, with some going so far as to simply number each bottle of medicine, which was prescribed based on the symptoms observed.

One story tells of a captain who, upon finding the book called for a dose from bottle number ten and finding it empty, solved the dilemma by simply prescribing a double dose of bottle number five instead.

MERRY DUN OF DOVER

An immense ship featured prominently in many galley yarns. It was so large, old salts claimed when she tried to pass through the Straits of Dover her jib-boom toppled the Calais steeple, while at the same time her ensign swept a flock of sheep from the Cliffs of Dover. It was said her masts were so high, that if the bosun ordered a young boy aloft to handle sail, he'd be an old man before he could climb back down again. *(The Straits of Ballam-bangjang)*

MESSAGE IN A BOTTLE

Long before Sting sang about it, communicating via messages placed in a sealed bottle was deemed an official mode of correspondence by none other than Her Majesty Queen Elizabeth I during the sixteenth century. Having received an intelligence report in this manner, she was so disturbed to find it had been opened by a Dover boatman that a royal "Uncorker of Bottles" was named, along with a decree stating anyone else opening them did so on pain of death. Robinson Crusoe types could only hope the official uncorker dude didn't have too much of a backlog at any given time.

THE MILKY WAY

I'll have to file this one in my "bet'cha didn't know that" category. Canned (or condensed) milk was developed by Gail Borden in 1856 in order to solve the problem of providing a reliable food source for infants aboard ship. Ever try milking a cow during a williwaw off the coast of Tierra del Fuego in the dead of winter?

"MIND YOUR P'S AND Q'S"

A couple of sufficiently salty explanations exist to explain the origins of this term, each dealing with the two things in a sailor's life that could cause both pleasure and unspeakable pain: alcohol and wives.

First explanation suggests the phrase came from those fastidious wives who cautioned their seagoing spouses against soiling their pea coats (P's) with their tar-tipped pigtails or queues (Q's). Sailors dipped the ends of their pigtails in tar to prevent them from unraveling.

The other explanation deals with strong drink and a night on the town. Sailors aboard government ships could always count on friendly waterfront tavern keepers to extend credit until payday. Refreshments of the day were served in pints or quarts, a running tally of which was kept on a scoreboard behind the bar. Here's where the "Mind your P's and Q's" part comes in. It could be directed at the barkeep (to make sure no drinks were omitted by accident from a patron's tally) or it could be sage advice to the sailor, who was wise to ensure the pint he ordered wasn't *accidentally* marked as a quart.

It's also possible the phrase was friendly (or otherwise) advice from the ship's bosun, who in his own caring way was warning Jack to take care the night's drinking didn't affect performance tomorrow. *(Bully-Boys, Chewing the Fat)*

MMM MMM GOOD!

Ever wonder about the common sailor's fare during the days of sail? The following was part of a letter from an eleven-year-old boy serving aboard one of His Majesty's ships:

> "We live on beef which has been ten or eleven years in corn and on biscuit which quite makes your throat cold in eating it owing to the maggots which are very cold when you eat them, like calves-foot jelly . . . We drink water of the colour of the bark of a pear-tree with plenty of little maggots and weevils in it and wine which is exactly like bullock's blood and sawdust mixed together."

Some other quotes I've found concerning the tasty culinary delights to be found aboard ship include "Tougher than the bosun's hide," and my favorite " . . . with the kind of flavor you'd expect an Egyptian mummy to give off if it were boiled."

THE MOB RULES

Long ago a tale was told concerning a band of buccaneers who unexpectedly arrived at the gates of heaven. Catching St. Peter unawares, the unruly mob forced the gates and began surveying paradise.

Not to be outdone, St. Peter (who was understandably apprehensive about his unwanted guests) devised a stratagem that would have made old Blackbeard himself laugh with approval.

"A sail! A sail!" he cried, pointing outside the pearly gates.

"Where away?" demanded the pirates, springing to their feet.

"To leeward, off the port bow!"

"Hoist sail! Man the cannon!" they shouted gleefully, rushing past the gates, which crafty old St. Peter quickly slammed and barred behind them. *(Buccaneer)*

MORE NORTHING!

Why, nothing less than old Jack's call for the barkeep to stop trying to poison him with water and add a few more degrees of spirits to the drinks! In sailorman vernacular, *due north* indicated a glass of pure spirits, while *due west* represented nothing but water. Any point between would be a mixture of the two, with a *northwester* being half water/half spirits. *(Black Tot Day, Grog, Grog-Blossom, Six-Water Grog, Splice the Main Brace)*

MOTHER CAREY'S CHICKENS

Sailor's name for the stormy petrel, whose presence, it was believed, foretold of inclement weather. No clear reason as to the name's origin is universally accepted. It's believed Mother Carey, derived from the Latin *mater cara*, is the guardian angel of sailors, who must surely have believed she personally watched over these tiny birds found so far from land. *(Kissed by Mother Carey, Stormy Petrel)*

MOURNING LINE

A blue line painted around a ship's hull signifying the death of some important member of the crew or company owning it; blue flags were often flown at the yardarms as well. Why blue? One possible explanation is that certain Middle Eastern cultures believed use of the color during mourning assured the departed spirit could more easily enter heaven. Regardless, it's where we get the phrase *feeling blue*. *(A-Cockbill, Half-Masting of Ensigns)*

NANTUCKET SLEIGH RIDE

The "exhilarating" ride experienced by a whaleboat crew once fast to a whale. Harpooned whales were known to tow whaleboats at a furious clip for miles, an experience many whalers compared to a brisk, winter sleigh ride back in their homeport of Nantucket, Massachusetts, the onetime whaling capital of the world. *(Jawing Up, Right Whale)*

NAVIGATION

A term used to describe the art or science of moving a vessel safely and efficiently from one location to another via water. It comes to us from the Latin words *navis* (a ship) and *agere*, meaning to drive.

NECK VERSE

Until 1536, English pirates sentenced to hang could escape the gallows by reading the first verse of the Fifty-first Psalm from a Latin manuscript. Afterward, the lax laws of the day enabled court officials (who more often than not were on the payroll of said pirates) the option of granting them "Benefit of Clergy" and therefore entitled to immunity from prosecution.

Based loosely on the passage in Chronicles stating "Touch not mine anointed and do my prophets no harm," the law itself was an effort by the church to declare its supremacy in all matters concerning members of the clergy, whether secular or civil in nature.

Didn't take long for those less savory in nature to corrupt it to the point that it encompassed not only church officials, but even those potentially capable of entering the priesthood by virtue of being able to read and write.

As such, the psalm, or "Neck Verse" as it was commonly known, was widely memorized by pirates in efforts to save their, well . . . necks.

THE NEW WORLD

When Columbus made landfall in San Salvador in 1492, he found "Indians" who slept suspended in baglike nets of cotton and "drank smoke" through a curious ritual of setting fire to the end of a tight roll of dried weeds and inhaling the smoke through their nostrils. The former became the standard seagoing bed for sailors, that being hammocks. The latter, of course, was tobacco.

The explorer was also intrigued by the corsage-like ornaments worn by both sexes in the West Indies—they were made of popcorn. *(I'll Eat My Hat, Quid of Tobacco)*

NEW YEAR'S AT SEA

Tradition dictates " . . . the oldest man in the ship, be he admiral or Jack-of-the-dust, strikes eight bells at midnight on 31 December." Immediately following are eight bells struck by the youngest member of the crew in order to usher in the New Year.

U.S. naval custom also dictates the ship's first log entry of the New Year be in verse. *(Eight Bells, Jack-of-the-Dust)*

NIGHT HAWK

A long, black streamer flown at the masthead of homeward bound American vessels while in a foreign port. Its presence signified that other vessels in the harbor could forward letters and such home via the ship displaying it.

NIGHTINGALE

Said of one who "sings out" when sweetened with the cat 'o nine tails, it being a point of honor amongst most tars not to cry out while being flogged. *(Cat O' Nine Tails, Checkered Shirt, Cold Burning, Cursing and the Cangue, Flogging Around the Fleet, Goose without Gravy, Killing the Cat, Marry the Gunner's Daughter, Salt Eel, To Flog or Not to Flog, Whipped and Pickled)*

NIP CHEESE

Nickname given the ship's purser, based on that gentleman's oft-believed practice of *nipping* or reducing Jack's ration of this (and any other item he disbursed to the crew) for his own monetary gain. *(Harness Cask, Making a Dead Man Chew)*

NO TICKEE, NO LAUNDRY

At the height of California's gold rush, labor was so scarce miners wishing to have their clothes laundered had to send them to Canton, China. Of course the gamey garments had to be sent via English ships, as the hundreds of American vessels dotting California's harbors lay rotting at anchor, their crews having long since deserted in search of gold.

It was this labor shortage that caused the great influx of Chinese (and Chinese laundries) to the California coast during the mid-1800s.

THE NOT-SO-LUCKY BAG

The *lucky bag* was actually a locker onboard ship where stray items were stored—basically a seagoing lost and found department. Each month the articles within were brought out by the master-at-arms and an effort was made to return them to their rightful owners.

Isn't that nice, you may be thinking, but there was a catch. For every item returned, the lucky owner was given three lashes in order to impress upon him the benefits of keeping track of his possessions.

OF WAR GALLEYS AND SHIPS-OF-THE-LINE

Early European naval battles were mostly fought between rag-tag assemblages of merchantmen and other such commandeered vessels, this due to the fact few countries at the time had the desire or required capital to maintain a regular navy. These ships were generally modified in some fashion to ready them for battle, usually with the addition of light guns mounted forward or possibly along the rails. Guns at this stage were considered an add-on feature, with most captains getting a warm and fuzzy if the erratic cannon of the

day did no more than frighten the opposition with noise while pelting them with a few rocks or other such crude missiles. Any order to fire that didn't result in explosion of the cannon itself was considered a success.

The ship's primary function, however, was to transport men. As early cannon were too weak to cripple or destroy an enemy vessel, most naval battles during this period were carried out by boarding and entering. It was in this respect that fighting galleys carried an inherent advantage, having the option of arming rowers to assist in the fray. This, coupled with their ability to move independent of the wind, made them the naval weapon of choice throughout the Greek and Roman eras and well into the early Middle Ages, as far as the Mediterranean nations were concerned.

A war galley's design (which required placement of rowers along both sides) and the standard "frontal assaul" battle strategy of the day meant the only feasible place heavy guns could be mounted was on a platform at the bows of the ship.

Sailing vessels also possessed raised structures forward, behind which the ship's archers, cross-bowmen, and later musketeers crouched while firing down upon the enemy. In fact, most shipbuilding towns of the day boasted a castle-wright guild—skilled craftsmen whose sole purpose was adding these structures to converted merchantmen in times of war. That's why the foredeck of a ship today is known as the forecastle or fo'c'sle.

It wasn't until the sixteenth century that technology was sufficiently advanced to allow the casting of guns light enough to be mounted aboard ship, yet powerful enough to actually sink an enemy. Due to their weight and recoil when fired, however, these newly developed *great guns* were unable to be mounted in those flimsy superstructures up forward.

Then came the simple, yet revolutionary, idea of moving them from the bows and mounting them along the ship's sides, lighter ones along the gun rails (or gunwales as they're known today) with the larger ones below decks firing through gunports cut in the ship's side. This development pretty much assured that the utilization of war galleys as a major naval asset went the way of the dodo. Due to their design, even the largest galley was able to mount at most only five or so great guns in the limited space forward—a first-class ship of the line during the eighteenth century could carry upward of a hundred.

Although used by Spain with indifferent success in the New World during the 1600s, galleys were never very popular outside the Mediterranean anyway, and they were especially unsuitable for the rough waters of the North Atlantic. Europe also lacked the numerous ports required to support a galley fleet, which would of necessity be forced to make frequent stops for supplies.

The English, who utilized these new advancements in weaponry while developing their heavily armed man-of-war during the mid-sixteenth century, developed new battle strategies as well. Previously, warships traveled abreast of each other into battle in order to utilize the ship's ram (as was the case with galleys) as well as any larger guns located forward. But new tactics called for them to travel in a line in order to gain maximum efficiency from the revised placement of their cannon. It was out of this new strategy the term "ship-of-the-line" came into being.

Below are a few fun facts concerning your basic eighteenth-century ship-of-the-line:

- A standard battleship carried seventy-four guns arranged on two decks, one above the other. A first-rate ship-of-the-line carried a hundred or more on three decks. No ship with fewer than sixty guns was considered fit to stand in the line.
- Took two years to build.
- Required more than 3,000 loads of oak. Each load contained 50 cubic feet, the basic yield from one large tree. This was in addition to the elm and pine required for construction of the keel, bottom planks, masts, and spars.
- Each needed 100 tons of wrought iron (in addition to the guns) as well as 40 tons of copper, plus thousands of feet of rope and cable.
- Each broadside could deliver half a ton of metal with devastating results to targets as far as a quarter-mile away.
- Broadsides were delivered in sequence, as few ships could stand the recoil of all guns firing at once. *(Great Guns)*

OFFICE OF THE SWABBER

A sailing ship's crew was divided into various disciplines—able seamen, ordinary seamen, ship's boys, cabin boys, and finally the wasters or swabbers. Swabbers were the weakest of a ship's complement, those seamen unable to perform duties aloft or at the guns. Their assignments consisted of the dirtier, menial tasks to be found aboard ship, they themselves being pretty much viewed as scavengers by the rest of the crew.

Masefield (see Bibliography) quotes a description of their duties in *On the Spanish Main*.

"The Office of the Swabber is to see the Ship kept neat and Clean, and that as well in the great Cabbin as everywhere else betwixt the Decks; to which end he is, at the least once or twice a week, if not every day, to cause the Ship to be well washed within Board and without above Water, and especially about the Gunnwalls [gunwales or gunnels, over which the guns once pointed] and the Chains and for prevention of Infection, to burn sometimes Pitch, or the like wholsom perfumes, between the Decks: He is also to have a regard to every private Man's Sleeping-place; [to clean the cabins of the petty officers in the nether orlop] and to admonish them all in general [it being dangerous perhaps, in a poor swabber, to admonish in particular] to be cleanly and handsom, and to complain to the Captain, of all such as will be any way nastie and offensive that way. Surely, if this Swabber doth thoroughly take care to discharge this his charge I easily believe that he may have his hands full, and especially if there chance to be any number of Landmen aboard."

Lowly though he may have been, even the ignoble swabber had someone to boss around, that being "the liar." This was a transitory rate held but for a week by one lucky mariner.

"He that is first taken with a Lie upon a Monday morning, is proclaimed at the Main-Mast with a general Crie, a Liar, a Liar, a Liar, and for that week he is under the Swabber."

An exceptionally bad liar could expect to be hoisted to the mainstay with a shovel and broom seized to his back, just to get him in the right frame of mind for cleaning. *(A.B., Waisters)*

OLD IRONSIDES

Launched in 1792, the 44-gun U.S. naval frigate *Constitution* is the oldest commissioned ship afloat. The nickname is credited to a gunner aboard the English frigate *Guerriere*, who witnessed cannon fire bounce from her live oaken hull during the war of 1812.

Constructed of more than 1,500 trees, she boasted copper fastenings from the foundry owned by Paul Revere, who also cast the 242-pound ship's bell.

"ON THE ACCOUNT"

A euphemism for piracy, *on the account* can be traced back to the early seventeenth-century practice of letting merchant ship crewmen bring along small amounts of goods to trade "on their own account" at the various ports the ship called at. Few sailors possessed the means to take advantage of the practice, however, and even those that could were eventually forced to stop as cargo space reached a premium. Even after the custom had ceased, nautical humor kept the term alive as a reference to piracy. *(Piratical Buss Words)*

"ONE HAND FOR THE SHIP, ONE HAND FOR YOURSELF"

Sage advice given new recruits by the old timers on board when working aloft. One trip to the yardarm during a howling gale of rain or snow to reef a flapping mass of wet, frozen canvas was all it took to validate this bit of wisdom.

Ol' Jack was often forced to "hold on with his eyelids" while working aloft, and is it any wonder a right good tar was said to possess a hand with "every hair a rope yarn, every finger a fish hook."

OOOOO! THAT SMELL!

West Indian sailors once believed storms were caused by soul-hungry demons who tracked their victims by sense of smell. Belief was if the captain removed his smelliest article of clothing and cast it leeward, the demon would rush after it, thereby leaving the ship in peace.

Fortunately for most sailors of the day, smelly garments were easy to come by.

THE OPIUM WAR

During the Opium War of 1839–1842 between China and England, China assumed victory was inevitable. After all, it was common knowledge that the sailors manning Britain's fleet would lose their eyesight when deprived of Chinese tea. Even more conclusive was the notion that ol' Jack couldn't have regular bowel movements without the help of Chinese rhubarb. How hard could it be to defeat an invading fleet of blind, constipated sailors?

It was during this conflict, basically a war fought to ensure drug-pushing English merchants could continue selling opium to the Chinese masses, that the HMS *Nemesis* saw battle. She was the first iron-hulled steamship in the Pacific. *(Cumshaw Artist)*

"OUT OR DOWN"

Warning given those slow to "tumble out" when called on deck for muster, follow-up being the bosun or one of his mates making rounds below and cutting the hammock strings of those still asleep.

Another tactic used by the fun-loving mates on late sleepers or those found sleeping on watch was called "Blowing the Grampus," a cure involving a sadistic bosun and a bucket of cold seawater poured over the offender's head, an act that caused such sputtering and blowing as to resemble the exhalation of a surfacing whale.

"OVER A BARREL"

In difficult or dire straits—from the practice of seizing a sailor over the barrel of a deck cannon in preparation for flogging.

PACIFIC OCEAN

So named by the Portuguese explorer Magellan, who found its waters decidedly calmer than those of the tempestuous straits he traversed prior to its discovery. It's derived from *pacificus*, the Latin word for peaceful.

"PAINT THE LION"

Another distraction whipped up by the old salts aboard when things about the deck were slow and the need for mirth great. It involved stripping one of the greenhorns aboard and slushing his entire body with tar. Who said sailors don't know how to have a good time? *(Gilding the Lion, King Arthur)*

PAINT WASHERS

Derisive term used by the hairy-torsoed, manly men of sailing vessels to describe crewmen aboard those lubberly new steam-powered vessels. They had to be called something and to them *sailor* wasn't it.

PALE ALE

Nickname given the drinking water placed in the scuttlebutt for the ship's crew. It was also known as "Adam's Ale." *(Scuttlebutt)*

PATAGONIA BY WAY OF TIERRA DEL FUEGO

Ever wonder what the name Magellan bestowed upon the southernmost region of South America actually means? *Patagonia*, which roughly conveys the sense of "dogs with large paws" in the various romance languages (Spanish, French, and Portuguese), was thought to have been derived from a Spanish chivalric poem, *Primaleon*, that was widely published throughout Europe in the early 1500s. Its hero, Primaleon, encounters an island of savages among whom was an exceptionally monstrous being named Patagone. The region Magellan discovered was populated by a race of giant natives as well, and the name alluded to their huge feet.

Tierra del Fuego, literally the "Land of Fire," was also named by Magellan during his circumnavigation, a reference to native signal fires he and his crew noted on the island at night. It's home to the guanaco, a new world camel/llama-type critter that grows up to 300 pounds and has the nasty habit of spitting at its enemies with an accuracy of up to 15 feet—even more nasty is the fact that this spit can be either saliva or the dreaded "green spit" consisting of stomach contents.

"PAY BOTTLE AND POUND"

This ceremony, performed when "crossing the line" (i.e., the equator), is a time-honored tradition amongst all seafaring nations. The festivities novitiates were (and are) obliged to endure were as varied as the sailors themselves, with no uninitiated crew members being exempted from paying tribute to the sea gods, from captain to the lowest hand.

One popular custom during the mid-1700s called for an initiate to "pay his bottle and pound" referring to a bottle of rum or brandy (to keep Neptune and his minions in a jolly mood) and a pound of sugar. Failure to comply, whether from reluctance or destitution, was punishable by dunking "sowse over head and ears in the water."

A rope was secured around the initiate's waist or ankle, by which he was immediately hoisted to the main or foreyard. He was then repeatedly dropped into the sea until " . . . the offender is as wet as a drowned rat. They [the crew] then take him in and as he has contributed so much to their mirth they suffer him to partake of their liquor till he is thoroughly drenched both inside and out."

"PAY 'EM WITH THE TOPSAIL"

Slang for absconding with goods or services from shore without payment, kind of like pay 'em with a view of your rapidly diminishing backside. Soldiers so inclined were said to pay with the drum (i.e., by marching away) while sailors leaving without paying for lodgings were said to "burn the town."

"PAY FOR YOUR FOOTING"

Old nautical custom in which those sailors present were *paid* a glass of grog by first-time visitors to the main topgallant masthead, an action that placed one on good footing or standing with his fellow shipmates.

PEA JACKET

"Did you know that's what it was for when you bought it?"

That question from Fred G. Sanford to son Lamont concerning the purchase of his new coat would have to be my favorite quote about the pea jacket. Two possibilities stand out concerning the origin of the name for this foul weather garment, a short, double-breasted jacket fashioned from heavy twilled blue cloth.

One source says the name is derived from pilot or "P" cloth, heavy, water-repellant wool commonly used in the jacket's construction. Another states it's a corruption of the Dutch word *pij* (pronounced pea), which was a similar material used by Dutch mariners.

The jacket was also called a *reefer*, as its shorter length made it better suited for going aloft while reefing or adjusting sails.

PETTICOAT ROW

Name given Center Street on the island of Nantucket, Massachusetts, during the 1800s, as most businesses at the time were managed by the wives of absent whalers.

THE PETTY TALLY

A chest of medicines and other such comforts provided the crew by some of the more humane captains in the days of sail. In his book *The Sea Man's Grammar* published in 1627, Captain John Smith provides a list of items contained in his petty tally:

"Fine wheat flower close and well-packed, Rice, Currants, Sugar, Prunes, Cynamon, Ginger, Pepper, Cloves, Green Ginger, Oil, Butter, Holland cheese or old Cheese, Wine-vinegar, Canarie-Sack, Aqua-vitae, the best Wines, the best Waters, the juyce of Limons for the scurvy, white Bisket, Oatmeal, Gammons of Bacons, dried Neats tongues, Beef packed up in Vineger, Legs of Mutton minced and stewed, and close packed up, with tried Sewet or Butter in Earth Pots. To entertain Strangers Marmalade, Suckets, Almonds, Comfits and such like."

Captain Smith goes on to justify providing such niceties to the crew, proving himself an exceptionally humane leader in an era when most were not known for such qualities.

"Some will say I would have men rather to feast than to fight. But I say the want of these necessaries occasions the loss of more men than any English Fleet hath been slain since 88. For when a man is ill, or at the point of death, I would know whether a dish of buttered Rice with a little Cynamon, Ginger and Sugar, a little minced meat, or rost Beef, a few stew'd Prunes, a race of green Ginger, a Flap-Jack, a Kan of fresh water brewed with a little Cynamon and Sugar be not better than a little poor John, or salt fish, with Oil and Mustard, or Bisket, Butter, Cheese, or Oatmeal-pottage on Fish-dayes, or on Flesh-days, Salt, Beef, Pork and Pease, with six shillings beer, this is your ordinary ship's allowance, and good for them are well if well conditioned [good for those of the crew in good health] which is not alwayes as Sea-men can witnesse. And after a storme, when poor men are all wet, and some have not so much as a cloth to shift them, shaking with cold, few of those but will tell you a little sack or Aqua-vitae is much better to keep them in health, than a little small Beer, or cold water although it be sweet. Now that every one should provide for himself, few of them have either that providence or means, and there is neither Ale-house, Tavern, nor Inne to burn a faggot in, neither Grocer, Poulterer, Apothecary nor Butcher's Shop, and therefore the use of this petty Tally is necessary, and thus to be employed as there is occasion."

(Scurvy, Slush Fund)

PIERRE LE GRAND

It just doesn't get any better than this seventeenth-century tale of brave men and daring-do. Le Grand, considered by many to be the first buccaneer, led twenty-eight companions in a successful attack upon one of the most fearsome dreadnoughts of the day, a treasure-laden Spanish ship-of-the-line. It was in fact the flagship of a Spanish treasure fleet lumbering its way back to Spain, and when Le Grand observed it straggling behind the others off the coast of western Hispaniola, he decided to attack.

Although greatly outnumbered, the pirates swore an oath to take her or die in the attempt. Armed with sword, musket, pistol, and ax, the twenty-nine Frenchman drew near the ship under cover of darkness. Bolstered by their oath (and the knowledge Le Grand had instructed the ship's surgeon to bore holes in the bottom of their own small craft prior to coming alongside) they scrambled up the side of the huge galleon and "overpowered" several hundred Spanish sailors and marines.

After finding little or no resistance from the crew, Le Grand made for the cabin. It was there the captain, upon finding his nightly card game so rudely interrupted by a hairy group of wild-eyed, pistol-waving Frenchmen, promptly surrendered.

After securing the ship Le Grand drafted some of the Spanish sailors, put the rest ashore, and sailed on to France and obscurity. *(Buccaneer, Know Your Pirates)*

PIPE ONE'S EYE

Why, to shed a tear, as in "Don't it pipe one's eye ta see tha little nippers scamper 'round, happy ta see their old man a'coming home from tha sea?"

PIRATES FOR HIGHER EDUCATION

In the fall of 1687, three men trying to cross the Chesapeake in a small boat were hauled aboard the HMS *Quaker*, part of a squadron sent from England earlier that year in an effort to suppress piracy.

Upon searching the boat, several sacks of gold coins and silver plate were discovered. The three were immediately taken to Jamestown gaol and identified to be none other than the pirate Edward Davies and two of his crew. The booty was seized by the crown and the men thrown in jail.

After a period of three years they were shipped to England (as was the law of the day) to be tried before the Admiralty court, where, after some complicated legal maneuvers, they were eventually acquitted due to lack of evidence. Bolstered by their good fortune, the pirates boldly petitioned the crown for return of their ill-gotten plunder, the balance of which was eventually returned, minus three hundred pounds.

That's the amount ordered set aside by the Treasury for construction of a new college in Williamsburg, Virginia—one founded on a generous "donation" of pirate loot . . . the College of William and Mary.

PIRATICAL BUZZ WORDS

Just in case you decide to turn pirate later on in life, here are a few terms you should be familiar with concerning your new profession.

"Gone on the account" was the generally recognized phrase for going *A-pyrating*.

"Finding their market" referred to the successful capture and plundering of a prize by pirates.

"Looking for merchandise consigned to them" described a pirate vessel cruising for victims, while the phrase "no prey, no pay" meant the crew received no pay unless a prize was captured. *(On the Account)*

PITCAIRN ISLAND

"Yeah, that's the one!" if the question was "On which island do the direct descendants of the HMS *Bounty* mutineers reside?"

It was here Fletcher Christian (a distant relative of William Wordsworth, by the way) and eight of his crew burned their vessel and settled on January 23, 1790, nine months after their infamous confrontation with Captain Bligh. Bligh and his eighteen loyal men were cast adrift in an open longboat and forced to endure a forty-seven day, 3,618 mile trek to safety.

After the mutiny, the remaining crew sailed the *Bounty* back to Tahiti, where sixteen of the crew opted to stay. These sixteen were later captured and transported to England for trial (seven were eventually acquitted, three others hanged).

Fletcher and his mixed crew of mutineers and Tahitians sailed off into the South Pacific and oblivion, their whereabouts a mystery to the world for over eighteen years.

Ahhh, tropical isles, beautiful native women . . . what more could a sailor ask for?

Sad to say, there must have been something missing from the equation if the *Lord of the Flies*–type society discovered by the American whaler *Topaz* upon landing there in 1808 was any indication. Murder and suicide had combined to usher eight of the nine mutineers into eternity.

The mutiny itself has become so shrouded by popular legend that most fail to realize it was not Bligh's temperament that drove the crew to rebellion so much as the eroding effects of Tahitian society on his men's discipline.

Sent at the suggestion of England's prestigious Royal Society, the *Bounty*'s mission was to gather breadfruit plants and transport them to the West

Indies, where it was hoped the fruit could be introduced as a staple for Negro slaves. The ship had to remain in Tahiti for over five months in order to give the breadfruit seedlings time to mature enough to pot and transport.

This was the longest period any significant number of Europeans had remained on the island, and the easy life ashore (coupled with the sirenian qualities of the Tahitian women themselves) was most likely the real impetus behind the mutiny. Granted, Bligh's high-handedness probably exacerbated the crisis, but the driving force remained the mutineers' desire to return to their Tahitian girls and that little grass shack on the beach.

Regardless of the mutiny's cause, Bligh's journey in that open boat remains one of the most remarkable feats of navigation in naval history. Of course being the protégé of arguably the greatest navigator of all time probably didn't hurt any—he served as ship's master for the *Resolution* under Captain James Cook during his last, ill-fated voyage to explore the North Pacific.

Oh, and the breadfruit experiment? Bligh eventually did manage to transport another cargo of seedlings via a second expedition. Unfortunately, the slaves despised the fruit, which found its only viable use as food for livestock.

On a side note, Captain Bligh's personality-induced dilemmas didn't end with the *Bounty*. After Nelson's victory at Copenhagen (during which Bligh was acclaimed a hero), he was sent out as governor to the Australian colony of Sydney, which was having troubles of its own with corruption and graft. Despite good intentions and a sensible approach to the situation, Bligh once again found himself deposed via mutiny, this time being shipped back to England in chains, where he was replaced with a more tactful administrator.

Below are a few fun facts concerning Pitcairn, one of the most remote, inhabited places on earth (data from 2004).

Background. Pitcairn was the first Pacific island to become a British colony (1838) and today remains the last vestige of that empire in the South Pacific. Outmigration, primarily to New Zealand, has thinned the population from a peak of 233 in 1937 to fewer than 50 today. Pitcairn is Britain's most isolated dependency; only the larger island of Pitcairn is inhabited but it has no port or natural harbor; supplies must be transported by rowed longboat from larger ships stationed offshore.

Location. Oceania, islands in the South Pacific Ocean, about midway between Peru and New Zealand (1,365 miles south of Tahiti).

Size. 47 sq km (about 0.3 times the size of Washington, DC).

Ethnic Groups. Descendants of the *Bounty* mutineers and their Tahitian wives.

Languages. English (official), Pitkern (mixture of an eighteenth-century English dialect and a Tahitian dialect).

Labor Force. Fifteen able-bodied men.

Economy. The inhabitants of this tiny isolated economy exist on fishing, subsistence farming, handicrafts, and postage stamps. The fertile soil of the valleys produces a wide variety of fruits and vegetables, including citrus, sugarcane, watermelons, bananas, yams, and beans. Bartering is an important part of the economy. The major sources of revenue are the sale of postage stamps to collectors and the sale of handicrafts to passing ships. In October 2004 more than one-quarter of Pitcairn's small labor force was arrested, putting the economy in a bind, since their services were required as lighter crew to load or unload passing ships.

Telephones—(main lines in use). One (there are seventeen telephones on one party line). *(Yarn of the* **Nancy Bell***)*

PLACING COINS BENEATH THE MAST

Copper coins are traditionally placed under a ship's mast prior to being stepped (raised) as payment to the gods in efforts to procure good luck and favorable winds. Seems sailors of wooden-masted boats made a little good luck of their own by doing this. As bilge water moisture penetrated the bottom of the mast, it allowed the copper of the coin to be leached upward into the mast itself, preventing fungal growth and rot.

Ensuring the coin is of the current year also lets the next person to unstep (lower) the mast know when it was last done.

THE PLANE! THE PLANE!

The first successful launch of a fixed-wing airplane from the deck of a ship occurred on November 14, 1910, in Hampton Roads, Virginia. It was there aviator Eugene Ely launched his Curtiss biplane (a Hudson Flyer) from the deck of the cruiser USS *Birmingham* as it floated peacefully in the waters of Chesapeake Bay.

The flight proved the feasibility of naval aviation warfare, and six years later the first navy ship modified to actually carry and operate aircraft arrived on the scene, the USS *North Carolina*. The first official United States Navy aircraft carrier, however, was the USS *Langley*, which began launching aircraft from its wooden flight deck on October 17, 1922.

"POLISH THE GOLDEN RIVET"

An order given to insure new recruits possessed the required amounts of humility and gullibility deemed necessary by the old salts on board.

This imaginary rivet, which was invariably located in the darkest, most inaccessible portion of the ship's bilge, arose from the keel-laying ceremony of the champion Nova Scotian schooner *Bluenose*, where the governor-general of Canada drove a gilded spike into its keel beam for good luck.

Other such errands given a greenhorn might be to lay aloft for "eggs from the crow's nest" or asking the bosun for fifty feet of shore line. Another would be placing ear to hull in order to "hear the dogfish bark." *(Crow's Nest)*

POLYPHEMUS

I've always been fascinated with the exploits of early seafaring legends like Jason and the Argonauts or Odysseus in Homer's epic poem the *Odyssey*. I'll have to admit, however, that the thing that really creeped me out as a teenager reading the *Odyssey* was the Cyclops dude named Polyphemus—you know, the one that was eating Odysseus' crewmen like popcorn shrimp at a seafood buffet. I always wondered how they came up with the Cyclops thing until reading an article on wooly mammoths. Come again? According to archaeologists, mammoth skulls are fairly common throughout the Mediterranean region. As the most unusual feature of a mammoth's skull is its large nasal cavity, theory is the ancient Greeks (few of which had seen a living elephant) mistook them for the skulls of a race of giant, one-eyed men.

PORTABLE BROTH

Portable broth was actually a solid in its portable stage, resembling a gelatinous slab of old-fashioned glue, the type that had to be heated before use. It was made by collecting and boiling down those indescribable little beef leftovers at the slaughterhouse (hoofs, snouts, and the like) to a viscous mass, where they were then formed into cakes and packed into 25-pound containers.

It was quite the hot item as far as shipboard victuals were concerned. To use, a piece was simply broken off and tossed into a pot of water, which was then brought to a slow boil. The resulting broth was considered quite nutritious and in fact was often used to make green vegetables more palatable in efforts to prevent scurvy.

POSH

The late nineteenth and early twentieth century witnessed the birth of the golden age of ocean travel. Huge, opulent luxury liners began crossing the globe, all constructed to provide the wealthy of the day a means of traveling about in style. Meals equal to the world's finest hotels, orchestras to provide music for dancing, a small army of stewards to wait on passengers hand and foot—there seemed no limit to the luxury offered or the amount the ultra-rich were willing to pay.

One perk available for those willing to shell out a little extra was found aboard the P&O steamship line, a major shipping company of the day serving China and India. The story goes that well-heeled travelers in the know always requested the cooler cabins located on the shady side of the ship while crossing the Indian Ocean, cabins that P&O charged a premium for in addition to the already substantial fare.

As port was the shady side on the outbound leg (with starboard being the sought-after side on the return or inbound portion of the trip) passengers who requested such cabins had the letters "POSH" (Port Outward, Starboard Homeward) printed on their tickets, introducing a new word for elegant or fashionable into the English language.

POTTING AND PIPING

Sailor's slang for becoming close friends. It referred to drinking pots of ale and smoking pipes of tobacco together, a tradition any sailor knows has to be observed or you really don't know Jack.

POWDER MONKEYS

Name given ship's boys assigned to supply the gun crews with powder cartridges from the magazine during battle.

PRESS-GANGS (THE ROYAL NAVY NEEDS YOU!)

Press-gangs once roamed the streets of every British port or harbor, recruiting with sword and club to supply badly needed manpower for England's navy. Armed men of the community, who served not out of civic pride so much as to prevent being impressed themselves, assisted officers in charge of recruitment for each area. As they scoured the streets seeking men (able-bodied or otherwise), everyone met was at risk, doubly so if he had the tell-tale gait or look of a seaman about him. Fishermen, merchantmen (who were supposed to be legally exempt), and even sailors on shore leave already in His Majesty's service could easily be cracked on the head and spirited away.

Generous tips were often paid to those informing on likely victims, a situation that ensured Jack Tar had to watch his step when dealing with just about everyone. A rival for his lady's fancy, an angry wife . . . all were aware of the press-gang's ability to tidily solve their problem and generate coin at the same time.

Press-gangs didn't limit themselves to citizens of the crown, either. During the early 1800s, American sailors were being seized with alarming frequency from both ships and third-nation ports. The news invoked cries of public outrage in the United States, one of the situations that eventually triggered the War of 1812.

Britain abolished the practice of impressment in 1815. *(Jack Tar, The King's Shilling, Shanghaied by the Crimps, Son of a Gun)*

PROJECT HABBAKUK

"Behold ye among the heathen, and regard and wonder marvelously: for I will work a work in your days, which ye will not believe, though it be told to you."

So proclaims a biblical quotation from the book of Habbakuk, namesake to one of the most bizarre naval experiments in history—a top-secret WWII project to build ships of ice.

Conceived by what eventually became known as Britain's "Department of Bright Ideas" (DBI), Project Habbakuk was designed to address the German U-boat threat and enjoyed backing from none other than British Prime Minister Sir Winston Churchill. The North Atlantic convoys from Canada were crucial to England's war effort, and while they could be reasonably protected near shore, once beyond the range of shore-based aircraft vessels were forced to run "U-boat alley," the stretch of open, unprotected ocean between the two continents.

Churchill felt increased aircraft coverage of the area was the key to allow more shipping to get through. Project Habbakuk called for creating a fleet of unsinkable landing strips of ice to allow planes to land and refuel on the open ocean. Each "carrier" was to be at least 1800 feet long, 270 feet wide, and up to 135 feet thick, and the beauty of it all was that if bombed or torpedoed, repairs could be quickly made by simply freezing water into place.

The hull itself would contain pipes of super cold air (to keep it from melting) and was to be constructed of PyKrete, a frozen mixture of water and wood pulp that is stronger, more stable, and less prone to melting than ice. It was named after Geoffrey Nathaniel Pyke, the eccentric genius (or nut-job, depending on who you asked) who authored the idea and constituted Churchill's one-man think tank of "creative" ideas and solutions.

The ice ships (covered in wood or cork) would resemble ordinary vessels, but be much larger—several times longer than the Queen Mary, the largest ship afloat at the time.

These larger ships were to serve as aircraft carriers and transports, while smaller vessels would be used to attack enemy ports. Enemy warships would be encased in ice by spraying them with super-cooled water, while the port itself would be sealed utilizing huge blocks of PyKrete. Once the port was secure, Mr. Freeze–type commandoes would terrorize the countryside, freezing railway tunnels and such, thereby disrupting transport and throwing the enemy into chaos.

The head of Combined Ops, Lord Mountbatten, was so enamored of the plan that he rushed into the prime minister's chambers and dropped a lump of PyKrete into his hot bath to demonstrate its resistance to melting. Similar theatrics were performed for a group of generals at the Quebec conference concerning the material's strength, where he produced a block of ice and a block of PyKrete while inviting an attendee to smash both with an axe. The ice shattered easily enough; however, a similar whack at the PyKrete produced a whelp of pain as the smashee's arms were nearly jarred from their sockets. In a further demonstration of its strength, Mountbatten pulled his revolver and shot the icy lump point blank—not such a good idea in hindsight, as the bullet ricocheted, nearly decapitating another general.

A prototype 1,000-ton PyKrete ship was actually built amid great secrecy on Canada's Patricia Lake in efforts to gather information on how feasible the idea really was. A handful of engineers constructed a 1:50 scale model in just two months, managing to keep it frozen during the entire summer of 1943. Cost and manpower estimates to build each ship (nearly 8,000 men, eight months, and over $70 million in 1940s dollars) were a choke point, and the project's relevancy became moot with the Normandy landings. British Combined Ops HQ quietly pulled the plug (literally), allowing the project to sink below the waters of the lake, where its remains to this day.

PUMP SHIP

To remove water from the ship via pumps; also sailorman slang for urinating.

"PUT ONE'S OAR IN"

Said of those offering unasked-for advice or meddling in another's affairs, as in "To be sure, old Jimmy Squarefoot here has to put his oar in!"

"PUT TO THE HOOP"

Whenever the youngsters on board (ship's boys, officers' servants, nippers, and the like) found themselves a bit of mischief, they were often "put to the hoop" as punishment. Each was stripped to the waist, tied by his left hand to a hoop (either of metal, such as from a cask, or a large rope grommet) and furnished with a piece of light line called a *knittle* to hold in the other.

With all in readiness, the bosun signaled commencement via a friendly lick from cane or knittle, at which point they began running in a circle, each boy striking the one before him. The blows began lightly at first, but each soon became so nettled at the lashing he was receiving from behind, they were soon flogging away in earnest.

Other occasions for dusting off the hoop for a little action would be when the ship was becalmed (it was thought to raise the wind) or when the happy crew just got bored. *(Making Chalks)*

QUARANTINE

The first recorded case of sequestering a ship for fear of disease occurred at Marseilles, France, during the Great Plague of fourteenth-century Europe. City officials ordered ship and crew isolated a total of forty days, a number of obvious biblical connotations. The term itself is derived from the French word *quarant*, meaning forty.

Origins of that bubonic plague can be traced to an eruption in the Gobi Desert during the late 1320s, where it continued to spread rapidly throughout the 1330s. As China was a major trading hub of the day, it rapidly spread via merchant ships and caravans to western Asia and Europe.

A fleet of Italian merchant vessels introduced it to Messina, Sicily, after returning from China in October 1347. So virulent was the disease that within days it spread to the city proper and the surrounding countryside. City officials discovered too late that many of the crew had perished prior to entering port, with the remainder continuing to die at an alarming rate. An eyewitness describes what happened next:

> "Realizing what a deadly disaster had come to them, the people quickly drove the Italians from their city. But the disease remained, and soon death was everywhere. Fathers abandoned their sick sons, Lawyers refused to come and make out wills for the dying. Friars and nuns were left to care for the sick, and monasteries and convents were soon deserted, as they were stricken, too. Bodies were left in empty houses, and there was no one to give them a Christian burial."

Physicians were stunned by the ferocity of the disease, which often killed its victims within a matter of hours. Indeed, it was said by the Italian chronicler Boccaccio that the sickness was so lethal victims literally "ate lunch with their friends and dinner with their ancestors in paradise."

Medieval medicines were powerless, with prescribed cures ranging from bathing in humane urine and excrement to drinking molten gold and powdered emeralds. Even that old standby, leeches, proved ineffective, despite additional admonishments for patients to chop up a snake every day and avoid falling asleep on the right side of their bed.

Of course it didn't help matters that those trying to combat the disease hadn't a clue as to how it spread. Common folk held it was caused by witches, which history tells us is partially true in a roundabout way. Many a harmless old crone was burned; however, what really caused ye olde feces to hit the rotary oscillator was the widespread killing of cats, known familiars of said conjurers. Not the best of moves in hindsight, especially as rodent-borne fleas were the main vehicles of dispersion. It covered Europe within the year.

In England it was labeled the *Black Death*, a name derived from the black spots appearing on the skin of those contracting the disease (a result of ruptured blood vessels and internal bleeding). *Bubonic plague*, its other name, referred to the appearance of buboes (swollen lymph nodes), which could reach the size of an orange during its final stages. Just how bad was it, you ask? From 1347 to 1353, the death toll in Europe alone was an estimated twenty-five million, almost one third of the continent's population.

OK, two more plague-induced tidbits and we'll let this one go by the board.

First of all, most people today believe the plague came, hung around a few years, killed folks, and left. Fact of the matter is plague was out and about long before the fourteenth century; Europe itself suffered an epidemic in the sixth century. Outbreaks were cyclical in nature, with dormant periods spanning months or centuries. Even during the Great Plague of the Middle Ages, it subsided during winter (when fleas became less active) only to begin killing anew in spring.

The Great Plague of London (1665) was England's last major bout with the disease. Outbreaks after the fifteenth century tended to be more localized in nature, affecting only a particular area or city, and this one was no exception. The upper crust moved to country estates to ride out the plague, while the poor pretty much stayed where they were and died.

Among those fleeing to distant estates was young Isaac Newton, a Cambridge professor who had some pretty neat ideas concerning the laws of gravity, but just couldn't find time to follow up on them. Seems the plague had at least one positive effect: it was during his almost two years in absentia from London to avoid it that Newton finally had time to solve the mathematical enigmas needed to support his theories on gravity.

Lastly, remember "Ring around the Rosie," that staple of childhood innocence immortalized by Mother Goose:

"Ring around the rosie . . .
. . . Pockets full of posies . . .
. . . Ashes, ashes, we all fall down . . . "

Sounds innocent enough, right? Unfortunately, as with most fairy tales and rhymes, we can trace this one to some pretty morbid medieval roots. First my disclaimer: there are those of the folklore community who dispute the below interpretation of the rhyme, based on the fact that written evidence of suitable age has not been found to substantiate it. Those who agree with this interpretation are just as numerous, however, so here we go.

"Ring around the rosie" referred to the sores accompanying the plague, a reddish-hued scab with a raised rim or ring around its edge.

"Pockets full of posies" concerns the numerous flowers carried about in efforts to mask the stench of those dead and dying (it was thought the plague was spread by these foul humors).

"Ashes, ashes, we all fall down" correlates with the biblical text "ashes to ashes, dust to dust," or perhaps the practice of burning the dead in an effort to prevent the plague from spreading.

As to falling down, this was said to have mimicked the almost 100 percent mortality rate associated with the pneumonic strain of the disease. Scary stuff . . . and don't even ask me to tell you about Peter, Peter, pumpkin eater. *(Clean Bill of Health, Yellow Jack)*

QUID OF TOBACCO

Jack's chaw of the leaf, quid being a corruption of *cud* (in reference to the chewing of a cow). Other names included fid and plug, both of which were derived from the small wad of hemp or jute used to plug a cannon's touchhole when not in use.

While we're on the subject, here's a little more tobacco trivia—the name itself comes from *tabaco*, a "Y" shaped pipe used by the Carib Indians of early Haiti.

And just so you know, anti-smoking sentiments are nothing new. James I penned "A Counterblaste to Tobacco" in 1604 basically for the purpose of stating the plant was "an invention of Satan." *(I'll Eat My Hat, The New World)*

"RECEIVE PAY ON CAPS"

Old British Navy rules called for enlisted men to receive their pay attached to the tops of their caps, in order that all could see and verify it was the correct amount. Upon his name being called the sailor stepped forward, hat in hand, repeated his name and number, and received his pay atop the hat extended to the officer. It's where we got the phrase "Hats off to (whomever)!" as a congratulatory expression for some fortunate occasion.

RED DECKS

As late as the 1700s, standard was the practice aboard warships of painting decks, inner bulwarks, and gun port lids red. This was done so that the delicate natures of new recruits wouldn't be unduly upset by the sight of blood splattered about during the height of battle.

RED DUSTER

Nickname for the British mercantile ensign.

RED-HANDED

Legend has it the Campbells and the Macdonalds both claimed ownership of Lismore Island, located in the Inner Hebrides of Scotland. The dispute raged back and forth for some time, until it was finally decided a boat race would settle the issue, with the first clan to reach the island being granted ownership.

There, in the bow of the Campbell boat stood the Duke of Argyll, tough old geezer that he was, bellowing out motivation to his boatmen while getting ready to jump ashore. But those Macdonalds were a fast lot, and he sees their boat will reach shore first unless something's done about it. Reaching around, he grabs the axe hanging from his belt, lays his hand on the thwart of the boat, and WHACK! Chops it off. Catching the severed hand he tosses it ashore, thus winning the race and the island.

Another version of the tale claims it was actually a fifth-century boat race between St. Moluag (the patron saint of Argyll) and rival St. Mulhac, with the first to land on Lismore having the right to found a monastery there. In this version, Moluag cut off his finger and threw it ashore, enabling him to claim victory.

THE REGIMENT OF INVALIDS

Regardless of how accurately the title may describe your own coworkers, this militia group was actually formed during the late 1600s in an effort to alleviate chronic manpower shortages faced by England. As England was constantly under the threat of invasion at the time, the crown decided to form companies of invalids from among the sick and infirm pensioners residing at the Royal Hospital Chelsea. These old war-horses were used to free the regular troops from the more mundane tasks of garrison duties and the like, enabling them to better ready themselves for field work.

In 1719 the *Regiment of Invalids* was officially formed, numbering the forty-first of the line. What could one expect with such a company under their command? The following inspection report gives some idea.

"The Officers are old and mostly wounded and infirm. Many have lost limbs, many of the men are stout (that'd be fat to you and me). One major was 82 years old and other officers not much younger. Two were stone blind and the average age was 50 to 60."

When the need arose to mobilize, outpatients were notified to report to Chelsea via press notices. Failure to appear meant a loss of retirement pension.

When war was declared between Great Britain and Spain in October 1739, a South Seas offensive was launched to "annoy the Spaniards" through harrowing shipping and commerce or outright capture of Spain's Pacific possessions. Captain George Anson, one of England's greatest unsung naval heroes, was chosen to command the effort.

During the initial phase of planning he was promised 1,500 marines to man his six ships in anticipation of land assaults and raids against Spanish settlements. Imagine his feelings when he was instead given 170 men and orders to receive 500 invalids to make up the difference. Despite vehement protests, military officials thought them quite adequate to participate in one of the most grueling naval voyages in history.

Regardless, only 259 came aboard to answer the call to muster (most of those being over 60 years of age, with some over 70). Upon learning the nature of their new assignment, the healthiest of these scurried out of town as fast as cane and wooden leg would permit, pension be damned. A smart move on their part—none of the invalids who stayed lived to see jolly old England again.

REMOVING HATS IN THE GALLEY

The galley—or eating area—on many warships was often converted to an operating room/infirmary in time of battle. Unwritten shipboard law calls for removal of one's hat upon entering the galley as a show of respect to those shipmates who have passed on (whether by wounds or food received).

REVERSAL OF RANK DURING NAVAL FUNERALS

" . . . The first shall be last, and the last first." So states the Bible and that's exactly where this practical application concerning the virtues of humility arose. At a funeral, the seaman leads the admiral, a fitting reminder to all that regardless of lofty positions attained in life, death awaits to place all on equal footing.

RIGHT WHALE

The right whale got its name from early Nantucket whalers, who deemed them the correct or "right" whales to hunt. It was a surface feeder, tended to be nonaggressive when harpooned, and had a high blubber content, which caused them to float when killed.

The sperm whale was a different matter altogether. They have teeth instead of baleen (50 to 60 of them 7 inches in length, set in a roughly 16-

foot lower jaw), are the deepest diving whales (8,000 feet or more by some accounts) and ornery to boot, often turning on their attackers, smashing whaleboats with their tails or crushing them in their massive jaws. One even rammed and sank the Nantucket whaling vessel *Essex* in November 1820 while it was cruising in one of the most remote areas of the South Pacific.

Considering the danger associated with sperm whales, why were they the most sought-after by the whaling fleets? The higher quality sperm whale oil produced a brighter, cleaner flame compared to other whales, while the upper portion of its huge head (called the *case*) contained a huge reservoir of even finer-quality oil. The case oil (once exposed to air) resembles seminal fluid, which is where the name spermaceti or sperm whale is said to have originated. *(Jawing Up, Nantucket Sleigh Ride)*

RMS *TITANIC*

While pretty much everyone's heard of the *Titanic*, most probably don't know what the letters RMS preceding it stand for. Royal Mail Ship (or Steamer) is a designation that's been used since the 1840s to identify a seagoing vessel contracted to carry mail for the British Royal Mail service.

Mail ships were originally operated by the British Admiralty, who began awarding contracts to private companies in the 1850s. As competition for the mail routes was fierce, the designation was considered a status symbol of sorts by ship owners, one indicative of quality and reliability (the mail had to be on time, after all).

Although the shift from oceanic to air transport has significantly reduced the number of ships that can claim the designation RMS, a few notable examples still exist, one being the *RMS Queen Mary II*. *(SOS, Why the **Titanic** was Doomed from the Start)*

THE ROARING FORTIES

A region of the southern ocean between 40 and 50 degrees latitude known for its extreme winter storms. The name is said to come from the peculiar roaring noise made by the prevailing westerly winds while blowing over the huge seas the area is infamous for. With no continents to intervene (save the spine of South America) the theoretical fetch for the roaring forties to roar over is almost 360 degrees around the world and over 12,000 miles.

ROPE YARN SUNDAY

Name given to a half-day holiday on Sunday, when the pipe "Make and mend" authorized crewmembers time to repair and make clothes. A "Negro's holiday" signified a Sunday filled with hard labor, just as those bestowed upon plantation workers.

ROSTRUM

A fancy Latin word for a speaker's platform or podium derived from the bronze beak or ram found aboard early Mediterranean war galleys. After a great naval victory in 338 BCE, rostra (the plural form of *rostrum*) from some of the captured ships were brought back to Rome as war trophies and placed on display at the speaker's stage of the forum (center of Rome's political, religious, business, and social life). Over time, the stage and speaker's platform became known as a rostrum.

ROUGE'S MARCH

The catchy tune played by the ship's drummer aboard British warships while floggings and other such punishment were being dispensed. It was used when someone was "flogged around the fleet," as well as during ceremonies in which a person was dismissed or expelled from the service, which is where the phrase to be *drummed* out of the navy originated. *(Flogging Around the Fleet)*

ROUGE'S YARN

Red or blue colored yarn woven into rope manufactured for the British Royal Navy in efforts to prevent its theft. Sails had similar thread woven into them for the same reason.

ROUNDABOUTS

Some sailors believed it unlucky to mention eggs by name while aboard ship, instead referring to them as *roundabouts*. Scottish seamen believed it imperative to crush the shell entirely after eating one, as witches would gather those left whole and use them as vessels to travel the seas, sinking the ships of honest sailors.

ROUND ROBIN

The bleak conditions aboard ship could easily reach unbearable levels when an unusually harsh captain entered the equation. When this happened, the crew would sometimes draft and sign a grievance petition, listing all points they considered unjust.

Eighteenth-century captains had the power to inflict severe penalties on ringleaders or inciters of such petitions, so no one wanted their name to be first seen by a most likely irate captain.

Round Robin, a corruption of the French words *rond* (round) and *rouban* (ribbon) was a practice happily stolen from the French by English sailors in an effort to avoid these penalties. By placing signatures on a ribbon encircling the petition, no one's name appeared at the top of the petition, thus eliminating the appearance of being the ringleader. It's the same reason that later, when sailors began signing the actual petitions, they did so in the shape of a wheel.

RUBBERNECKER

Although drivers may more readily associate it with their daily commute, the expression rubbernecker is actually of nautical origin. It was originally used to describe a sailor who stood by and looked on as his shipmates worked.

RUMBULLION

The original name for that favorite refreshment of all seafaring men: rum. Sailors who first drank it on the island of Barbados labeled it "a hott, hellish, and terrible liquor." Pirates named it *kill devil*, another testimony to its potency.

RUMGAGGERS

Long-winded braggarts who told fantastic tales of hardship and misery they endured during some famous naval battle or campaign.

RUMMAGE

More venerable sea lingo washed ashore, this one comes from the French word *arrimage* meaning ship's cargo or the packing of it in the vessel's hold. The yard-sale-type association of the term arises from the fact that damaged cargo was often sold at a "rummage sale," a clearing-out sale of unclaimed goods at the dock. *(Junk)*

"RUNNING THE GAUNTLET"

To this day thieves are still universally despised by sailors—discovering one aboard ship generates more hate and discontent amongst the crew than most anything else. After all, what could be worse than stealing from one's mates, the very men you ate, slept, and worked with 24 hours a day? The fact that most sailors were unable to secure their valuables under lock and key made such an offense doubly villainous.

Major theft was a flogging offense aboard ships of the British Royal Navy, and it speaks the seriousness of the charge when one realizes it was the only crime for which the cat o' nine tails was knotted (three at three-inch intervals for each strand). Charles Nordhoff (see Bibliography) relates the following instance of theft aboard a ship of the line in his book *Man-of-War Life: A Boy's Experience in the U.S. Navy.*

> "He was found with several pieces of clothing in his clothes-bag, belonging to others. The crime was plainly and patiently proven on him; and then came the punishment: first confinement in the brig, in irons, for two weeks; then a dozen with the 'thieves cat,' an instrument made of heavier

line than the common 'cat,' and soaked in stiff brine for a week before it is used, which makes each strand hard and stiff as a piece of wire; and, finally, he was sentenced to mess alone, and to wear upon his back, for six months, a placard containing, in conspicuous letters, the word 'thief.' . . . "

He goes on to say,

"Poor fellow, base as was his offense, his punishment was enough to raise pity in the hardest breast. It was impossible for anyone to commiserate with him, for everyone knew his punishment was just. But no one molested him, and, during the time he remained on board, he moved about among the ship's company [some 800 men] shunned by all, and as much alone as though left on a desert island. He was kept on board until the day before leaving our next port, when he disappeared, having received, it was said, an intimation to the effect, that if he could get ashore, he would not be sought for."

Petty theft was more often punished by "running the gauntlet," a term derived from the Dutch word *gauntelope* (*gaunte*, or all, and *loopen*, meaning to run). All hands helped mete out punishment in this form of discipline, each finding a length of rope and forming two opposing lines, facing each other. The perpetrator was then stripped to the waist and forced to walk between the lines as his shipmates whipped him.

On English men-of-war, the master-at-arms walked in front, his cutlass touching the man's stomach (to prevent too fast a pace) while a marine walked behind with his bayonet against the perpetrator's back to prevent hesitation. The British Royal Navy abolished the practice in 1806. *(Blooding and Sweating, Cat O' Nine Tails, The Locked Sea Chest, Making Chalk)*

"SAIL BEFORE THE MAST"

The term applied to those shipping out as a common seaman or deckhand (as opposed to an officer). The crew was normally quartered in the fo'c'sle, which was indeed literally before the mast. *(A.B., Hand)*

SAILOR'S VAPORS

Name given a sailor's affliction that in essence amounted to seagoing cabin fever. Fatigue, brutal treatment, and miserable living conditions often combined to create an atmosphere of hostility so tense that shipmates slit each other's ears, noses, or throats with little or no provocation.

Even Captain James Cook, a leader noted for his humane treatment of subordinates, recorded instances of "the vapors" during his more lengthy expeditions. In one such incident a clerk by the name of May Orton fell into a drunken sleep, only to awake and find someone had cut off his ears! Tough as life may have been aboard ship in the eighteenth century, this particularly brutal act both shocked and outraged Cook, prompting him to offer fifteen guineas and fifteen gallons of Arrack (a strong alcoholic drink distilled from fermented palm sap, rice, or molasses) for information leading to the culprit. Even this, an incredibly rich reward for the day, failed to produce results.

Despite this lack of cooperation from the crew, Cook's suspicions fell on Patrick Saunders, one of his midshipmen. Though not formally charged, it's interesting to note Midshipman Saunders later deserted when the ship reached port.

SALAMANDER

A cannonball with attached handle that was heated, then hung up by sailors aboard ship for warmth. The name is in reference to an old belief that salamanders lived in or could tolerate fire.

SALLY SHIP

A method of loosening ice-bound vessels in which the crew is assembled on deck and instructed to run from side to side, thus causing the ship to roll and hopefully break herself free. A *sally* is defined as a sudden leap or rush.

SALMAGUNDI

A "whatever's handy" type pirate dish consisting of any precooked or marinated meat combined with eggs, pickled vegetables, olives, etc., all heavily seasoned with salt, pepper, garlic, oil, ginger, or any other spice the cook could find.

SALT EEL

"You shall have salt eel for supper," was said of one to be flogged with a rope end soaked in brine. It's a carryover from the days when whips were fashioned from eel skin.

"Claws for breakfast," on the other hand, indicated punishment with the cat o' nine tails. (*Cat O' Nine Tails, Checkered Shirt, Cold Burning, Cursing and the Cangue, Flogging Around the Fleet, Goose without Gravy, Killing the Cat, Marry the Gunner's Daughter, Nightingale, To Flog or Not to Flog, Whipped and Pickled*)

SALT JUNK

Regardless the weather, a ship's captain could always find busy work for the crew in the form of picking oakum or *junk*, old rope unraveled and used as caulking for hull and deck seams.

Salt Junk was slang for the rations of corned beef served the crew, a term indicative of both taste and texture. (*Junk*)

SALTY TALK 101

No one who's ever heard an old salt describe a scene or event, no matter how mundane, can ever view it in the same light again. Take the following excerpt from *Etchings of a Whaling Cruise* in which one sailor describes losing his hat and subsequently falling off his horse during an outing ashore.

> "Shiver me, if I've ever been athwart such a craft, shipmates. You're just in time. I've lost my main-top-gallant-sail, and hauled back in distress. The lubberly-rigged thing wouldn't lay-to, so I had to fetch her short up, and run her off a point or two to leeward of her course; but she made so much leeway that I had to haul her to port again. Then she wriggled like she'd shipped a heavy sea, and pitched me on my beam-ends. I righted up, I tell you, in pretty short order, and here I am with my main rigging hanging by the board, and my union-jack at the mizzen-peak!"

Or how about these simple, how-to instructions from the days of wooden ships and iron men:

> "Lift the skin up, and put into the bunt the slack of the clews (not too taut), the leech and foot-rope, and body of the sail; being careful not to let it get forward under or hang down abaft. Then haul your bunt well up on the yard, smoothing the skin and bringing it down well abaft, and make fast the bunt gasket round the mast, and the jugger, if there be one, to the tie."

Sounds kind of nasty.

SCHOONER ON THE ROCKS

Old salts' slang for roasted joint of beef surrounded by potatoes.

SCOUSE

A hearty, stick-to-your-ribs, artery-clogging stew of hard tack biscuits (also known as pilot biscuits) and chopped salt pork seasoned with pepper. Add potatoes and onions for your more elegant lobscouse.

SCRIMSHARKER

Old British naval term bestowed upon those of the crew especially adept at avoiding work of any kind. It's thought to be the word scrimshaw was derived from, as sailors often practiced this art in times of idleness.

SCUPPERED

Canned; shelved; cast aside. The term itself comes from the practice of hurriedly placing dead and wounded crew in the scuppers, thus clearing the gun deck for further action.

"They'll be blood in the scuppers" was a term predicting violence of some sort.

SCURVY

Of the many hazards encountered by sailors, disease was feared above all others. It was estimated that for every sailor killed in battle, up to 40 succumbed to some form of fatal malady. One such threat was scurvy, a disorder brought on by lack of vitamin C. It was especially devastating on long sea voyages, where the crew's diet consisted mainly of salt beef or pork, hard tack, and the like.

Doctors of the day were both horrified and amazed by the disease, as is evident by the following observations made during Captain George Anson's circumnavigation of the globe (1740–1744).

"Its symptoms are inconstant and innumerable, and its progress and effects extremely irregular; for scarcely any two persons have the same complaints and where there hath been found some conformity in the symptoms, the order of their appearance has been totally different . . . The common appearances are large discoloured spots over the whole surface of the body, swelled legs, putrid gums, and above all, an extraordinary lassitude of the whole body, especially after any exercise, however inconsiderable. And this lassitude at last degenerates into a proneness to swoon on the least exertion of strength, or even the least motion.

". . . At other times, the whole body but more especially the legs, were subject to ulcers of the worst kind, attended with rotten bones, and such a luxuriancy of fungous flesh as yielded to no remedy. But a most extraordinary circumstance, and what would be scarcely credible upon any single evidence, is that the scars of wounds which had been for many years healed, were forced open again by this violent distemper: of this, there was a remarkable instance in one of the invalids on board the *Centurion*, who had been wounded above fifty years before at the Battle of the Boyne; for although he was cured soon after, and had continued well for a great number of years past, yet in his being attacked by the Scurvy, his wounds, in the progress of his disease, broke out afresh, and appeared as if they had never been healed: Nay what is still more astonishing, the callous of a broken bone, which had been completely formed for a long time, was found to be hereby dissolved, and the fracture seemed as it had never been consolidated. Indeed, the effects of this disease were in almost every instance wonderful; for many of our people, though confined to their hammocks, appeared to have no inconsiderable share of health, for they ate and drank heartily, were cheerful, and talked with much seeming vigour, and with a loud strong tone of voice: and yet on their being the least moved, though it was only from one part of the ship to another, and that in their hammocks, they have died before they could well reach the deck: and it was no uncommon thing for those who were able to walk the deck and do some kind of duty, to drop dead in an instant on any endeavour to act with their utmost vigour, many of our people having perished in this manner during the course of the voyage."

Of the over 1,300 casualties during this military expedition only four were lost in battle, the rest succumbing to disease and other such hazards of shipboard life. *(First Ships to Cross the Antarctic Circle, Limeys, The Petty Tally, The Regiment of Invalids)*

SCUTTLEBUTT

The scuttlebutt was a small cask (called a butt) of water placed on deck each day for members of the crew to drink from, normally by dipping a chained tin mug through a small hole or scuttle cut into the barrel's side. The men could drink as often as they liked, but were allowed only one cup per trip in order to conserve water. Another conservation practice was doing away with the scuttle entirely, with the crew drinking from the cask via an old musket barrel shoved through the bung.

As noise had to be kept to a minimum on deck (so commands for sail handling and general orders could be heard) and below decks as well (where off-watches were often trying to sleep) the scuttlebutt was one of the few common areas where a sailor could relax a bit while mulling over the day's events and exchanging views with fellow Tars. As such, the word itself eventually came to mean rumors or gossip. *(The Dipper is Hoisted)*

SEAHORSES?

In 1794 French revolutionary forces invaded the Netherlands, reaching Amsterdam by mid-winter. Receiving intelligence of a Dutch fleet stationed to the north off the nearby town of Den Helder, French General Charles Piche-gru dispatched a cavalry brigade to assess the situation. Finding the Dutch ships frozen fast in the harbor, the French hussars urged their horses onto the ice, capturing the entire fleet.

SEA LAWYER

Not one of those beloved members of the land-based legal fraternity, but instead a prophet of pessimism and declarer of doom aboard ship who is forever arguing his views concerning any and everything, from how to properly complete any task (without involving any action on his part, of course) to his views on what's wrong with the fleet and what needs be done to correct it.

In *The Sailor's Word Book* (1867) he's described by Admiral William Smyth as "an idle, litigious long-shorer, more given to questioning orders than obeying them. One of the pests of the navy as well as mercantile marine."

SEAT OF LIFE

At one time the "Seat of Life" was considered to reside in the liver. Based on this, Grand Banks fishermen tossed cod livers into a cask while cleaning their catch, drinking a cup of liquid from said barrel each morning.

Eventually, someone in the scientific community noticed how healthy the fisherman remained despite the bleak climate of the region. Thus were the virtues of cod liver oil introduced to millions of joyful children.

THE SEVEN, ER, FOURTEEN SEAS

Although most folks know of the *Seven Seas*, many would be hard-pressed to name them. That being the case, how would they fare if called upon to name the *Fourteen Seas*?

The original seven seas were those described by ancients of the Mediterranean world, who believed the world's oceans consisted of the seven large bodies of water they were familiar with—the Mediterranean, Red, China, West Africa, East Africa, Indian Ocean, and Persian Gulf. Everyone was pretty much good with this until the age of exploration, when it was discovered there was a lot more water than the ancients ever dreamed of. As these new seas were discovered and subsequently named, the term *Seven Seas* fell out of use for a number of centuries.

It wasn't until Rudyard Kipling settled on the name *The Seven Seas* for his new book of poetry that the term came into vogue again. As such, geographers of the day (who most likely feared calling Kipling a liar and subsequently being torn to bits by his fans) divided the oceans of the world into seven parts: the Arctic, Antarctic, North Atlantic, South Atlantic, North Pacific, South Pacific, and Indian Ocean.

"SHAKE A LEG"

Until the practice was abolished in 1840, a sailor's "wife" or sweetheart could live aboard ship while in port, sometimes even accompanying him underway. This was granted as a form of redress to the crew, as liberty was routinely denied for fear of desertion.

The following passage is taken from *The Adventures of John Wetherell* as edited by C.S. Forester. Wetherell served as seaman in the British Navy during the Napoleonic Wars and this excerpt from his journal describes a typical port call during the early 1800s.

> June 1, 1803 "In the course of an hour the ship was surrounded with shore boats. First the Married men had liberty to take their wives on board then the young Men had their girls come off and took them on board, a curious sight to see boats crowded with blooming young girls all for sale. Our crew were mostly young Men and caused the boatmen to have a quick dispatch or as we usually term it a ready market; this business over, nothing particular occurred that day. Next morning it was found there was two more women than men on board...a mighty Jovial crew 661 souls on board."

While making his morning rounds the bosun's mate, upon finding a slumbering form still occupying a hammock after muster was called, would cry "show a leg" or "shake a leg there." If said leg presented for inspection was hairless or clad in stockings, it was presumed to belong to a member of the fairer sex, who was allowed to continue sleeping.

A hairy, heavily tattooed leg (hopefully) denoted a male member of the crew, who was then turned out for the day's work. *(Son of a Gun)*

SHANGHAIED BY THE CRIMPS

A crimp (the civilian counterpart of the navy's infamous press-gang) made his living by bribing, coercing, drugging, or just plain knocking sailors over the head and kidnapping them in order to supply merchant ships with crewmembers. While the practice was widespread, the term *shanghaied* actually originated along California's infamous Barbary Coast, where sailors so recruited often wound up in Shanghai, China, a major trading hub in the days of sail. *(The King's Shilling, Press-Gangs, Son of a Gun)*

SHELLBACK

A hardened sailor of such vast nautical experience that seashells were said to grow upon his exceptionally salty hide. They were also said to be able to converse with seabirds, coming back as one themselves upon death.

SHE WAS SLOW AND DIDN'T POINT WELL TO WINDWARD . . .

Few know that ancient Rome's famous Colosseum employed a specially designed canvas roof called the *velarium*, which was raised and lowered by an elite team of Roman sailors, each renowned for their skill in rigging the ships of the empire. It was reportedly along the lines of a circus big top, with a huge hole in the middle that could be opened or closed to let in light or keep out rain. Here are a few other little know Colosseum factoids:

- The Colosseum is properly known as the *Flavian Amphitheatre* (not after Flavor Flav, but because it was constructed by emperors of the Flavian dynasty).
- Nero never gave the thumbs down, thumbs up, middle finger, or anything else in the Colosseum. Its construction was planned as part of a larger, more lavish palace complex (that was never completed) but Nero kicked-off before it was opened in AD 80.
- The word *Colosseum* is actually derived from a "colossal" statue of Nero once located near the stadium.
- The emperor Titus marked the opening of the Coliseum in AD 80 with 100 days of games in which 9,000 animals were killed for sport and amusement (take that, PETA).
- Seating capacity was around 50,000—commoners, slaves, and foreigners (those who didn't hold Roman citizenship) were seated in the nose-bleed sections directly beneath the velarium, which coincidentally were the hottest seats as well.
- *Arena* is a Latin word for sand, which was spread about the fighting pit to soak up blood from the festivities.

SHIFTING BALLAST

A term used by sailors to describe marines, passengers, and other such folk aboard ship who served no visible purpose.

SHIP IN A BOTTLE

In the early days of seafaring history, stone amulets bearing images of ships where carried as protection against shipwrecks. This ship-inspired theme continued into more modern times through other media, such as embroidery, tattoos, and scrimshaw.

Land-bound artists may favor a ship running fast before a howling gale; however, sailors definitely did not. In their eyes authoring such scenes, like calling the devil by name, could very well cause them to appear. They chose tranquil scenes, a ship sailing gracefully through seas of blue or peacefully swinging at anchor in some secure harbor. Placing a ship within the protective confines of a bottle signified the sailor was, in effect, securing fair winds and following seas for his own safety. Such models were often left with family or friends in order to ensure a safe return.

This is also the origin of the phrase "bottled up," a naval term describing the results of forcing an enemy fleet into a position from which they have no room to maneuver.

SHIP OF FOOLS

Although I sailed on a number of these during my U.S. Coast Guard career, I never really knew the term's origin. Seems city fathers of fifteenth-century Germany had a novel way of addressing that nasty issue of crazy folk roaming the streets—the *Narrenschiffs* or *ships of fools*. The mad were routinely gathered up and imprisoned on riverboats, a move that, according to Michel Foucault's book *Madness and Civilization,* served dual purpose.

"To hand a madman over to sailors was to be permanently sure he would not be prowling beneath the city walls," while also serving to address society's changing view of madness itself.

The insane were historically viewed as being "touched by the gods" and as such played many important roles in fables as well as learned literature (think the fool in *King Lear*). In such tales the mad not only knew the truth, but were allowed to speak it without consequence because of their madness—insanity enjoyed the status of divine wisdom.

This sentiment began to change, however, and by the end of the Middle Ages the mad were viewed as a dangerous element, one that had to be both expelled and contained. The insane were viewed as having lost their souls and it was the ships of fools that served to carry "cargoes of madmen in search of their reason."

SHIP'S BELL

Few items onboard account for more nautical lore than the ship's bell. Gold and silver were often added as it was cast (to sweeten its tone) and it was said to be the very voice of the ship herself, tolling mournfully if she were to sink, no matter how well secured beforehand.

Old salts believed if an accidentally struck glass produced a bell-like tone within a sailor's home or upon the mess deck, drownings were sure to follow unless the sound was stopped (in which case the devil would claim two soldiers instead).

It was considered extremely bad luck to re-engrave a ship's bell upon renaming a vessel, and numerical errors while striking the bell was a harbinger of misfortune, requiring the stroke be muffled and countered by a backward stroke. *(Eight Bells)*

SHIPSHAPE

A term used originally in reference not to a vessel's tidiness, but rather to the sail plan she carried, one fully- or ship-rigged as opposed to a jury-rig (a makeshift or temporary rig set up by the crew to replace one lost or carried away).

SHIP'S HUSBAND

Traditionally, the term used to describe the shipyard foreman who oversaw the ship's repairs while in the yards. A ship may have many such husbands in the course of her life, but as all old salts will attest, her true love was reserved for the men who sailed her.

"SHOOT CHARLEY NOBLE"

A *Charley Noble* is the galley stove's chimney, said to have been so nicknamed by the crew serving under British merchant Captain Charles Noble. Seems after discovering the smokestack was made of copper, the good captain was stricken with a severe case of anal retentiveness and thereafter ordered the chimney be kept brightly polished.

"Shoot Charley Noble" was the order given to clean the smokestack of soot and ash via shots from a pistol.

SHORTEST NAVAL BRIEF IN HISTORY?

Story goes that a British admiral had difficulty keeping his fleet busy during a lull in the war with France. Not wanting to keep so many ships in port, he directed Lieutenant Percival Brown, commander of the eighteen-gun brig *Rattlesnake*, to sail for such and such a latitude and longitude. Once there, he was to open his sealed orders and proceed accordingly. Upon arriving at the designated position (somewhere in the Bay of Biscay) the orders were opened, revealing the nature of his mission: proceed to the Island of Tierra del Fuego, there to make a study of the manners and customs of the natives.

After several months in the frigid, storm-swept waters of the Magellan Straits and those surrounding the inhospitable island itself (where she was almost lost a dozen times), HMS *Rattlesnake* turned north, dropping anchor off Spithead nearly three months later.

Upon arriving to brief the admiral, who had pretty much forgotten the *Rattlesnake* and was in a bad mood to boot, he was curtly instructed to file a very brief report, in fact the briefer the better. Below is the report that followed:

Report of Lieutenant Percival Brown
Commanding H.M.S. eighteen gun brig *Rattlesnake*
On the manners and customs of the natives of Tierra del Fuego
Manners: None   Customs: Beastly
(Signed) Lieutenant Percival Brown

SHOT IN THE LOCKER

Naval slang for a sailor having a bit of cash on hand or holding some type of resource in reserve.

SHOT ROLLING

Ships in the British Royal Navy on the verge of mutiny (normally brought about by too harsh a captain) were called *shot rolling ships*. Disgruntled crewmembers would oft times try to bowl over unwary officers by rolling cannonballs along the decks.

SICK BAY

From sailing ships to the Starship *Enterprise*, crewmembers afflicted with anything from cutlass wounds to Klingon acne were whisked off to sick bay to receive medical attention and treatment. For centuries, sick and wounded seamen were sent to *sick berths*, compartments located aft in the rounded stern section of the ship, a location affording a smoother ride. Theory is, as the curved contour of the stern resembled a bay, sailors began calling it *sick bay*. *(Loblolly Boy)*

SIX-WATER GROG

Why, nothing less than the most impuissant ration of grog ever forced upon an honest sailor! With a ratio of six parts water to one part rum it's easy to see why Jack often commented that only the devil himself would have rhyme or reason to concoct such a wretched brew. It was, in fact, often served as a form of punishment to the crew. *(Black Tot Day, Grog, Grog-Blossom, More Northing!, Splice the Main Brace)*

SKIPPER

From the Dutch (literally *schipper*), a term generally used to describe the captain of a small pleasure or trading vessel.

SKIPPER'S DAUGHTERS

Tall, white-crested waves, such as are seen in windy weather; white caps: "It was gray, harsh, easterly weather, the swell ran pretty high, and out in the open there were 'skipper's daughters'" from Robert Louis Stevenson's "Education of an Engineer."

SKYLARKING

To "go on a lark" is to enjoy a bit of roguish merrymaking. It can be traced to the nautical term *skylarking*, a form of amusement in which seamen climbed to the highest point possible on the mast and slid down the rigging.

Lark is thought to be a corruption of the ancient word *lac*, meaning "to play."

SKY PILOT

A priest who administered to the needs of sailors, so named because he piloted them through the treacherous shoals of sin, helping them navigate a course to heaven.

Devil-dodger was another nickname, although my favorite would have to be *fire escape*. Get it? Fire escape—as in an escape route that kept one from getting roasted in the flames of eternal hellfire. Can I get an amen and a $25 love offering? *(The Man in Black)*

THE SLAUGHTER HOUSE

Nickname for the lower deck of a warship near the mainmast, so called by sailors as it was a focal point for enemy fire during battle.

SLOPS

Generic term for the cheap (as in quality, not price) ready-made, one-size-fits-all-type work clothes each ship carried for the crew to purchase as needed, the name itself being indicative of the quality one could expect when rummaging in the "slop chest" for duds. The term is derived from *sloppe* (old English for breeches) and was used in sailorman vernacular as early as 1691.

SLUMGULLION

Originally a term describing the offal and innards of a whale after it had been "cut in," slumgullion came to be a vulgar name for any type of meat stew served aboard ship. I don't have the exact ingredients, but judging from the terminology (*slum* being an archaic word for slime, while *gullion* is old slang for stomachache) I don't especially want to know.

SLUSH FUND

Meals aboard ship during the age of sail were monotonous at best, as the types of foodstuff that would keep without refrigeration during long voyages was limited. One such staple was *salt pork*, which was fried pork stored in barrels and preserved with salt. *Slush* was the yellow grease or fat that melted out as the meat was boiled, a necessary step in removing the salt to render it edible.

The cook (who was often nicknamed *Slushy*) saved this residue in small casks or barrels, where it was later used to grease the mast (so the hoops holding the sails would slide up and down more easily) or sold to the crew to spread on their biscuits or mix with their pudding. Regulations and instructions forbade old Slushy from the latter aboard British Royal Navy ships, however, as it was understood "scarcely anything more unwholesome or likely to produce scurvy can be eaten."

Upon returning to port, the remaining slush was sold to soap and candle makers. The moneys were then placed in a "slush fund," or general account, which was traditionally used to purchase special comforts or niceties for the crew.

SMOKING SHIP

Basically a good old-fashioned vermin killin' via fumigation. All hatches, ports, scuttles, etc., were sealed, while smoke-producing pots containing a slow-burning mixture of charcoal and brimstone were placed throughout the ship. Burning pitch or a concoction of gunpowder, vinegar, and water could also be used.

SNAKE'S HONEYMOON

An unruly mass of line or rigging, the sight of which resembled a group of amorous, intertwined snakes. "Snake" in nautical terms is to tightly wrap or wind small stuff around something, such as when seizing a line.

SNOTTY

A midshipman, based on those young sailors' unsavory habit of using their shirtsleeve as a makeshift snot rag while pining for home and dear old mum. *(Brass-Bounder)*

SOJER (SOLDIER)

A derogatory term applied to those on board who pulled less than a regular Jack Tar's share of work. It denoted a shirker or goldbricker, one who always stands clear of work or hangs back when there's duty to be done. Marines aboard ship acted as soldiers and although they performed sentry duty and the like, they had no real involvement with the actual working of the ship. They were also used as a quasi armed police force over the sailors, who hated them beyond measure. As such, *sojer* and *marine* were interchangeable when used to describe crewmen viewed as lazy or ignorant of a sailor's work and therefore fit only "to keep the bread from moulding."

When used by your real Tar, sojer was about as stinging a rejoinder of contempt as could be mustered. The old sailor's adage "a messmate before a shipmate, a shipmate before a stranger, a stranger before a dog, but a dog before a sojer," pretty much sums it up. *(Jack Tar, Soldier's Mast, Tell It to the Marines)*

SOLDIER'S MAST

Derisive term used by old salts to describe the puny, sailless, auxiliary masts found aboard early steamers. Sailors considered both the mast and their namesake to be equally useless aboard ship. *(Sojer, Tell It to the Marines)*

SO LONG

A sailor's term for goodbye. It's reportedly a mispronunciation of the East Indian term *salaam*, a salutation or ceremonial greeting performed by bowing very low and placing the right palm on the forehead.

"SON OF A GUN"

The life of a sailor was particularly harsh and brutal. Given the scarcity of volunteers in the early part of the nineteenth century, as many as half the crew of any given ship in the British Royal Navy was likely impressed or forced into the service. Captains were reluctant to grant shore leave due to extremely high desertion rates, often denying it even to those sailors who could be trusted for fear they would be impressed by other vessels in port.

As consolation for liberty denied the crew, a sailor's "wife" was often allowed to live aboard while in port (a policy that prompted the saying "sailors had a wife in every port") and in many cases allowed these women to accompany their husbands to sea.

It doesn't take much imagination to picture the goings-on such an arrangement fostered below decks, or its inevitable consequences (i.e., the patter of little feet in the fo'c'sle). The only place these women could give birth with some semblance of privacy was behind a canvas curtain or shelter hastily erected between cannons on the gun deck. If doubts existed concerning the paternity of a male child (prostitution was often rampant), he was fastidiously entered into the ship's log as a "son of a gun." *(The King's Shilling, Press-Gangs, Shake a Leg, Shanghaied by the Crimps)*

"SON OF A SEA COOK"

Another phrase reflecting on one of the more unappreciated folks aboard, that being the ship's cook. However, where "son of a gun" was used to express admiration, referring to someone as a "son of a sea cook" was definitely not.

SOOJE MOOGE

An acid-based cleaning mixture used by the crew to remove dirt and such from painted surfaces (bulwarks, deckhouses, etc.)—probably of Japanese origin. It reportedly did a pretty good job on skin too—taking it off, I mean.

SOS

Nope, not "Save Our Ship" or even "Save our Souls" for that matter. In fact, the letters themselves stand for nothing at all. Originally adopted in 1906 at the second International Radiotelegraphic Convention held in Berlin, Germany, the letters were chosen as the Morse code maritime distress signal based on their simplicity (three dots, three dashes, three dots) and due to the fact that regardless of at what point a listener began hearing the signal, he could distinguish what it was.

At that international convention, SOS officially replaced one of the first radio distress signals, CQD, which was adopted for radio use based on the land telegraph signal CQ (*sécu*, from the French word *sécurité*). CQ was originally used as an identifying header for alert or precautionary messages of interest to all stations along a telegraph line. As there was no general emergency signal or "general call" for maritime radio use, in a 1904 operations publication the Marconi company announced the addition of a "D" (for Distress) to create the emergency call CQD, which was defined as "All stations: distress."

It's reported that in 1912, RMS *Titanic* radio operator Jack Phillips originally sent CQD once directed to send a distress signal (as it was still widely used by British ships), but began alternating between the two when junior radio operator Harold Bride jokingly reminded Phillips that SOS was the new call and that ". . . it may be your last chance to send it." Turns out it was, as Phillips perished. *(RMS* Titanic, Why the Titanic *was Doomed from the Start)*

SO 'TIS TRUE, YOUNG MASTER HAWKINS . . .

In 1720, pirates captured a heavily armed Indiaman (a British East India Company ship) in a lonely bay near Madagascar. The captain and loyal crew remaining (those who hadn't joined the pirates) were about to have their throats slit, when amid the commotion a giant of a man "with a terrible pair of whiskers and a wooden leg, being struck round with pistols, like the man in the Almanack with darts" thumped forward and stopped the butchery.

Grasping the Indiaman's captain by the hand, he swore amid a shower of oaths to kill the first man who offered to do him harm. Seems he had formerly sailed under Captain Macrae (the Indiaman's captain) and found him a decent, honest fellow.

Upon this real-life seadog was based Robert Louis Stevenson's Long John Silver.

SPANISH MAIN

The "Spanish Main" (or "Terra Firma" as it was known by the Spanish) were originally the Spanish possessions located along the northern coast of South America, between Orinoco and the Isthmus of Panama. Not until the end of the seventeenth century were the islands of the Caribbean included as well.

SPIKE CANNON

In order to disable artillery left behind during retreat or after capture, the order to *spike* or *nail cannon* was often given. The procedure involved driving a pin or headless nail into the touchhole till flush, making it incapable of being fired and therefore useless to the enemy.

SPIRIT SHIPS

Sailors from the West Indies believed a ship that sank with no loss of life would invariably rise to the surface, endlessly searching for a crew to man her. In order to prevent such phantom craft from terrorizing the living, captains sometimes "failed" to rescue their entire crew in order that some could accompany the ship to her final resting-place.

"SPLICE THE MAIN BRACE"

The order given to issue an extra ration of grog to the crew as reward for some difficult or unusual service. On sailing ships, the main brace was a line crucial to many evolutions and one subject to considerable strain. If damaged, standard practice was replacement rather than splicing, as a line so repaired was never considered as strong as the original. As such, splicing the main brace was a rare event indeed, one probably coinciding with the sailor's view of how often he received that extra ration of rum. *(Black Tot Day, Grog, Grog-Blossom, More Northing!, Six-Water Grog)*

SPOUTER

Contemptuous nickname given whalers by *real* sailors—"Blubber Hunter" would be another.

"SQUARE MEAL"

A solid, hearty meal, said to be derived from the square, wooden platters hot meals were served upon aboard ship in good weather.

STARBOARD IS THE RIGHT SIDE

Approaching boats traditionally hail each other from the starboard side (the right-hand side when facing the bow). Ancient sailing vessels were steered by a huge oar fastened to that side, which was also where the master was customarily stationed so as to more easily distinguish those approaching and give appropriate welcome or warning.

Starboard (a corruption of the Old English word *steorbord*) is a term meaning steering paddle or board. Over time it came to mean not only the oar, but the right side of the vessel as well.

Why so much emphasis on the right side? It stems from the belief that anything associated with the right side of the body was superior to the left, the right hand as compared to the left, for example. It was a common perception in Christianity as well, where the saints are placed on the right hand side of God in most paintings and it's the right hand that gives blessing and is used to make the sign of the cross. According to one source, there are over a hundred positive references to the right hand (The right hand of the lord doeth valiantly, the right hand of the lord is exalted, Psalm 118 v 15-16), compared with over twenty-five unfavorable mentions for the left hand, which is derived from the Latin word *sinister*, meaning ill omen or foreboding.

The same is true in Islam, where the left hand and everything associated with it is viewed as unclean (from the Middle Eastern custom of using the left hand for personal hygiene).

Right-hand man? Left-handed dealings? Coincidence? Could be, or maybe the steering oar was placed on the right side for the more mundane reason that most people are right-handed and that location provided better control.

Port is substituted for *left* aboard ship, which was the side a vessel normally moored to when entering (you guessed it) port. This was done to protect the steering oar while docking—rear mounted rudders didn't show up until the mid-twelfth century.

Originally called larboard (from the Medieval English word laddebord or loading side), it was later changed to port after mishaps caused by crewmen mistaking larboard for starboard commands while maneuvering or during adverse weather conditions.

STEADY AS SHE BLOWS!

Here's a good one to stump Biff Spiffington down at the yacht club bar: What's the difference between a *veering* wind and a *backing* wind? A veering wind is one shifting in a clockwise direction, while a backing wind is shifting counterclockwise.

STEAMPOWER HEADS OFFSHORE

The first steamship to venture offshore was the American paddle wheeler *Phoenix*, which traveled the 150 miles from New Jersey to Delaware in April 1808. Its builder and owner, John Stevens, decided to move her in order to avoid competition with rival steamship owners Fulton and Livingston.

The first steamship to cross the Atlantic was the *Savannah*, which chugged into Liverpool, England, on June 20, 1819, after a twenty-one-day trip from Savannah, Georgia. She sailed most of the journey, utilizing the engines for a total of only 8 hours, and smoked so much upon entering port a British cruiser was dispatched to assist her, thinking she was on fire.

The first ship to make the entire Atlantic crossing under steam was the 178-foot *Sirius*. She departed Cork, Ireland, on April 4, 1838, and arrived in New York after a trip of 18 days, 4 hours, and 22 minutes (a normal west-bound passage via sailing packet by comparison was 40 days).

Her two-cylinder steam engine produced a total of 500 indicated horse-power and drove two paddle wheels for a maximum speed of 12 knots. She was also one of the first steamships built with a condenser, which enabled her to use fresh water (avoiding the need to periodically shut down her boilers at sea for cleaning) but also resulted in high coal consumption. During the crossing she burned not only all of her coal, but her cabin doors, furniture, and even one mast as well.

STEAM-PROPELLED WARSHIPS

During the War of 1812, New Yorkers became acutely aware of how suscep-tible their fair city was from an attack by the British fleet. Enter the cen-ter-wheel steam battery *Demologos,* or "Voice of the People."

Constructed by Robert Fulton (of steamship fame) *Demologos* was more floating fortress than man-of-war, designed as it was to move about the calm waters of New York Harbor in the event of a British offensive. A hundred and fifty-six feet in length, it was driven by a single paddle wheel (mounted between twin hulls for protection against enemy fire) and boasted thirty-four 36-pound cannons, each designed to fire red-hot shot in efforts to set enemy ships aflame. It also featured a steam-driven hose to douse the enemy's guns, rendering them unable to fire. Completed too late to take part in the war (and eventually blowing up in a dockyard explosion), she was nonetheless the first steam-driven battleship.

The U.S. Navy's first steam-propelled man-of-war to actually engage in warfare was the side wheel gunboat *Sea Gull*, a converted Connecticut ferry initially launched as the river steamer *Enterprise*. Armed and fitted with sails for ocean passage, she first saw action against Caribbean pirates while serv-ing with Commodore David Porter's West India Squadron from 1823 to 1825.

The first Navy ship constructed as a steamer from the keel up was the sloop-of-war *Fulton*, a side wheeler commissioned on December 13, 1837, with Captain Matthew C. Perry in command.

Screw-propelled warships made their debut on October 16, 1843, with the launching of the USS *Princeton*. It was constructed according to plans submitted by the Swedish inventor John Ericsson, designer of the Civil War ironclad *Monitor.* *(Commodore Matthew Calbraith Perry and the Opening of Japan, First Ironclad Battleship, Hunki-Dori, Tycoon, Who Said "Don't Give up the Ship"?)*

STEWARD

Modern stewards will note a special irony when contemplating the origin of their title, particularly as it relates to their duties concerning the welfare of the passengers in their charge. It's derived from the Saxon term *Stig-weard* (*Stigo*, a sty and *weard*, a ward or keeper), literally "keeper of the pigs."

STONE FRIGATE

Sailor's slang for a shoreside prison or jail. Another would be calaboose, from the Spanish word *calabozo* (via the French *calabouse*). *(Brig)*

STORMY PETRELS

Also known as "foul-weather birds," these small seabirds are often observed hovering in the smooth wake of the ship, close to the stern, during times of inclement weather. The name itself is derived from their habit of patting the water with their feet while skimming across its surface, *petrel* being a reference to St. Peter's walking upon the Lake of Gennesareth (a.k.a. the Sea of Galilee) with Christ. The Sea of Galilee is the lowest freshwater lake on Earth and second-lowest lake overall after the Dead Sea (which is a saltwater lake). (Also known as storm petrels.) *(Mother Carey's Chickens)*

STRAIGHTS CAPTAIN

Name given the *master cannoneer* or officer aboard a seventeenth-century man-of-war in command of the gunner's mates and their ordinance.

THE STRAITS OF BALLAMBANGJANG

A strait prominently featured in many sea stories due to its narrowness. 'Twas said ships were forced to place their yards a-cockbill in order to pass through, which was just as well—old salts claimed the monkeys inhabiting the trees lining its rocky cliffs were so numerous, their tails invariably jammed the brace blocks each time the order to square away the yards was given. *(A-Cockbill, Merry Dun of Dover)*

STRANDED

A ship (or sailor) that's beached, aground, or otherwise high and dry in a strange, unfamiliar place without sufficient funds or means to depart. It's derived from *strand*, the Dutch word for beach or embankment.

STRAPPADO

A shipboard punishment in which the offender was hoisted aloft by a rope tied to his wrists. Not particularly scary? Did I mention the wrists were lashed behind his back? How about the part where he was allowed to free fall toward the deck and then jerked to a halt a couple of times before reaching it, often dislocating his arms and shoulder joints in the process? *(Bosun! Keel Haul Him, Cat O' Nine Tails)*

STRIKE

The order "strike sail" means to lower or take down yards. During disagreements with the captain, disgruntled sailors would sometimes strike or remove the sails until their demands were met, giving us the phrase "to go on strike."

STRIKE ME BLIND

Sailor's nickname for rice pudding with raisins, the implication being you would be struck blind trying to find the raisins supposedly in there. What few raisins there were did double duty, however, as they helped hide the weevils often inhabiting the ingredients. *(Dandy Funk)*

"SUCK THE MONKEY"

Not quite as nasty as it sounds, the term actually describes the clandestine siphoning of spirits from one of the ship's casks via a straw or other such tube. The word monkey has always been used in nautical vernacular to describe something diminutive in size, in this case the small wooden butt that contained the crew's grog ration.

Captain Marryat (see Bibliography) states the term was originally applied to the ruse of replacing a coconut's milk with rum, thus enabling a sailor to get hammered while strolling about the decks, innocently sucking on a coconut. Worked pretty well too, until the officers noted an alarming increase in drunkenness due to "bad" coconut milk.

The practice was also known as "Tapping the Admiral" after the brandy-filled cask used to transport Admiral Nelson's body to England after his death reportedly required topping off a couple of times prior to its arrival. Scholars say the missing brandy was absorbed by the admiral's body. However, those familiar with the ways of thirsty sailors have other theories . . . *(Scuttlebutt)*

"SWALLOW THE ANCHOR"

"He swallowed the anchor" is a term used to describe an old salt who retired ashore, forever giving up his life at sea.

"SWEATING THE GLASS"

Come fair weather or foul, the need for watches aboard ship never ceased (nor the grumblings of those forced to stand them). Old salts swore warming the half-hour glass (used to time watches) in one's hand caused the neck to expand and allowed the sand to flow faster, thus shortening the watch.

"Flogging the glass" was a similar ploy in which a watch stander actually shook the glass in an effort to hurry the sand. A more modern form of the ruse is "flogging the clock," where sailors move the clock hands forward. *(Dogwatch, Eight Bells, Hot Bed)*

"SWINGING FROM THE GIBBET"

For over four centuries, England's Execution Dock (on the northern bank of the Thames) was the place scores of condemned pirates had the burden of a sinful life lifted from their weary shoulders. Until passage of the "Act For More Effectual Suppression Of Piracy" in 1700, English law decreed all cases of piracy occurring within the High Court of the Admiralty's jurisdiction (the high seas, ports, rivers, and other waters belonging to the crown) be heard by the Lord High Admiral himself. This meant captured pirates that colonial governors felt deserved a little neck-stretching had to be transported to England in order to stand trial.

After due process of law the condemned was marched to the gallows at Execution Dock, a simple affair consisting of two posts and a crosspiece located near the low tide mark. The location of the gallows within the marks of ebb and flow served to stress that those being punished had committed

crimes within the Lord High Admiral's domain, civil courts holding sway above the tide line.

It was there those sentenced *"to be hanged by the neck until severely dead, dead, dead"* were led up a ladder, noosed, and pushed into space. It was of course considered immodest to hang women so convicted (for obvious reasons) so they were afforded the more decent option of being drawn to the gallows and burnt at the stake, buried alive, or perhaps caged at the low water mark, there to drown with the rising tide.

OK, I'll tell you the obvious reason women weren't hanged—lack of underwear. Undergarments as we know them today (i.e., bloomers or panties) weren't worn by women until the late eighteenth century. The courts felt that what could become exposed to view while hanging warranted a more modest form of execution, one in keeping with a lady's dignity.

As to the hanging itself—unlike those quickies in westerns you watched as a kid—it was a slow, humiliating death by strangulation, with each twitch and spasm of the hangee being cheered by the fun-loving crowd. As the short drop from the gallows was rarely sufficient to effect a quick, clean death, it wasn't uncommon for friends or relatives to pull on the legs of the condemned in order to shorten their suffering.

Yes, it was a kinder, simpler time as far as public entertainment was concerned and while there might not be as much screaming and flailing about as one would find, say, at a good witch burning, public hangings were quite the popular attraction—doubly so when a notorious pirate was on the marquee.

Upon justice being served, the bodies of those so punished were placed at the low water mark, there to be covered and exposed by the murky waters of the Thames until three high tides had passed. Bodies of the more infamous pirates were then displayed in a prominent location via the gibbet (an upright post with a projecting arm upon which the body was hung) to serve as a gruesome reminder to those of the maritime community that the rewards of piracy weren't limited to warm tropical islands, dusky island beauties, pieces of eight, and drinks with those little umbrellas in them.

In order to keep the corpse intact as long as possible (while continuing to serve as a deterrent) they were coated with tar and placed in a specially constructed harness or cage of iron hoops and chains. The bodies of those lacking in notoriety were normally whisked off to Surgeon's Hall, where they served medical students as cadavers for dissection. *(Dance the Hempen Jig, The Deadly Nevergreen, Jack's Kitchen, Turning a Profit with the Upright Man, You'll Grin in a Glass Case)*

TAILWINDS

Ancient sailors believed nailing a shark's tail to the mast or hoisting one aloft assured favorable winds throughout the voyage. Along the same lines, German U-boats sported porpoise tails for good luck while patrolling the South Atlantic during WWII (probably because they were easier to acquire than the requisite shark tail).

Based on the war's outcome, seems the sea gods aren't too fond of convenient substitutions. *(Blue Monday, Making Wind)*

"TAKE A CAULK"

Sailor slang for snatching what today would be called a power nap. Deck seams or caulks ran fore and aft, the same alignment sailors aspired to attain within their hammocks or upon some out-of-the-way deck. Had to be careful about that latter choice in hotter climates, however—softened pitch stained the well-known pattern of deck seams onto ol' Jack's clothes, proclaiming to all he'd been napping.

"TAKE A HAIR OF THE DOG THAT BIT YOU"

Common advice both afloat and ashore to those who enjoyed too much spirituous liquor the night before. John Nicol, cooper for the British ship *King James* during a trip to China in 1787, relates in his memoirs an incident that occurred while ashore outside Canton, which possibly sheds light on its origin.

> "One day a boy was meddling rather freely with the articles belonging to me. Neptune [the ship's Newfoundland dog] bit him. I was extremely sorry for it, and after beating him dressed the boy's hurt which was not severe. I gave the boy a few cass [a Chinese coin], who went away quite pleased. In a short time after I saw him coming back, and his father leading him. I looked for squalls, but the father only asked a few hairs out from under Neptune's foreleg, close to the body. He would take them from no other part, and stuck them all over the wound [a home remedy to prevent rabies?]. He went away content. I had often heard, when a person had been tipsy the evening before, people tell him to take a hair of the dog that bit him, but never saw it in the literal sense before."

"TAKE IN ONE'S COALS"

Said of a sailor who contracted venereal disease, a condition guaranteed to keep him "hot" for some time afterward. Those so infected were said to have been *burned,* and just to prove I am somewhat cultured, I'll point out a pun on this in Shakespeare's *King Lear*: "No heretics burned, but wenches' suitors." *(A Pox on Ye!, Dock, Fire Ship, To Go into Dock)*

TARPAULIN MUSTER

Sailors have always taken fierce pride in loyalty to their shipmates, individuals who they worked, ate, slept, and caroused with pretty much twenty-four hours a day. At any given time a sailor's life could rest within the hands of his messmates, which is why crimes that destroyed that trust (stealing, for example) were sure to garner the harshest punishments from the crew.

By the same token, a crewmember finding himself in dire straits knew shipmates could be counted on to see him through. If the difficulty was financial in nature, a "tarpaulin muster" was often the answer. This involved rigging a tarpaulin catch-net near the mast, after which the ship's company filed past, each donating what money he could to help. *(The Locked Sea Chest)*

TARWATER

A panacea of Scotch pine tar and water devised by none other than George Berkeley, erstwhile philosopher and Bishop of Cloyne (1685–1753). Touted as a curative for just about any ailment a sailorman could suffer, it was said to be especially effective for internal disorders, regardless of whether administered via orifices above or below the belt. *(Iron Water)*

TATTOOS

The first skin art sailors encountered adorned the bodies of South Pacific islanders, who referred to them as *tatau*, a Tahitian word meaning "to mark." It was first described by Captain James Cook in a 1769 account of his first voyage, where he used the word *tattaw* to describe the markings. Sydney Parkinson (the expedition's artist) described three Maori who visited the *Endeavour* on October 12, 1769:

> "Most of them had their hair tied up on the crown of their heads in a knot
> . . . Their faces were tataowed, or marked either all over, or on one side, in
> a very curious manner, some of them in fine spiral directions . . . "

Sailors promptly called them *tattoos*, no doubt due not only to the similarity of the two words, but additionally to the rapid, tapping sounds produced by the native implements used (a bamboo needle struck with a small, wooden mallet). Tattoo is derived from the Dutch word *tap-too*, a rhythmic, seventeenth-century drum signal given to call soldiers back to quarters and notify tavern keepers it was time to close their taps. Talking heads of the day suggested *tatau* itself was an onomatopoeic word, with "tat" referring to the above-mentioned tapping and "au" to the cries of pain from the tattooee.

It's interesting to note that European missionaries to the islands branded tattoos an affront to God, quoting Leviticus 19:28: "Do not cut your bodies for the dead or put marks on yourselves."

Oh, but how to get the mark of Satan out? Well, necessity may be the mother of invention, but religious zealots can hold their own when there's evil afoot. They noticed (no doubt on the long sail to the islands) that the sandstone blocks or holystones sailors used to scrub the ship's deck worked mighty fine to rid them of dirt and grime—thus, the *dermabrasion* method of tattoo removal was born.

Despite (or in *spite* of) the stated religious implications of tattoos, sailors soon copied this art form themselves, using needles along with ink, ash, or brick dust (for red) to prick out designs. These coloring materials required a binding or mixing agent to work properly—early tattooists sometimes used their own spit, but urine was popular as well.

In an age when most could neither read nor write, the ability to prove one's identity by having an anchor on your burly arm or a full-rigged clipper sailing in all its glory across your hairy, manly man's chest meant something. It also served as a pictorial logbook of a sailor's experiences. An anchor denoted he'd sailed in the Atlantic Ocean, while a full-rigged ship indicated passage around Cape Horn; a shellback turtle was proof he'd crossed the equator, whereas a dragon similarly indicated service on a China station.

With their growth in popularity, tattoos soon expanded beyond their initial role as decorations and into the realm of practical usage. Sailors often had images of Christ or the cross inked upon their backs in an effort to make the bosun soften the blows of the lash.

Hold tattooed above the knuckles of one hand along with *Fast* on the other was said to allow a sailor to grip the rigging better, while certain tattoos on and around the genitalia were said to protect the bearer from contracting venereal diseases.

A pig and cockerel tattooed on the left instep or knee protected ol' Jack against drowning and hunger—both animals hate water and it could truly be said a sailor so tattooed always carried his "ham and eggs" with him. *(Drownproofing, Holystoning the Decks)*

"TELL IT TO THE MARINES"

This expression, approved by the Royal Marines, was reportedly coined by King Charles II of England concerning his newly created "Marine Regiment of Foot" (forerunner of today's Royal Marines). Seems His Majesty was considered somewhat of a dullard by his contemporaries and, after finding himself the royal butt of many a courtly jest, developed a justifiably cynical outlook on tales brought before his court.

Story goes, after issuance of a royal guffaw upon being told of fish that flew by some of his "soldiers of the Royal Navy," they promptly produced one brought back for just such cases of disbelief, prompting the king to exclaim "Henceforth, ere we cast doubts upon a tale that lacks likelihood, we will first tell it to the Marines!" From that point on (the story goes), as a way of testing a statement's validity His Majesty would in essence remark, "Tell it to the Marines, as they have surely seen everything."

This all sounds well and good, but other sources state that this version was actually invented by W.P. Drury (a retired lieutenant colonel of the Royal Marines turned writer) in the 1900s.

Regardless of its origin, the phrase eventually took a derogatory turn as old England's sailors didn't quite hold the Marines stationed aboard their ships in such high regard. While they may have some use as cannon fodder and the like, Marines were otherwise considered downright gullible by their more worldly shipmates.

As tales of mermaids, birds that flew backwards, and all other manner of fantastical creatures were accepted with equal enthusiasm by the naïve soldiers, "Tell it to the Marines" eventually became synonymous with "Don't expect me to believe that whopper, but you're welcome to try it on Private Parts over there."

This derogatory form of reference is also mentioned in an early work of anonymous naval fiction, *The Post Captain; or The Wooden Walls Well Manned* (London, 1806). In it, Captain Brilliant of HMS *Desdemona* was credited with commenting (when a tale got too tall), "You may tell that to the Marines, but I'll be d——d if the Sailors will believe it!" *(Sojer, Soldier's Mast)*

TELL-TALE COMPASS

Not a work by Edgar Allan Poe, but a downward facing compass mounted in the overhead of the captain's cabin. It enabled the captain to keep an eye on the helmsman's course without going on deck.

THANK GOD IT'S FRIDAY?

Bad vibes abounded for undertaking just about any enterprise within the nautical realm of things on a Friday (beginning a voyage, launchings, etc.). Biblical events said to have occurred on that day (thus rendering it unlucky for any endeavor) include man's temptation and subsequent fall from Eden, the flood, and the crucifixion of Christ.

It was also known as "Hangman's Day" (from the American and English custom of hanging criminals on Friday), a nickname that didn't exactly scream "Lucky day, lucky day!"

Mondays didn't fare too well either. The first Monday in April is said to be Cain's birthday (as well as the day of Abel's death) while the second Monday in April is pegged as the day Sodom and Gomorrah were destroyed. December 31 was to be avoided as well, that being the day Judas committed suicide.

"THERE'S A RAT IN YOUR FORE-CHAINS!"

The ultimate insult when commenting on a sloppy ship. The origin of the term itself is unclear, but it positively reeks of unseaman-like innuendoes.

THIEVES' KNOT

Almost identical in appearance to the reef knot, a thieves' knot was often used by sailors in an effort to indicate theft. Theory was a careless thief would retie a pilfered sea bag with a reef knot, thereby leaving evidence of the crime.

"THREE SHEETS TO THE WIND"

Nautical lingo for someone who's staggering drunk. Sheets are the lines used to trim a vessel's sails, and *to the wind* refers to a sail flapping in the wind due to the sheets (lines) being cast loose or allowed to run free. With this, the ship loses momentum and becomes uncontrollable, which is where the analogy to the staggering walk of an inebriated sailor comes into play.

As to the three sheets part, it could be a corruption of "free sheets to the wind" (implying a lubberly handling of lines) or a reference to how uncontrollable a sail would be with three of its sheets free to the wind. *(Beating up Against an Ale-Head Wind, Lubber)*

THE THREE SISTERS

One group of ladies sailors did their best to avoid, they being three canes tied together and used for flogging. *(To Flog or Not to Flog)*

TIDEWALKER

Term used to describe a water-saturated log with only one end floating above water. Sailors from the steamship community called them a "propeller inspector." When used to describe a person, it meant a drifter or scalawag.

TIDY

The seaport of Bristol, England, has been a major commercial hub and port of entry for goods the world over since the twelfth century. During the seventeenth and eighteenth centuries it played a major part in the transatlantic slave trade or Triangle Trade (an historical term describing trade between three ports or regions). In this case, ships outfitted in Bristol departed for Africa laden with trade items (copper, guns, cloth, trinkets, and the like), which were sold or bartered for slaves. The slaves were then transported to the New World, where they were sold or traded in the Caribbean or American colonies for goods such as sugar, rum, and tobacco, which (along with slaves in many cases) were in turn transported back to Bristol for sale, completing the triangle.

During the height of the slave trade (1700 to 1807) over 2,000 slave ships were outfitted in the port of Bristol alone, transporting roughly half a million people from Africa to the Americas. Due to the horrid stench of these vessels and the risks they posed of disease, they were not allowed into port until

thoroughly cleaned and *tidy*, a word derived from the neat, orderly predictability of the tide. It's also where we get the term "Bristol fashion," meaning shipshape.

TIP A PERSON ONE'S FLIPPER

To shake hands, flipper being the nautical term for hand.

"TO BOX THE JESUIT AND GET COCK ROACHES"

I'll let Captain Grose (see Bibliography) tackle this one: "A sea term for masturbation; a crime, it is said, much practiced by the revered fathers of that [the Jesuit] society."

Partridge comments in his *Dictionary of Slang and Unconventional English* that it is "An unsavoury pun on cock and a too true criticism of nautical and cloistered life."

Insanity, torpor (fancy talk for apathy or laziness), blindness, hair loss, even death were just a few of the horrors awaiting those who succumbed to such sinful behavior according to the pious and learned.

While self-love didn't seem to bother the ancients (Egyptian queens were buried with all the paraphernalia they needed in the afterlife—jewelry, clothes, and—most notably—dildos), the practice fell out of favor across Europe with the birth of Christianity, and by the Victorian era even doctors began blaming it for pretty much everything wrong with the world.

Sylvester Graham (1794–1851) concocted his originally bland graham crackers "in part to reduce the body's passionate urges toward self-love," while health guru Dr. John Kellogg of Battle Creek, Michigan (yep, the guy who invented corn flakes), devoted much of his time crusading against the evils of masturbation amongst womenfolk of the day. His course of therapy to quench such fiery passions included a regimen of cool baths and soothing, daily enemas containing (I'm not making this up, by the way) cornflakes . . . and that's all I have to say about that.

"TOE THE LINE"

Sailors called to muster were told by the bosun to toe the line, meaning they were to form up in a straight line, toes to one of the ship's deck seams.

TO FLOG OR NOT TO FLOG

Although flogging was an effective means of discipline, it was a serious, formal punishment that disrupted the ship's daily routine. As such, sailors found guilty of minor infractions were often subjected to other less disruptive, but equally creative, forms of punishment.

A sailor could be "clapped in irons," ankles bound in sliding shackles attached to a long iron bar (called a *bilboe*), which forced him to sit upright or lie flat on his back. Bilboes were placed on some exposed deck for all to see, as use of such punishments relied on public embarrassment as much as physical discomfort in deterring misbehavior.

"Seizing to the shrouds" consisted of tying the convicted spread eagle to the ropes supporting the mast, while "the capstan" was a punishment in which the arms were fastened to a capstan bar placed atop the shoulders and a heavy weight was fastened about the neck.

As smoking presented too much of a fire hazard aboard ship, sailors chewed tobacco instead. Those who spat on deck were tied up with a spidkid (spittoon) around their necks, which their shipmates then used for target practice. Nordhoff (see Bibliography) relates the following:

> "Woe betide the careless fellow whom the lynx-eyed first lieutenant, or his worthy coadjutor, the boatswain, has caught spitting upon the deck. He is condemned for the next month, to carry about with him a spittoon, for the convenience of such of his shipmates as may indulge in the luxury of chewing tobacco: a perambulating spit-box, at the command of every passer by."

Often the punishment was made to fit the crime. A crewman who talked back to an officer "got a gagging," a punishment in which the offender's hands were lashed behind his back and an iron bar secured firmly in his mouth. Dirty speech was similarly rewarded, with the offending tongue being cleansed not with soap, but via a good scrubbing with sand and canvas.

Sleeping on watch was another infraction that had to be dealt with to the satisfaction of captain and crew, as 40 winks endangered not only the vessel, but all aboard her as well. A sailor of the early eighteenth century faced being doused with a bucket of seawater for a first-time offense, while punishment for a second was being tied up by the wrists and having water poured down his sleeves.

Reward for a third infraction was seizing the culprit to the mast, with a heavy bag of shot often tied around his neck for good measure. I guess after the fourth offense they pretty much gave up on you. Punishment was placing the individual out on the bowsprit with a small ration of rum, water, and food, there to remain until dying of hunger and thirst, or until falling off and drowning.

Finally, a captain could punish the crew by denying them their daily ration of grog—oddly enough, it was here the drunkards were better off than shipmates who practiced temperance. Unlike the former, who could be punished for minor infractions by having their ration withheld, those of "the people" (the term officers used to describe the crew) who were teetotalers really had no way of being disciplined other than by flogging or one of the others mentioned above. *(Cat O' Nine Tails, Checkered Shirt, Cold Burning, Cursing and the Cangue, Flogging Around the Fleet, Goose without Gravy, I'll Eat My Hat, Killing the Cat, Marry the Gunner's Daughter, Nightingale, Salt Eel, Whipped and Pickled)*

"TO GET SPLICED"

Nautical slang for marriage, an allusion to the joining of two lines via splicing. To "be bent on a splice" described a sailor who was looking for a wife. Both terms are kind of odd, considering splice comes from the German word *spleissen*, to split or divide.

"TO GO INTO DOCK"

Said of a sailor who found God's word, the inference being his soul was (like a ship in dry dock) being repaired and fitted out to better serve his master. Ironically, it was also slang for hospitalized sailors being treated for venereal disease. *(A Pox on Ye!, Dock, Fire Ship, Take in One's Coals)*

"TO HAVE NO MILK IN THE COCONUT"

Said of a sailor deemed crazy or *cracked*, coconut in this case being a euphemism for head. References between coconut and head are understandable, due to their similarities in size and shape. The name itself is derived from the Portuguese word coco or "grinning face" (as in a specter or goblin) in reference to the three dark hollows resembling eyes and a nose found at a coconut's base.

More useless coconut trivia as follows:

- Coconuts are the world's largest seed.

- Known as *cocos nucifera* in the scientific community, coconut palms grow to a height of 80 feet, produce around 50 coconuts per year (beginning at five years of age), and can continue producing coconuts for the next 50 years.

- They were first introduced into Europe by Marco Polo.
- Yes, I really do know a guy who was actually hit on the head by one while resting beneath a coconut tree (if he ever reads this, he'll know who he is).

TOM PEPPER

Nickname for a habitual liar, who was so called for his *hot* tongue. (*Office of the Swabber*)

TOP-LOCKER

Why, old Jack's noggin, such as in the sentence, "I ransacked my top-locker for the proper knot to bend on the main top-gallant-stern sail, but I couldn't recollect it."

"TO THE BITTER END"

Bitts are perpendicular pieces of timber or metal going through the deck, used to secure a ship's anchor line. The bitter end of an anchor line or cable is the inboard side or end attached to the bitt (and aptly named too, as any boater will attest you feel mighty bitter when it goes over the side).

"Holding on to the bitter end" refers to the practice of letting out as much rode as possible in bad weather, thereby increasing the scope and hopefully the holding power of the anchor.

"TOUCH AND GO"

Often used to describe a tricky or delicate situation, this phrase refers to a ship touching bottom with her keel, but being able to continue without grounding solidly. It especially high-lights those suspenseful few seconds all boat owners experience at some point—that period of alternating curses and prayers between touching bottom and reaching the safety of deeper water.

"TOUCH BUN FOR LUCK"

Just what it sounds like—the sailor's practice of copping a feel from some unsuspecting lass for good luck prior to getting underway.

"TURN A BLIND EYE"

Admiral Horatio Nelson was undoubtedly England's greatest naval hero. His long years of war with the French cost him an arm and the loss of sight in one eye. While engaged in the 1801 Battle of Copenhagen as second in command under Admiral Sir Hyde Parker, he knowingly held his telescope up to his blind eye in order to ignore a signal to retreat, thus winning the battle and giving England a great victory. Nelson later commented he possessed a blind eye and reserved the right to use it on occasion.

TURNING A PROFIT WITH THE UPRIGHT MAN

Condemned pirates were often housed at Newgate, London's most infamous prison. As *Ordinary* to the prison, members of the clergy so assigned were provided the last earthly opportunity to save these roguish souls from the clutches of Satan.

Sad to say, many of the priests were concerned less with turning wicked men toward God than with turning a wicked profit. Not a few recorded the heinous, well-embellished confessions and last words of condemned pirates in order to sell them, along with vivid, eyewitness accounts of their final hours before "dancing the hempen jig."

After King William III's "Act For More Effectual Suppression Of Piracy" in 1700 allowed Admiralty courts to convene outside England, certain members of the clergy proved once again good business is where you find it. One in particular, the Reverend Cotton Mather (minister of the Old North Church in Boston, Massachusetts) became known far and wide for his catchpenny descriptions of the final hours of sundry rogues and pirates.

Mather (1663–1728) seemed to relish such distressing events, using them as opportunities to deliver soul-shaking orations of hellfire and brimstone to the condemned on execution day, later followed up with printed versions of the sermon and accompanying events made available to the common man (for a nominal charge, of course).

One such pamphlet, titled *A Discourse occasioned by a Tragical Spectacle in a Number of Miserables under sentence of Death for Piracy* began:

"We have told you often, we have told you weeping, that you have by sin undone yourselves; That you were born Sinners, That you have lived Sinners, That your Sins have been many and mighty, and that the Sins for which you are now to Dy are of no common aggravation . . . "

Pirates of the day jokingly commented that fellow shipmates who were forced to listen to the good Reverend prior to hanging "died with Cotton in their ears." *(Dance the Hempen Jig, The Deadly Nevergreen, Jack's Kitchen, Swinging from the Gibbet, You'll Grin in a Glass Case)*

TURTLE

The English name for tortoise—it's believed to have been coined by sailors and influenced by the word turkey, in reference to the long, stringy necks both possess.

TWO FAMOUS SOLDERS THAT ALMOST WEREN'T

Few know that America's first president was initially destined for a midshipman's berth in the Royal Navy. The Washington family had close ties with British Admiral Edward Vernon via George's half-brother Lawrence, who served under him in the early 1740s during The War of Jenkins' Ear (Lawrence later changed the Washington family home to "Mount Vernon" in his honor). With Vernon's influence young George was a shoo-in for a naval career in the service of good King George, until his widowed mother Mary Washington (described as a tough, driven woman) voiced fears over his proposed occupational path and squashed the idea.

A naval career almost claimed Napoleon Bonaparte as well. An islander by heritage (he was born on Corsica), his family originally sought a place for him at the French Naval Academy.

The death of his benefactor Count Marbeuf (the French governor of Corsica and *really* close friend of his mother), coupled with the popularity of naval service with the aristocracy of France, forced young Bonaparte to instead apply to the Military School of Paris in 1784 at the tender age of 15. He was accepted and specialized in artillery, a skill that apparently served him well if history is any indication. *(The War of Jenkins' Ear)*

TWO-HEADED ANGEL

A hollow cannonball divided into halves and joined by a short length of chain. They were used to destroy an enemy's mast, rigging, or sails, thus reducing his mobility. *(Langrage)*

TYCOON

Among the many other results of Commodore Matthew Perry's visit to Japan during his 1852–54 expedition was the introduction of this word into the English language. *Taikun,* or "Great Prince," was the descriptive Japanese title of the *shogun* or commander in chief of the army. While being absorbed into English it was appropriately mangled (in both spelling and meaning) to tycoon, a word used to describe someone who displays real or imagined power, particularly within the business world. *(Commodore Matthew Calbraith Perry and the Opening of Japan, Hunki-Dori, Steam-propelled Warships, Who Said "Don't Give up the Ship"?)*

"UNDER THE WEATHER"

Although the modern sense describes someone who's feeling ill or poorly, the term itself originates from the discomfort sailors standing the forward watch often had to endure. A watch stationed on the weather side of the bow was subjected to the effects of both wind and wave, placing the sailor literally "under the weather."

"UP ALL HAMMOCKS"

This order, which was given as a naval ship prepared for battle, called for the crew's tightly rolled hammocks to be placed along the decks as shielding against musket fire. They were also used to cover bulkheads and cabin walls in efforts to prevent splinters caused by cannon fire, which were feared as much as the projectiles themselves.

On warships, sailors heading on deck to relieve the watch or turn to the day's work were required to pass their rolled hammocks through an iron ring suspended from the overhead, which was done to ensure uniformity and compactness. The hoop also just happened to be the size of your basic cannonball, meaning if the ship received a shot below the waterline the hammock could be jammed in the hole as a make-shift plug.

"UP THE POLE"

Said of one showing reckless disregard for personal safety, the pole in this case being the upper portion of the mast extending beyond the rigging, a place no sane man would venture to climb.

U.S. COAST GUARD CUTTER *ITASCA*

It was during routine supply operations in the central Pacific that the USCGC *Itasca* made the last-known radio contact with Amelia Earhart and co-pilot Fred Noonan on July 2, 1933. The *Itasca* later assisted in the Navy-led search for the aircraft, which continued until July 17, 1933. No trace of the aircraft or its occupants was ever found.

THE U.S. EXPLORING EXPEDITION

America's first exploring expedition, an event marking the entrance of the United States into the age of exploration that was carried out more in the name of science than military purposes. Between the years of 1838 and 1842 this squadron of six small ships (the only U.S. exploring expedition conducted under sail) logged an incredible 87,000 sea miles and surveyed some 280 islands. The charts they drafted during the expedition were of such accuracy many remained in use by the military as late as World War II.

The assemblage of artifacts gathered during the cruise was so immense it eventually formed the basis for the United States National Museum at the Smithsonian Institution. Had the expedition's commander not been forced to abandon plans to visit Japan in the later stages of the voyage, it could very well have succeeded in opening that island country to western dialogue over a decade before Commodore Perry's own expedition of 1853. (**Commodore Matthew Calbraith Perry and the Opening of Japan**)

VENETIAN WAR GALLEYS

At its height during the Middle Ages, the famous Arsenal of Venice located in Northern Italy could "prefabricate" a galley of over 1,000 pieces in two hours. Its development of the moving assembly line (galleys were floated along a canal during construction, allowing them to be brought to the workers and materials, instead of the other way around) predated Henry Ford's modern version of the assembly line by almost 700 years.

VIKING LONG SHIPS

Common law directed Viking captains to take down the ferocious, gilded figureheads of dragons and serpents adorning their warships prior to entering home waters. Consensus was the figureheads used to terrorize victims into submission would also frighten benevolent, local spirits as well. The entire ship, in fact, was constructed to resemble a sea serpent (head at the bow, tail at the stern, oars mimicking legs) in efforts to subdue storms and frighten malevolent creatures of the deep. Viking, by the way, is old Norse for pirate or sea rover.

WALKING THE PLANK

Probably no other image has been more universally associated with pirates (and less substantiated) than that of forcing condemned prisoners to "walk the plank."

Although dramatic, which probably accounts for its inclusion in practically every pirate movie ever made, the fact remains it just wasn't very practical. Every source I've researched indicates pirates wanting to rid themselves of prisoners would simply have thrown them over the side and been done with it.

With that said, it is possible the notion came from the so-called "Classical Period" of piracy, a time when people, not goods, aboard captured vessels were considered the booty. Ships were much smaller then, as was their cargo-carrying capacity. Consequently, most money realized by pirates was made by ransoming a ship's passengers and crew. Those of poor means were often forcefully invited to jump overboard and "walk" home.

Buccaneers of the Spanish Main also ransomed hostages taken from captured Spanish ships and towns for money, food, and supplies. If Spanish officials were lethargic in negotiating or paying said ransom (and they frequently were), the pirates forced their captives to throw dice in order to ascertain which heads would accompany the note protesting the authority's lack of action. *(Buccaneer, Know Your Pirates, Marooners, Spanish Main)*

THE WAR OF JENKINS' EAR

Yep, you *heard* me right. This war between Spain and England in 1739 actually erupted over the chafing trade restrictions England was forced to endure concerning the New World. The final straw materialized in the form of Robert Jenkins, an English captain who appeared before the House of Commons in 1738, claiming Spaniards boarded his ship while in the West Indies and cut off his ear. Some historians place doubts on Jenkins's story; however, he *had* lost an ear somewhere and he *was* waving about a jar containing something that looked like one for all to see, so war it was.

A missing ear is bad, but it could have been much worse. During a similar incident in which another English crew was captured and branded pirates, the Spaniards reportedly "cut off the hands, feet, noses and ears of the crew and smeared them with honey, and tied them to the trees to be tortured by flies and other insects."

WAISTERS

The old, disabled, or unskilled landsmen aboard who were unable to work aloft and thus normally gathered or mustered on deck at the "waist" or center of the ship during the workday or shipboard evolutions. Waisters were the lowest members of the shipboard pecking order and thus objects of derision to the rest of the crew. They were assigned the most menial of tasks aboard ship, such as cleaning, swabbing, mess cooking, and the like. The name itself comes from the foul bilge accumulations of deck water, garbage, cargo sweat, etc., that found its way into the center or "waist" of the vessel, there to cause nothing but trouble to real seaman.

"WATER BEWITCHED AND TEA BEGRUDGED"

A watery version of tea and molasses served the crew, more for being inexpensive than for good taste. If you've a hankering to whip up a batch for your hands, just follow the recipe below.

> 1 pint of tea
> 1½ pints of molasses
> 3 gallons of water

Place the above in a large pot and boil down to the coppers. Be sure to place a stick in the pot so each crewmember can stir it up prior to getting his one cup (to ensure each gets a fair share of the tea leaves and sweetener).

"Water bewitched" was also used in general to describe exceptionally weak or diluted spirits.

WATER, WATER, EVERYWHERE, NOR ANY DROP TO DRINK

Arguably one of the most famous works of maritime literature, who can read *The Rime of the Ancient Mariner* without peering uneasily between the lines and into a world of abject hopelessness and utter despair, some of which paralleled actual events.

The shooting of the albatross and subsequent shortage of water were based on notes concerning a voyage of the privateering vessel *Speedwell*. While rounding Cape Horn in October 1719 (the worst time of year for such a passage) she was battered for nearly a month by "the continued series of contrary tempestuous winds which oppressed us ever since we got into this sea."

The "gloomy, dismal waters" of the Cape so dispirited First Officer Simon Hatley that, according to the captain's journal, he shot the only other living creature to be seen, "a disconsolate black albatross who accompanied us for several days as if lost himself."

The passages concerning the incident were later brought to Coleridge's attention while strolling with a friend one day in 1797—some guy he knew by the name of William Wordsworth.

Speaking of water, the ration normally allocated each man aboard ship in the days of sail was three pints per day. They could either drink or wash with it—I'll leave it up to you to decide what most did. *(Booty Call, Give 'em the Bird)*

WELL BLOW ME DOWN!

Everyone knows Popeye the sailorman, right? Some people assume he's in the U.S. Navy, while others claim it's the U.S. Coast Guard (the answer you'll get depends upon which branch of the service the questionee is in).

I've always heard it was the Coast Guard and (as a retiree of the 5th armed service) I just assumed that was the case. It made sense—the Coast Guard transferred to the Department of the Navy in times of war (as was the case in WWII, when Popeye was so popular). Get the picture? Feisty little Popeye (Coast Guard) invariably linked with the larger, hulking Bluto (Navy).

I didn't really give it much credit, though, until I heard Popeye say "Stop in the name of the Coast Guard!" during a fight scene on one of my daughter's DVDs.

Aha! I thought with glee. There's the proof! Now I can razz those squids, er . . . Navy guys about having "Popeye the Coastie" adorning their imagined salty hides.

But, in order to verify it for inclusion here, I did a little more research on the subject (as inquiring minds want to know) and my Indiana Jones–type search led me to The Official Popeye Fan Club website and its "all the more shocking because it's true" answer.

Coast Guard? Navy? The correct answer is . . . none of the above.

Popeye's creator, Elzie Crisler Segar, originally conceived the squinty-eyed spinach addict as a civilian. The word sailor doesn't necessarily denote membership in any service, being synonymous with any of the maritime community (note the civilian yachting cap in the original cartoons).

Although the cartoon bigwigs drafted him into various services during WWII, Mr. Segar passed away in 1938, so we'll never know with certainty where he would have taken Popeye. Any Coastie can give you a pretty good guess, though.

One last bit of Popeye trivia as long as we're on the subject. Hats off to Jack Mercer (1910–1984), the voice of Popeye for over forty-five years. His qualifies as the longest voice characterization gig in cartoon history.

WETTING DOWN

The "wetting down" of an officer's commission is a time-honored tradition in which shipmates reflect upon and celebrate a companion's achievements, but mostly drink free booze at his expense. Why is it called a wetting down (other than the obvious reason of wetting one's throat with the aforementioned refreshments)?

In earlier times an officer's commission consisted of a hand-written proclamation penned on heavy parchment. Some sources say that during the course of the meal (which was customarily hosted by the newly commissioned or promoted officer) the new commission was rolled into the shape of a cone, forming a cup from which all present drank and toasted the new officer.

Other sources take a more literal stance, with the guest of honor donning his new uniform and being liberally christened with the traditional liquid refreshments.

WHAT DO YOU DO WITH A DRUNKEN SAILOR . . .

Ah yes, a thirsty sailor was indeed the mother of invention when it came to getting "loaded to the gunn'ls." *Rumfustian*, a traditional drink of pirates, consisted of cinnamon, nutmeg, raw eggs, sugar, beer, gin, and sherry, all heated together and served hot (probably got its name because rum was about the only thing not thrown in).

Care for a tankard of *Hipsy*, an amalgam of wine, water, brandy, and sugar? This particular mixture was also nicknamed "meat, drink, and clothing" as it was believed to be pretty much all a man needed.

How about a draught of *BumBoo*, a drink consisting of rum, water, sugar, and nutmeg, or maybe just plain old *Rumbo*, a half-and-half mixture of rum and water sweetened with crude sugar? Don't forget a mug of *Dog's nose*, a mix of beer and gin (or ale and rum, depending on the company you kept).

Flip (a heated mixture of small beer, rum or brandy, and sugar) was so named due to the belief a sailor could vault over the mizzenmast after consuming two pots—the mainmast after four.

Blackbeard favored a blend of rum and gunpowder, another popular choice among pirates. Accounts say he lit his before drinking it, flames and all. And if no liquor was to be had, a delicious concoction of seawater and gunpowder was whipped up to be enjoyed by all, incentive enough for a thirsty pirate crew to keep an extra sharp lookout for the next potential victim. *(Rumbullion)*

WHAT IS THIS CHIT?

"Chit" is a remnant of the days when Hindu merchants used a signed voucher or *chitti* for goods and services, thereby eliminating the need to carry cumbersome bags of gold and silver. It was shortened to *chit* by British sailors, who readily adopted it for various uses aboard ship (requests, mess vouchers, etc.).

While chits are still commonly used in modern naval services for requesting such things as leave or liberty, the term can be correctly applied to most any piece of paper requesting some privilege.

WHAT'S THE NAME OF THAT THING?

A traditional sailor's dress uniform has a square flap extending downward from the collar, covering the upper portion of the shirt. Sailors once used tar to secure the ends of their pigtails, and the purpose of the removable flap was to protect the more expensive material of the uniform below from stains. As for the name, unofficial U.S. Navy slang terms it a "jumper flap."

WHEEL STEERING

It wasn't until the early eighteenth century that a fancy new labor-saving device made its way aboard ship, that being wheel steering. Tillers were used up until that point and as ships became larger, tillers had to be made longer to provide leverage to move the rudder, often to the point that it took five to six men just to control it while steering the ship in rough seas.

WHERE'S NED LAND (OR KIRK DOUGLAS FOR THAT MATTER) WHEN YOU NEED HIM?

Jules Verne would have thought it rocked! Not only is the fastest round-the-world yacht race named after him (think *Around the World in 80 Days*) but one of the vessels competing in the 2003 race found itself grappling with a giant squid—just like Verne's fictional submarine *Nautilus* in his novel *Twenty Thousand Leagues Under the Sea*.

The squid latched on to the trimaran *Geronimo*, skippered by Olivier de Kersauson one night off the Straits of Gibraltar. After *Geronimo* slowed mysteriously and experienced strange vibrations, de Kersauson sent Chief Mate Didier Ragot below in an effort to find what the problem was.

"Suddenly he saw something moving," de Kersauson said. "It was tentacles."

Peering through a porthole, Ragot saw the squid clinging to the hull and rudder.

"It was impressive," he later recounted, "the tentacles were as thick as my arm wearing an oil-skin, and I immediately thought of the damage it could do . . . when we saw it behind the boat it must have been seven, eight or nine metres long."

The squid held on for an hour before releasing the vessel and heading off into the depths, presumably in search of something a little more edible.

"The squid was pulling really hard," commented de Kersauson, who was at the helm at the time, "so we put the boat about and when we came to a stop the tentacles let go. We saw it behind the boat—and it was enormous. I have been sailing for 40 years, and I have never seen the like." *Geronimo* continued on, undamaged.

The 26,000-mile Jules Verne Trophy race follows the old trade route taken by early twentieth-century windjammers plying the grain trade between London and Australia—captains who opted to plunge south, then east to harness the winds of the Roaring Forties (shaving months off their voyage) rather than follow the westerly China to Britain route of the old tea clippers.

The official course for the race starts and finishes between England's Lizard Point and Ushant (off the coast of France), taking competitors past South Africa's Cape of Good Hope, Australia's Cape Leeuwin, and Cape Horn off South America. *(The Roaring Forties)*

"WHIPPED AND PICKLED"

Term used to describe a sound flogging followed by a dousing of seawater. *(Cat O' Nine Tails, Checkered Shirt, Cold Burning, Cursing and the Cangue, Flogging Around the Fleet, Goose without Gravy, Killing the Cat, Marry the Gunner's Daughter, Nightingale, Salt Eel, To Flog or Not to Flog)*

WHISTLING FOR A WIND

Sailors often try to whistle up a wind upon finding themselves becalmed, this in reference to the sound of wind whistling through the rigging. Basic rules were never to whistle while on watch (as this signified boredom and may tempt the gods of the sea into sending a nice hurricane to keep you busy) and always face the direction you wanted the wind to come from.

These rules didn't apply to bosuns, however, who were known by all to be minions of the devil. *(Bos'n)*

"WHISTLING PSALMS TO THE TAFFRAIL"

A nautical phrase describing the giving of good advice to a shipmate that, unfortunately, has little chance of being followed.

WHO SAID "DON'T GIVE UP THE SHIP"?

Although most often associated with U.S. Naval Commodore Oliver Hazard Perry (who did indeed have this slogan on his battle flag), it was originally spoken by his friend Captain James Lawrence during the battle between his ship *Chesapeake* and the British frigate *Shannon* on June 1, 1813. Upon being told his ship was lost, the mortally wounded Lawrence reportedly replied, "Keep the guns going and fight the ship till she sinks . . . don't give up the ship. Blow her up."

The Navy later adopted it as their official slogan. Don't feel bad for Commodore Perry, though—he was credited with his own famous quote, one taken from a dispatch following a later conflict with the British on Lake Erie.

"We have met the enemy and they are ours . . . " *(Commodore Matthew Calbraith Perry and the Opening of Japan, Hunki-Dori, Steam-propelled Warships, Tycoon)*

WHO'S THE CAT IN THE HAT?

"Cocked hats" were once a required part of every officer's ceremonial uniform. You know the one, that honker Captain Crunch–style chapeau also referred to as the "fore and aft" hat, a name also denoting the manner worn. It was originally worn parallel to the shoulders up until the 1800s (à la Napoleon), but was then modified to be worn with points in the front and rear. It remained a part of the U.S. naval uniform until 1942.

WHY THE *TITANIC* WAS DOOMED FROM THE START

Any ship with a name that challenges the elements or boasts supremacy over the gods of wind and wave is just asking for trouble. Monikers like *Ocean Master* or *Wind Conqueror* do nothing but tempt the mercy of these gods, who favor names more humble in nature (just like sailors should be while traversing their domain).

Along those lines a ship named *Titanic*, a word used to describe something of immense strength and power, would surely be a tempting target to those gods who felt the need to take those uppity mortals down a peg or two. The fact she was launched without a proper naming ceremony probably didn't do much to endear her to Poseidon either; however, there are other reasons the name itself would be an affront to the god of the sea.

Greek mythology states the first ruler of the universe was Uranus, father of the twelve Titans. One of these Titans was Kronos, who at the urging of his mother, Gaia, castrated Uranus with a scythe and tossed his genitals into the sea. This shifted power to the Titans, who eventually chose Kronos as their leader. After wedding his sister Rhea, Kronos sired Zeus and the rest of the Olympians, the next generation of gods (which included Poseidon), who eventually defeated and ousted the Titans.

Kronos was a fearful, jealous god who ate each of his offspring after birth

in an effort to foil a prophecy stating he would be dethroned by one of his children. Evidently this routine got a little old for Rhea. After giving birth to Zeus, she tricked Kronos into swallowing a rock instead of the infant. It was Zeus who later ambushed his father, kicking him so hard he vomited forth the previously swallowed Olympians, now fully grown and pretty ticked-off over the entire affair. Uniting, they ousted Kronos and the rest of the Titans, afterward casting lots to divide the spoils (which is how Poseidon gained sovereignty over the seas).

And so, you can see how a ship that brought back memories of being eaten at birth and having to clean up old Grampa Uranus's mangled genitalia probably wouldn't be received all that well by the God of the Sea. *(RMS Titanic, SOS)*

WIDOW'S WALK

Name given the roof-top balconies of many shoreside homes located within the American whaling towns of New England. It was there that wives kept their lonely vigil, scanning the horizon in hopes of spotting the sails heralding their loved one's return from the sea.

WILL THE REAL DISCOVERER OF AMERICA PLEASE STAND UP?

The debate pitting Columbus against Leif Ericsson as the first to discover America is pretty well known, but what about poor Bjarni Herjólfsson? When does he get his due?

Seems Bjarni, a Norwegian captain, told Leif about some unknown landfalls he once made after his trading vessel missed its initial destination of Greenland. He described two areas he found (one level, the other a wilderness) before sailing east and finally hitting one of the Norse settlements in Greenland. Afterward, Bjarni even loaned Leif his ship to organize an expedition to the new lands.

Although neither Bjarni nor his crew went ashore, there are those who feel he's still the undisputed, first European discoverer of America.

WINDFALL

Used to describe an unexpected stroke of good fortune, this is another popular term that has its roots in nautical language. During Britain's emergence as a growing naval power, the crown proclaimed all standing trees of a certain size located within His Majesty's realm belonged to the Admiralty, to ensure an adequate supply of wood for shipbuilding.

Landowners were forbidden to touch trees so designated; however, if one was blown down via an act of god, the owner was free to claim and use this *wind fall* as he saw fit.

WINDJAMMER

In its earliest English form, a term said to have been used in reference to a horn player, possibly from the German word for wind followed by the verb *jammer*, meaning to moan, cry, or wail loudly. Thus, an exceptionally bad horn player (who was probably considered to be making some pretty horrendous noises with his wind) was said to be a *windjammer*.

Add to that the second oldest meaning of the word, "a talkative person; a windbag or blowhard" and you set the stage for the most common usage, a disparaging term used to describe the great clipper ships of the nineteenth century. Best guess is the hairy-chested, manly men of the clippers boasted so loudly the benefits of sail to the steamship community, the term became synonymous with them and their vessels.

WNA AND THE PLIMSOLL LINE

All modern ships are required to have Plimsoll marks located on their hulls in order to gauge how much cargo/weight can be carried safely. The marks themselves have been in use since 1875 and give a visual indication of the depth to which a vessel may be safely loaded, depending on such variables as the area to be traveled and expected conditions.

They're named after Samuel Plimsoll (a.k.a. "the sailor's friend"), a philanthropist from the seaport of Bristol, England, who championed maritime safety laws during the late 1800s. Working aboard a merchant marine ship of the nineteenth century was dangerous business. An 1876 report from the Board of Trade stated that 856 British merchant ships were lost within ten miles of the British coast, all in conditions no worse than a strong breeze.

Plimsoll was shocked by the overloaded, unseaworthy merchant vessels of the day (known by seamen as coffin ships) and successfully fought for use of the compulsory load line that bears his name.

As to WNA, probably no ocean delivers more punishment to a ship than the North Atlantic, a place where shrieking gales and mist-enshrouded icebergs push man and ship to the extreme.

The lowest mark (which correlates to the lightest loading of cargo) is labeled "WNA" for "Winter North Atlantic." *(Tidy)*

WOMEN ONBOARD

Although they occupied many a lonely sailor's thoughts and dreams, women and ships were always considered an unlucky combination. In fact, many old salts believed the only thing worse than shipping out with a woman was having a priest onboard.

"Aye, might'n as well lower tha gang plank and help ol' Davy Jones hisself aboard!"

Redheads were especially feared, due to their strong will and fiery disposition, as well as those who were cross-eyed. Fishermen believed a woman's touch would curse their nets and during menstruation they would bring misfortune to anything they came in contact with. The only exception in the matter was a pregnant woman, who with her glow of birth and new life was considered lucky to have aboard, more so if a male child was born on the first night out.

The only other benefit of having the gentler sex aboard might be to help out during bad weather, though not in the way you may imagine. Storms were said to be calmed by a woman exposing herself to the howling gale à la naked, the reason many a ship's figurehead was of a nude or bare-breasted woman—probably didn't hurt morale any either. *(Davy Jones' Locker, The Eyes Have It, Family-Head, Fiddlehead, Go Figure . . ., Son of a Gun)*

WOODEN SHIPS AND IRON MEN

Being a proper shipwright in the days of sail went far beyond the typical woodworking skills one was expected to possess. You had to be knowledgeable in selecting the correct types of wood for each application, as well as the pros and cons of your decision from both a practical and supernatural standpoint.

Ash and dogwood warded off your basic witches and the like, while apple and holly were associated with fairies. Chestnut added speed, but black walnut was to be avoided, as it was thought to attract lightning.

WOODING

Another form of persuasion used by early English and French pirates while raiding Spanish settlements in search of gold. It involved tying a cord around a captive's head and, with the aid of a wooden block, twisting it until a confession of where they had hidden their gold was obtained (often to the point of eyes being forced from their sockets). *(Blooding and Sweating)*

"WORKING THEIR OLD IRON UP"

Another term for hazing. A harsh captain often punished his crew by constantly supplying them with meaningless busywork, the worst of which might even continue through Sunday (the sailor's traditional day of ease or liberty ashore). The iron part most likely comes from the hated task of chipping rust off the ship's ironworks prior to painting.

"WORK TOM COXE'S TRAVERSE"

The serpentine, wandering route taken aboard ship by those trying to avoid issuance of work or while dragging out tasks assigned. If the crew felt they were being ill-treated by the officers or kept at work for nothing (*humbugged* in nautical terms), Tom Coxe's Traverse became the order of the day.

"Three turns round the longboat, and a pull at the scuttled butt" during every phase of a job assured all work done (if any) was an up-hill battle. " . . . up one hatch and down the other" they would go, hiding in voids and other places "a greased rat would have trouble navigating." *(Scuttlebutt)*

"X" MARKS THE SPOT

What pirate tale worth its salt would be complete without a rum-stained treasure map, a requisite bloody *X* scrawled across its yellowed parchment? Unfortunately, this mainstay of pirate lore is fictitious.

"The devil!" you may exclaim in disbelief, but 'tis true. Credit *Treasure Island*, the Holy Grail of pirate adventures, for introducing that bit of nautical lore.

YARN OF THE *NANCY BELL*

"The Yarn of the *Nancy Bell*" is a poem by Sir William S. Gilbert that addressed a practice once so widely followed by those of the maritime community that by the late 1900s the general populous pretty much accepted it as "a custom of the sea." The tale begins with a riddle told by "an elderly naval man" who, like Coleridge's *Ancient Mariner*, is seemingly compelled to tell his story to all he meets.

> *"Oh, I am a cook and a captain bold,*
> *And the mate of the Nancy brig,*
> *And a bo'sun tight, and a midshipmite,*
> *And the crew of the captain's gig."*

Can you answer the riddle or do you feel like the young man listening to his tale?

> *And he shook his fist and he tore his hair,*
> *Till I really felt afraid,*
> *For I couldn't help thinking the man had been drinking,*
> *And so I simply said,*
> *"Oh, elderly man, it's little I know*
> *Of the duties of men of the sea,*
> *But I'll eat my hand if I understand*
> *How you can possibly be,*
> *At once a cook, and a captain bold,*
> *And the mate of the Nancy brig,*
> *And a bo'sun tight, and a midshipmite,*
> *And the crew of the captain's gig."*

Yep, can you say survival cannibalism? Along with the rise of shipping throughout the late eighteenth and nineteenth centuries came the inevitable increase in shipwrecks and instances of castaways forced to ask "the delicate question 'which'."

To entertain thoughts of cannibalism requires survivors to overcome a taboo at once ancient and powerful, and while consuming the bodies of those dying of natural causes is repugnant enough, imagine the moral and social dilemmas facing those forced to choose and kill one among their number to sustain the rest.

Yet that was often the case, and the practice became so routine as to be universally accepted not only by the folks back home, but by the courts as well. Accepted, that is, if the victim was chosen by some manner that guaranteed all stood an equal chance of selection.

The use of a lottery or similar game of chance to solve problems associated with shipwrecks can be traced to antiquity. Debates raged among Roman philosophers over questions arising from survival-at-sea situations. Marcus Tullius Cicero put forth the following line of reasoning in 44 BCE, the same year he was engaged in a power struggle with none other than Marc Antony.

If a ship sinks, leaving two shipwrecked survivors alone in the water with a single plank large enough to support only one, who gets it? Is the wiser of the two justified in pushing off the foolish man by virtue of his higher intellect? No, states Cicero (to whom wisdom was almost sacred) as that would be an unjust act and one not in keeping with what wise folks were supposed to do.

If one was the captain, does he have the right to claim what's left of his vessel? No again, as a paying passenger is seen as chartering his vessel, in essence meaning he owns the ship until her destination is reached.

The final discussion revolved around a situation in which both men are equally wise and their lives are of equal worth. Cicero sets precedence for centuries to come, stating "One will give place to the other, as if the point were decided by lot or by a game of [chance]."

It was a convenient solution to an unpleasant dilemma, particularly for the winners, who upon their return would be accepted by civilized society

without fear of ostracism or prosecution, as all participated voluntarily and had equal chance of selection (survivors were in fact often welcomed home as heroes). If chicanery or other such skullduggery came to light, however, those involved could be charged with murder. Charged, but rarely convicted.

Case in point would be the *Euxine*, which was abandoned by her crew some 850 miles southwest of St. Helena on August 8, 1874, when her cargo of coal spontaneously ignited. The crew was divided into three boats, but one became separated from the other two during the first night. Occupants of this lone boat decided to strike out for St. Helena, but after their attempts to locate it failed, they headed toward Brazil. The boat capsized several times in heavy weather, resulting in the drowning of two crewmembers, as well as the loss of all navigation instruments, food, and water.

Choices were made and lots cast, resulting in the killing of one crewmember to feed the rest. Unfortunately, inconsistencies in the survivors' stories arose that cast doubt on the fairness of the selection, not the least of which was the fact that the victim just happened to be the only non-English-speaking member of the crew. Survivors said they even held a second lottery to ensure fairness, with the same result. I guess you don't have to speak English to see you're getting shafted—later rumors stated that the victim, upon seeing the results of the two lotteries, jumped into the sea rather than provide sustenance for his dishonest shipmates. They allegedly fished him out, afterward cutting his throat with such force that he was decapitated.

The whole thing caused quite a stink back in England. British authorities feared failure to prosecute would give sailors the green light to murder passengers and weaker members of the crew in survival situations, resulting in a drastic reduction in the life expectancy of ship's boys. Such courts of inquiry often faced strong opposition from the public, however, with even the relatives of those chosen to sustain the rest often supporting the survivors. It showed just how reluctant terrestrial authorities were in claiming jurisdiction on the high seas and punishing those who followed its customs. Jailed for a time, the *Euxine* survivors involved were eventually released and allowed to continue their profession.

Historians observe that the chances of survival for castaways increased dramatically with the presence of a competent officer among them, a symbol of authority in a situation that could easily devolve into a brutish, downward spiral of petty squabbles, murder, or worse. The HMS *Bounty* mutiny illustrates this concept beautifully. When Fletcher and his crew of mutineers were finally located some eighteen years later on Pitcairn Island, all but one of the nine mutineers had exited this worldly plane via murder or suicide.

Not too good a ratio, especially when you consider only one of the eighteen loyal men cast adrift in that open boat with Captain Bligh didn't survive their ordeal. In a craft so severely loaded it possessed only inches of freeboard, Bligh managed to guide his remaining crew safely through a forty-seven day, 3,618-mile trek to Timor, besting exposure, storms, and hostile natives along the way. In fact, Bligh's one casualty occurred not at sea, but during a clash with the latter.

Thus, Bligh and those in his charge survived, while Fletcher and his crew succumbed to what essayist Milton Rugoff describes as a situation in which men of "dubious character . . . found themselves on an island, without responsibility, free of law and restraint, beset by sensual temptation, and most corrupting of all, without hope of ever returning to civilization."

Detractors of the noble officer theory of castaway survival, however, are quick to cry the academic equivalent of foul! They note it was the ship's officers who possessed training in the art of navigation and the tools needed to accomplish it; therefore, it's no surprise the survival rate of castaways in their boats was higher.

Written accounts of such incidents often portray officers as heroes, but this too is a point of contention, as most were written by the officers themselves. If accounts were told as seen through the eyes of the common, more often than not illiterate sailor, a very different view of the general conduct of officers in such situations might have been told.

That being said, maritime cannibalism wasn't a practice limited to castaways. When Magellan's fleet arrived at Guam during his famed circumnavigation, the natives' theft of a small boat forced him to arm forty men and go ashore in an effort to retrieve it. Many of the sick amongst the crew were said to have begged for the entrails of any natives killed " . . . as they would recover immediately."

Luckily, we modern folk don't have to worry about trying to make sure the fat guy is assigned to our life raft, what with modern search and rescue organizations and technology such as EPIRBs, satellite phones, and prepackaged food. We and our humanity are safe . . . unless, of course, we get in a bind like the survivors of the Andes plane crash back in 1972, a true story of survival cannibalism that was the basis for the book and movie *Alive! (Pitcairn Island, Water, Water Everywhere, Nor Any Drop to Drink)*

YELLOW JACK

The quarantine flag, which was also flown by ships carrying yellow fever. *(Clean Bill of Health, Quarantine)*

YO HO! YO HO! A PIRATE'S LIFE FOR ME!

OK, I'll admit I always ride "Pirates of the Caribbean" a plethora of times when taking my kids to Disney World. Who can resist seeing those lovable scalawags doing all the piratical-type things we'd not only like to do ourselves when pulling into that next liberty port, but have also been conditioned to expect via popular tales and Hollywood?

Who can forget that one thrilling scene integral to every pirate movie worth its rum? You know, the one showing a wildly cheering crew casting off the tyrannical yoke of their oppressive captain, hoisting the Jolly Roger, and setting sail in search of adventure and fortune?

The earliest pirate flags were usually solid black in color, black being the traditional color of renegades in the Mediterranean and West Indies. The red flag (symbolic of blood) was another popular choice among seventeenth-century Caribbean and Madagascar pirates.

During the later part of the 1690s the black flag once again fell into vogue, this time embellished with some form of gruesome design crafted to instill fear and compliance amongst potential victims, more often than not some play on the skeletal theme (bones, multiple skulls, and the like). While earlier pirates such as Henry Every were said to have used a variation of it, the first *documented* use of the familiar skull and crossed bones was by the French pirate Emanuel Wynne, who flew what was destined to become the classic "Jolly Roger" during an encounter with a British man-of-war off the west coast of Africa in 1700.

Terminology-wise, *roger* was an eighteenth-century word for rouge, while "Old Roge" was a nickname for the Devil. As to the jolly part, I guess it proves even pirates kept a sense of humor while looting and killing.

Another possibility is that the name originated in the eastern seas, where the chiefs among the notorious Cannonore pirates assumed the title *Ali Raja*

(King of the Sea), a term easily corrupted to Jolly Roger by the English, who probably thought the title referred to the flag itself. Still others suggest the name was derived from *joli rouge*, the name French buccaneers gave the red flag they initially used.

While the skull and crossed bones became most widely known, there were many other variations among pirate flags. Each had the same purpose, however—to strike so much fear into a potential victim's captain and crew that they surrendered without a struggle. Your basic pirate was a pragmatist at heart, one who avoided a fight whenever possible, knowing full well he could die in battle as easily as his quarry.

Which brings me to another Hollywood-induced myth. Tinsel-town invariably portrays the Jolly Roger as a flag of death, when actually it was an offer that all aboard would be spared and the ship set free—if its cargo was given up without resistance. The standard that brought a shudder to even the most hardened captain was the red flag, which promised an all-out, no-quarter-given fight to the death. *(Buccaneer, Know Your Pirates, Give No Quarter)*

"YOU'LL GRIN IN A GLASS CASE"

Said of pirates and other such brigands who, after being hanged, were anatomized (their skeletons displayed in glass cases at Surgeon's Hall). *(Dance the Hempen Jig, The Deadly Nevergreen, Jack's Kitchen, Swinging from the Gibbet, Turning a Profit with the Upright Man)*

YOU PUT YOUR RIGHT FOOT IN . . .

Some fishermen believed bringing a right boot aboard in their nets signified good luck and promptly nailed them to the mast. A left boot, however, was considered unlucky and quickly returned to the sea.

YOU SAY TRONADA, I SAY TAI-FUNG

Tornado is a sailor's corruption of the Spanish word *tronada* (thunder), a term used to describe any powerful cyclical storm of limited area and short duration. Typhoon (another mangled foreign word) comes from *tai-fung*, the Chinese word for hurricanes occurring in the South China Sea and throughout the islands of the Pacific.

Bibliography

Books

Bailey, Nathan. *An Universal Etymological English Dictionary; Seventeenth Edition, with Considerable Improvements.* Gale ECCO, Print Editions, 2010.

Baker, Margaret. *The Folklore of the Sea.* David & Charles, 1979.

Beck, Horace. *Folklore and the Sea.* Stephen Greene Press, 1983.

Biesty, Stephen. *Stephen Biesty's Incredible Cross-sections: Stowaway.* DK Publishing, 1995.

Brewer, Ebenezer Cobham. *Dictionary of Phrase and Fable.* Henry Altemus Company, 1898.

Browne, J. Ross. *Etchings of a Whaling Cruise.* 1846; reprint, Harvard University Press, Belknap Press, 1968.

Canby, Courtlandt. *A History of Ships and Seafaring.* Hawthorn Books, 1963.

The Century Dictionary. Century Company, 1889–91, 1911.

Chase, Owen. *Shipwreck of the Whaleship* Essex. 1821; reprint, Lyons Press, 1999.

Chichester, Francis. *Along the Clipper Way.* Pan, 1966.

Clary, James. *Superstitions of the Sea.* Maritime History in Art, 1994.

Cloud, Enoch Carter. *Enoch's Voyage: Life on a Whale Ship, 1851–1854.* Moyer Bell, 1995.

Cochran, Hamilton. *Freebooters of the Red Sea: Pirates, Politicians, and Pieces of Eight.* Bobbs-Merrill, 1965.

Colcord, Joanna Carver. *Sea Language Comes Ashore.* Cornell Maritime Press, 1945, 1974.

Cook, Peter. *You Wouldn't Want to Sail on a 19th Century Whaling Ship.* Children's Press, 2004.

Cordingly, David. *Under the Black Flag.* Random House, 2006.

Dana, Richard Henry. *Two Years Before the Mast.* World Publishing Company, 1946.

Dening, Greg. *Mr. Bligh's Bad Language.* Cambridge University Press, 1994.

Durant, John and Alice Durant. *Pictorial History of American Ships on the High Seas and Inland Waters.* A.S. Barnes, 1953.

The Encyclopedia of Discovery and Exploration: Pacific Voyages. Doubleday, 1973.

Esquemeling, John. *The Buccaneers of America.* 1969; reprint, Cosimo Classics, 2007.

Farmer, John Stephen and William Ernest Henley. *Slang and Its Analogues Past and Present: A Dictionary.* Harrison & Sons, 1891.

Felton, Bruce and Mark Fowler. *The Best, Worst and Most Unusual.* Galahad Books, 1976.

Foucault, Michel. *Madness and Civilization: A History of Insanity in the Age of Reason.* Vintage, 1988.

Freuchen, Peter. *Book of the Seven Seas.* Messner, 1957.

Funk, Charles Earle. *Horsefeathers & Other Curious Words.* Harper & Row, 1986.

Funk, Charles Earle. *Thereby Hangs a Tale.* Harper & Row, 1950.

Gibson, Gregory. *Demon of the Waters: The True Story of the Mutiny on the Whaleship Globe.* Little, Brown & Company, 2002.

Gosse, Philip. *The History of Piracy.* Longmans, Green & Co., 1932.

Green, Alfred John. *Jottings from a Cruise.* Kelly Printing Co., 1947.

Grose, Francis. *A Classical Dictionary of the Vulgar Tongue,* 3rd ed. Edited by Eric Partridge. 1796; reprint, Barnes & Noble, 1963.

Guinness World Records 2000. Guinness World Records Ltd., 1999.

Harland, John H. *Seamanship in the Age of Sail.* Naval Institute Press, 1984.

Harlow, Frederick Pease. *The Making of a Sailor, or, Sea Life Aboard a Yankee Square-Rigger.* Dover Publications, 1988.

Hotten, J.C. *The Slang Dictionary.* 1887; reprint, EP Publishing, 1972.

Irwin, Godfrey. *American Tramp and Underworld Slang.* 1931; reprint, Gale Group, 1971.

Isil, Olivia A. *When a Loose Cannon Flogs a Dead Horse There's the Devil to Pay: Seafaring Words in Everyday Speech.* International Marine, 1996.

Johnson, Charles and Daniel Defoe. *A General History of the Robberies & Murders of the Most Notorious Pirates.* Garland Publishing, 1972.

Kemp, Peter. *The History of Ships.* Orbis Publishing, 1978.

Kemp, Peter and Christopher Lloyd. *Brethren of the Coast.* St Martin's Press, 1961.

Kerchove, René de. *International Maritime Dictionary.* Van Nostrand, 1961.

King, Dean. *A Sea of Words.* Henry Holt, 1997.

Koning, Hans. *Columbus: His Enterprise.* Monthly Review Press, 1976.

Leslie, Edward E. *Desperate Journeys, Abandoned Souls.* Mariner Books, 1998.

Lind, Lew. *Sea Jargon.* Patrick Stephens, 1982.

MacLiesh, Fleming. *The Privateers.* Random House, 1962.

Marryat, Frederick. *Peter Simple. Or, The Adventures of a Midshipman.* University of California Libraries, 1838.

Masefield, John. *On theSpanish Main.* Macmillan, 1906.

McDougall, Walter A. *Let the Sea Make a Noise.* Harper Perennial, 2004.

McEwen, William A. and A.H. Lewis. *Encyclopedia of Nautical Knowledge.* Cornell Maritime Press, 1953.

McLain, Bill. *Do Fish Drink Water?* Quill, 2000.

Merriam-Webster's Collegiate Dictionary, 10th ed. Merriam-Webster, 1999.

Mingo, Jack. *How the Cadillac Got its Fins and Other True Tales from the Annals of Business and Marketing.* HarperCollins, 1994.

Moorehead, Alan. *The Fatal Impact: The Invasion of the South Pacific, 1767–1840.* HarperCollins, 1990.

Morison, Samuel Eliot. *Sailor Historian: The Best of Samuel Eliot Morison.* Houghton Mifflin, 1977.

Mulder, Kenneth W. *Piracy: Days of Long Ago.* Hillsboro Printing, 1998.

Nicol, John. *The Life and Adventures of John Nicol, Mariner.* Edited by Tim Flannery. Grove Press, 2000.

Nordhoff, Charles. *Life on the Ocean: Being Sketches of Personal Experience in the United States Naval Service, the American and British Merchant Marine, and the Whaling Service.* Wilstach, Baldwin & Co., 1874.

_____ *Man-of-War Life: A Boy's Experience in the U.S. Navy.*

Parry, J.H. *The Establishment of the European Hegemony, 1415-1715: Trade and Exploration in the Age of the Renaissance.* Harper & Row, 1961.

——— *Romance of the Sea.* National Geographic Society, 1981.

Partridge, Eric. *A Dictionary of Slang and Unconventional English.* MacMillian, 1956.

Pigafetta, Antonio. *The First Voyage around the World.* University of Toronto Press, 2007.

Pope, Dudley. *Life in Nelson's Navy.* Naval Institute Press, 1996.

Radford, Edwin. *Unusual Words and How They Came About.* Philosophical Library, 1946.

The Random House College Dictionary. Random House Reference, 2000.

Rankin, Hugh F. *The Golden Age of Piracy.* Henry Holt, 1969.

Raveneau de Lussan. *Journal of a Voyage into the South Seas in 1684 and the Following Years with the Filibusters.* A. H. Clark Company, 1930.

Rogers, John G. *Origins of Sea Terms.* Nimrod Press, 1985.

Rovin, Jeff. *Did You Ever Wonder.* Globe Communications Corp., 1997.

Sanders, Diedre, Dick Girling, Derek Davies, and Rick Sanders. *Would You Believe It, Again?* Pinnacle Books, 1977.

Shenkman, Richard. *Legends, Lies, and Cherished Myths of American History.* William Morrow, 1988.

Shepard, Birse. *Lore of the Wreckers.* Beacon Press, 1961.

Sherry, Frank. *Raiders and Rebels: The Golden Age of Piracy.* HarperCollins, 2009.

Smyth, William H. *The Sailor's Word Book: An Alphabetical Digest of Nautical Terms, Including Some More Especially Military and Scientific, but Useful to Seaman; as Well as Archaisms of Earlier Voyages.* [Orig 1867.] Conway Maritime Press, 1996.

Snow, Edward Rowe. *Unsolved Mysteries of Sea and Shore.* Dodd, Mead, 1963.

Spaven, William. *The Seaman's Narrative.* Sheardown and Son, 1796.

Spectorsky, A.C. *The Book of the Sea.* Grosset & Dunlap, 1954.

Stanton, William Ragan. *The Great United States Exploring Expedition of 1838-1842.* University of California Press, 1975.

Van Loon, Hendrik Willem. *Ships and How They Sailed the Seven Seas (5000 BC–AD 1935).* Simon & Schuster, 1935.

Vigor, John. *The Practical Mariner's Book of Knowledge.* International Marine, 1994.

Voss, John Claus. *The Venturesome Voyages of Captain Voss.* Gray's Publishing, 1976.

Waring, Philippa. *A Dictionary of Omens and Superstitions.* Souvenir Press, 1997.

Wetherell, John Porrit. *The Adventures of John Wetherell*. Penguin Books, 1995.
Whedbee, Charles Harry. *Legends of the Outer Banks and Tar Heel Tidewater*. John F. Blair, 1966.
Wilcox, L.A. *Anson's Voyage*. HarperCollins, 1969.
Williams, Neville. *Captains Outrageous*. Barrie and Rockliff, 1961.
Woodbury, George. *The Great Days of Piracy in the West Indies*. Norton, 1951.
Zacks, Richard. *An Underground Education*. Anchor, 1999.

Websites

Architecture in Ancient Roman [sic]. http://www.crystalinks.com/romearchitecture.html.
The Bounty, Pitcairn Island, and Fletcher Christian's Descendants. Brunner, Borgna. http://www.infoplease.com/spot/pitcairn.html.
Captain Cook Society. http://www.captaincooksociety.com/home.
Constitution: America's Ship of State. U.S. Navy. http://www.history.navy.mil/ussconstitution/.
George Washington's Mount Vernon. Mount Vernon Ladies' Association. http://www.mountvernon.org/mansion/10facts.
History of Western Civilization. Knox, E.L. Skip. Boise State University. http://europeanhistory.boisestate.edu/westciv.
Lloyds of London. http://www.lloyds.com/
Markham, J. David. "Napoleon: Educating a Genius." Napoleon for Dummies. http://www.dummies.com/how-to/content/napoleon-educating-a-genius.html
Medieval online. http://medievalonline.bizland.com/customs.chtml [site discontinued]
Naval History & Heritage Command. U.S. Navy. http://www.history.navy.mil/.
Official Popeye Fan Club. http://www.popeyethesailor.com/.
"Samuel Plimsoll—the seaman's friend." BBC. http://www.bbc.co.uk/bristol/content/articles/2008/05/14/plimsoll_feature.shtml.
Turks and Caicos National Museum. http://tcmuseum.org/.
U.S. Coast Guard Historian's Office. U.S. Department of Homeland Security.http://www.uscg.mil/history/ .
Yacht Crew Suckered by Giant Squid's Advances. Cape Town News, January 16, 2003. http://www.capetimes.com

Magazines

48° North (April 1994 issue)
Century Magazine, 1881–1915: illustrations.

Index

Made in the USA
Las Vegas, NV
16 February 2021